LIVING LANGUAGE IN KAZAKHSTAN

CENTRAL EURASIA IN CONTEXT SERIES
Douglas Northrop, EDITOR

LIVING LANGUAGE
IN KAZAKHSTAN

THE DIALOGIC EMERGENCE OF AN ANCESTRAL WORLDVIEW

EVA-MARIE DUBUISSON

UNIVERSITY OF PITTSBURGH PRESS

Published by the University of Pittsburgh Press, Pittsburgh, Pa., 15260
Copyright © 2017, University of Pittsburgh Press
All rights reserved
Manufactured in the United States of America
Printed on acid-free paper
10 9 8 7 6 5 4 3 2 1

Cataloging-in-Publication data is available from the Library of Congress

ISBN 13: 978-0-8229-6460-5
ISBN 10: 0-8229-6460-0

Cover art: Saule Suleimenova, *Bata*
Cover design by Joel W. Coggins

This book is dedicated with love and gratitude to all the friends and family in Kazakhstan who shared their time, energy, and knowledge with me; it is only because of them that any of this writing was possible.

CONTENTS

ACKNOWLEDGMENTS
ix

A NOTE ON THE COVER ART
xi

A NOTE ON TRANSCRIPTION AND TRANSLITERATION
xiii

A NOTE ON FIELDWORK AND METHOD
xv

INTRODUCTION. An Ancestral Worldview
3

ONE. *Bata* and Blessing
25

TWO. Guardians of the Ancestors
56

THREE. Ancestry in *Aitys* Poetry
84

FOUR. Dialogic Authority
106

CONCLUSION. Participatory Politics
133

NOTES
145

REFERENCES
157

INDEX
169

ACKNOWLEDGMENTS

THE RESEARCH and writing represented by this book spanned more than a decade, and during that time I received help from a significant number of people without whom this project never would have been finished. My initial fieldwork of 2004–6 was supported by research fellowships from the Fulbright-Hays Program and the Wenner Gren Foundation. I am grateful to Bakhytnur Otarbayeva, Balzhan Suzhikova, and Aliya Kuryshzhanova for their guidance in my *aitys* research and for their continued friendship, as well as Asiyat Suleimenova at the Fulbright Program in Kazakhstan. To the families and friends with whom I lived during all of my research years, I am profoundly grateful; I do not include their names, as I want to protect their identity, but this book certainly represents their experience and perspective. I would particularly like to thank the three grandmothers of the families with whom I lived, especially the woman I called "Saltanat" (*Apai!*) and her daughter for quite literally making this book possible. I hope that they will be happy with what I have written.

I am thankful to the aitys community in Kazakhstan for allowing me to work with them; I am in awe of their talent and vision! In particular I wish to thank the poets Kenzhebai, Karima, Marzhan, Aibek, Renat, and the departed Orazaly for their inspiration, help, and friendship; I hope that they would be proud of the way I have represented their words and performances here. I would like to thank Margarita Madanova and the Academy of Literature and Arts in Almaty, Murzatai Zholdasbekov and the Department of Aitys Research at Eurasia University, Zhulduzai Karibaeva and the Office of Cultural Affairs in Kyzylorda, all of whom provided the institutional backbone of my aitys research. I also owe thanks to all of my research assistants and translators over the years, particularly Zaure Batayeva and Murat Abdi, and to Bota Zhunussova and Naubet Bissenov for their translation assistance.

My dissertation writing period was supported by the Department of Anthropology at the University of Michigan, a year of residence at the Institute for the Humanities (IH) at the University of Michigan, and a Eurasia Dissertation write-up fellowship from the Social Science Research Council (2008–9). I am grateful for the support of the fellows at IH, which I still call upon to see me through the emotional wear and tear of work and writing. I owe my graduate committee special thanks for their patience and continued encouragement through the years, particularly Douglas Northrop, Alaina Lemon, and my advisor, Judith T. Irvine.

I also owe a thank you to the Department of Anthropology at the University of California, Berkeley, where I held a Mellon Postdoctoral Fellowship and completed my first publication projects, and another to Valentina Pagliai, for being the first editor to show me that publication was possible! Thanks also go to Bogazici University and to my students and colleagues there for their support in recent years. My research and writing in Turkey has been supported by a grant from the Marie Curie Framework Seven Program of the European Commission (2012–16).

I am so grateful to the colleagues, readers, coauthors, and friends whose feedback and collaboration have made the conditions of research and writing possible and successful over the years, including Anna Genina, Zhanara Nauruzbayeva, Marielle Debos, Jessica Robbins, and Aksana Ismailbekova. Thanks also go to Svetlana Jacquesson, Madeleine Reeves, and Jeanne Feaux de la Croix, for creating workshop spaces in which my work and knowledge developed and for their vision and generosity. I owe a very special thank you to Madeleine Reeves for her strong support and constant spirit and for being such an inspiration. In my very first year of research in Kazakhstan I met the soul-friend with whom I have since shared the journey of work and writing in two worlds: Bagila Bukharbayeva, and to her I owe my love and gratitude. Thanks also go out to Susan Rottmann and Ayse Parla for our ethnographic writing group in Istanbul and for believing that this book was possible! Thanks go to Peter Kracht and Douglas Northrop and the team at the University of Pittsburgh Press for including my book in their series and for working with me so patiently, to the anonymous reviewers whose suggestions greatly improved and strengthened my work, and to the freelance copy editor, Maureen Bemko, for such clear and careful editing.

Finally, I would like to thank my family (and my family-in-law) for their love and support all these years. I particularly want to thank my husband, Atilla Yilmaz, who often throws his hands up in frustration at my "writing process" (which consists mostly of stress) but who walks around proudly in his bright blue "Kazakhstan" jacket, because he has always been a supporter of my fieldwork and anthropology—my efforts toward what he calls "meaning making" in the world.

A NOTE ON THE COVER ART

THE GIFTED artist Saule Suleimenova has graciously allowed her graphic painting *Bata* to be included here as cover art. This is a piece from her series entitled *Aru-akhtar* (Ancestor Spirits), in which she explores how the spirits of those who have passed continue to inhabit and observe the contradictions of modern life. Each image in that series contains a backdrop of a gritty urban landscape—from construction projects to graffiti—invoking the hardness of street life in the post-Soviet city (namely Almaty, Kazakhstan). Atop these images—of future, change, reversal, failure—float the ethereal specters of ancestral figures, so that we see the city quite literally through their bodies. These figures come from portrait photographs the artist found in a historical archive, of real individuals living a century ago. When I first stood in her studio and looked at these paintings, I was completely overcome with emotion, because these images contain exactly what I struggle to express in words about life in Kazakhstan.

Suleimenova is a prolific and active artist in Kazakhstan, and her work and vision are a cornerstone of the contemporary art scene.[1] In addition, she has helped to create large-scale public art installations, including one for the annual Art Fest in Astana, as well as the Topographica project at American University of Central Asia in Bishkek, Kyrgyzstan. Suleimenova is committed to using her position to promote contemporary art as an involved and multifaceted aspect of the country, as well as to challenge and influence the worldview of contemporary culture.[2] A previous collection of paintings, *I'm Kazakh*, interrogates the casual realness of ethnic identity: the look, the attitudes, and the relationships inside that category (see Suleimenova 2009). The series *Ancestor Spirits* continues that exploration; the faces and characters inhabiting these images reflect her own experience as an urban Kazakh, trying to stay connected to the people who have passed over this ground before and whose presence still lingers here. I think her perspective is that of someone who also tries—with compassion and humor in equal share—to make sense of what we inherit from the past in the conditions of the present. Suleimenova is explicitly interested in making those struggles and contradictions *part* of the conversation about "national identity," rather than hiding them under the unity of national symbols.[3] As an artist, she wants to inform and shape national ideology and the role of art therein, as well as to actively shape the conversations and relationships of being and belonging in the messy reality of the everyday, rather than the polished halls of power.[4]

I wish to convey my deep and abiding gratefulness to Saule and to her vision and inspiration, and particularly for her permission to use the painting *Bata*, which bears an obvious connection to my own work and themes and in which I see the visual echoes of care so clearly. The presence of this painting on the cover of my book is a blessing in itself, and I would like to thank Joel W. Coggins for this artistic realization. I would also like to express my love and gratitude to the very wonderful person who introduced us, Zhanara Nauruzbayeva, who first understood the possibilities for this collaboration.

A NOTE ON TRANSCRIPTION AND TRANSLITERATION

THE TRANSCRIBED material in this volume is presented in two different ways. For both poetry and blessings (*bata*), I have provided, side by side, both the original Kazakh as well as an English translation. These translations are all the result of collaborative efforts and help from native speakers, but I take full responsibility for any mistake or lack of clarity in the final result. I have chosen to represent Kazakh in the Cyrillic script, as it is the script that people in Kazakhstan would actually encounter both today and during the period of my research. Given that there are debates in Kazakhstan about the respective ideological consequences of using Latin (and Arabic) scripts, I feel that converting to a latinized script might add an extra and unnecessary layer of opacity to the language I present here. For the everyday conversations occurring between myself and interlocutors in the field, I have been encouraged by manuscript readers to create a simplified and readable English-language transcript that does not include extra information or technical detail, for ease of comprehension for readers less familiar with the cultural and linguistic landscape. Similarly, for single words or terms throughout the text, as well as for bibliographic references, I have chosen to provide brief latinized translations. For written Kazakh in all scripts I follow the conventions set by the University of Indiana Center for the Languages of the Central Asian Region (CELAR), including the IPA phonetic romanization of all alphabet characters with the single exception of the Cyrillic letter /ы/, which I have chosen to transliterate using the roman character /y/ for English-language expressions.

A NOTE ON FIELDWORK AND METHOD

AITYS RESEARCH AND THE NATIONAL NETWORK

One of the central methodological premises of this book—that meaning comes from conversation and dialogue in encounter—was born not only from a theoretical perspective but also from practical and methodological issues emerging after years in the field. The material I present in chapters three and four on the contemporary oral tradition of *aitys* was gathered during the years of my doctoral research (2004–6). I worked primarily with a national network of poets, cultural organizers, and sponsors described at length in this volume, all of whom collaborated to stage performances around the country in a conscious effort to build and revive this form of poetry as a national tradition in the post-Soviet period.[1]

Over my years of research on this oral tradition, I traveled widely throughout Kazakhstan, as well as to Kyrgyzstan and to Russia, by train and by car to attend dozens of performances. Given my enthusiasm and long-term presence, my research position was something like that of a groupie in the community; I became like one of the many journalists and writers who tend to hang around poets and to form a community of support and interest. My knowledge of Kazakh was only intermediate—enough to grasp the literal content, and even the metaphor of poetry sometimes, but not colloquialisms or complete contextual comprehension; my understanding necessarily remained partial. Most members of the aitys community spoke a mix of Kazakh and Russian with me, although they preferred to speak Kazakh, and this was also an ideological position, given the context of nationalist politics. For these reasons, I almost always worked with long-term research assistants who helped interpret to me in English. I owe a great deal in this regard to both Zaure Batayeva and Murat Abdi, whose patience and perspective greatly affected my own, as we spent a great deal of time together, and without whom there would be no research project at all. My research assistants and I went backstage and on trips together, taking photographs, speaking informally with other audience members, and giving interviews to local newspapers. We also simply spent a great deal of time in and with the aitys community and conducted personal interviews with people at all levels of the network in order to contextualize their words and experiences.

Renat was the first *akhyn* (poet) I interviewed, the first to take a chance on me, to come to my home and be awkwardly served tea (made with tea bags) and cakes in the kitchen (these were my silly attempts at Kazakh hospitality, in which the table is supposed to be in the formal room, piled with things to eat, and the tea should be freshly brewed). He was a very polite guest, but when we talked years later he laughed and said he'd thought it was pretty funny. He was nineteen when I met him, and even then he was a star. We talked for two hours straight. I asked him all the questions I'd fretfully prepared, and Renat answered them each seriously and thoughtfully. "I have a gift," he said. "My purpose is to voice the truth of the people."

Over the years I worked in the aitys community, interviewing participants, there came to be a few questions I asked of everyone: Why do you do what you do? What is the point of aitys? How do you know aitys has been successful? Aman Zhol, a poet from Astana who has participated in the televised national aitys competitions for more than a decade, explained that he should reach people's hearts and leave something there: "Even if someone's only [at aitys] for an hour, [they] will listen to beautiful, strong words," which he hopes will influence people by generating different ideas about the situations and issues they face in their lives. The well-known poet Balghymbek, also from Astana, told me that aitys *akhyns* exist to raise the social and political consciousness of the people. The particular genre of *zhek pe zhek* (one on one, which he also refers to simply as *shyndykh,* or truth) allows poets to do just that, because they can relay information about current events, "who is who and what is happening." As a result of aitys, he noted, people living in the country now have access to a lot of new information. If a poet does not tell the truth and make an effort to relay real circumstances, a poet is not an akhyn. The success of that effort depends on your opponent, explains Balghymbek—if two poets go in different directions, they bore the people.

Here, he means literally the people in the live audience, upon whom the success of every aitys depends. All the poets have explained this to me, how they feel the audience and sense their response, how audience support is palpable, how it brings confidence and happiness, how it can make the muses come faster. Poets feel the audience react—during performance they must make a connection. What is the point of all of this—how do we know aitys has been successful? Every single person I ever interviewed had the same answer: *because it is satisfying.* Balghymbek explained the connection between performance and politics in this way: "It's of course important to inform authorities in our country, but [here] you can't criticize openly. But [poets] try, of course, try to say something important for the people. If people hear it, about the problems *they* think about, they're very satisfied—you can tell from their reaction." Reflecting on this point, his friend Dauletkere, a fellow poet from Astana, told me he likes it when people recognize him: "It's a great pleasure because they don't just recognize *you,* it means they recognized your *words,* it means you can influence people toward something." But on whom and how can a poet's words have influence?

National sponsors are hoping that poets and their audiences can have some effect on the broader politics of the country: from within the frame of ethnic nationalism, they hope to popularize Kazakh language and culture, as well as to use these categories metaphorically to criticize other government leaders who do not take the concerns of the Kazakh people seriously. Since the late Soviet years, lead organizers have intensely focused their efforts on publicizing modern aitys performances. In addition to encouraging large live audiences with reasonably priced tickets and advance advertising, organizers also work to televise and record performances—a new series of videos and DVDs of notable aitys performances was already available for purchase in local bazaars by the time of my research. The editorial office of the Kazakh writers' union in Almaty was one official entity heavily involved in recording and transcribing performances into text. Some of the excerpts I present here come from their collection, which they were incredibly generous to copy for me.

The efforts of the aitys community itself in turn very much shaped how I came to create my own collection of materials. In addition to collecting books and DVDs, I also traveled to Astana to work for a short time in the fall of 2004 with historians and poets at the Aitys Research Center run by Murzatai Zholdasbekov and housed at the Eurasian National University in Astana. From conversations there, I was able to understand the place of poetry within a broader historiographical and ideological imagination, undergirding the project of political nationalism. In Almaty, with the help of the comparative literature scholar Margarita Madanova, I was able to work for a time in the archive of aitys materials housed at the Academy of Literature and Arts in Almaty. This was essential to understanding the context of aitys during the Soviet period, as well as to identifying those scholars who had made writing about this oral tradition the object of their own research in Kazakh folklore at the academy, as well as to seeing the ways in which the approach of the academy differed from that of the contemporary national network. In the last year of my research, I was also able to visit the audio archive at Kazakhstan's national radio station and listen to historical recordings of Soviet-era aitys performances preserved there as part of the Altyn (Golden) trust.

Working with the national network was at once productive and alienating. I felt that I was "chasing" my research subject in an almost journalistic fashion, rather than functioning as an ethnographer. My research often felt like my "day job" when I worked with research assistants and interpreters/translators in all my travels and interviews. While I did find friends among poets, sponsors, and cultural organizers and while I did tend to have close relationships with those working as assistants, ultimately my work life during those years overlapped with but often tended to be separate from my "home life," the day-to-day living I shared with friends and families in the field. I couldn't always seem to integrate especially well these two spheres of my experience. But over the years it was always clear that my own understanding of the impact and importance of the aitys tradition was being shaped significantly not just by poets or sponsors but by all the people with whom I spent time, even if we were not always directly discussing poetry or performance.

In my second and third years of research, I made a conscious decision to leave the national network and move out to live with families and cultural communities in different regions of the country, to pursue my research about the meaning of aitys poetry in a more holistic fashion.

REGIONAL FAMILIES AND COLLABORATION

All national poets move from training and performance at the regional level to national and international competitions. To study this progression, and to examine the influence of regional organizers and sponsors on performances, in my second and third years of research (2005–6), I moved to regional capitals in the west, the south, and the north of the country for periods of three to six months to work as a participant observer in regional cultural affairs offices. These offices recruit and judge local poets for competitions, channel government and private sponsorship monies, and advertise and stage competitions. With the help of office directors and staff, I gathered a wealth of textual documentation of present-day as well as Soviet-era aitys performances. With their help and connections, I was also able to go on cultural pilgrimages and to visit Soviet era poets' homes and shrines, a practice carried on by most currently performing poets today. Doing so deeply enriched my ethnographic understanding of the aitys tradition and led me to subsequent work on sacred site visitation as a fundamental part of an ancestral worldview, described in chapter two.

In my third and final year of research, I was extremely fortunate to become a participant observer at a school for the artistically gifted in a southern regional capital where aitys is taught, as well as later in an aitys mentorship network in a northern regional capital. In both, experienced poets serve as administrators and teachers, helping to channel younger poets into public performances and into relationships with cultural affairs offices and sponsors. I attended classes with young poets and musicians, watched rehearsals, accompanied them to public performances, and became a regular group photographer and happy fan. From interviews with regional sponsors, as well as from visits to their business enterprises, I learned that by cooperating with "cultural projects" such as aitys, the regional political elite could simultaneously act to voice dissent from the national government while gaining popular prestige. Their patronage allowed young poets to work their way through school and/or support their families; the relationship between poets and their sponsors is mutually beneficial.

During the second and third years of my research, I lived with multigenerational Kazakh families in each of the regions where I worked, which allowed me to stay current with local concerns and gossip, as well as to develop a lived sense of familial responsibility, daily gendered economies, and religious practices. These experiences deeply enriched my understanding of poets' jokes and metaphors and also allowed me to experience the country's cultural and political events as part of a televisual (imagined) audience. At home, outside the aitys community itself, my families and other friends found my research topic interesting and were generally happy to talk about it or to watch aitys shows together when they came on television. This poetry tradition is stereotyped as "entertainment for grandparents," but I found that younger folks who tended to dismiss aitys as old-fashioned kitsch were often surprised at the humor and the political undertones of performances. An equally significant observation was that my research topic often provoked quiet but heated discussions of local and national politics. People were frustrated by their own social and economic conditions, as well as with leaders who seemed to be self-interested and nepotistic rather than serving the population's interests; these were audiences who were therefore warmly receptive to poets' criticism, whether outspoken or veiled, of government and sociological dynamics.

The aitys tradition and the context of my research ultimately seemed to create a space in which people could take pride in Kazakh language and culture and in their home country but simultaneously air their concerns over palpable forms of social inequality and their opinions of a government they perceived as corrupt and unable to solve problems. Given my work with sponsors and politicians, I could also see the very same concerns resonating at high levels of government and business and taking the form of a cultural nationalism. I recognized that it was only by enfolding my "home" and "work" life into the same story that I could begin to explain the dynamics I wanted to understand.

Although I had so many people around me during fieldwork, I always harbored the sinking feeling that the analysis of all the material and experiences we collected and shared should ultimately be a solitary task, mine alone. More than valuing any success, I felt weighted by small failures, most notably by my own lack of literary fluency in the Kazakh language, which I experienced as a personal and moral failing because I was working with poetry. I knew that my own solitary interpretation would be entirely insufficient to allow my readers to experience the richness of that poetic world. I left Kazakhstan after two and a half years of an utterly aitys-centered worldview and tried to reacclimate to graduate school and the United States. However, I soon realized that there was simply no proper (or possible!) way to "analyze" the material I had so painstakingly gathered by myself; that process also needed to happen "in the field" with native speakers. I therefore undertook one final research trip for the aitys project in the summer of 2008. Three student research assistants and I worked together to transcribe and translate the final set of materials from my collection of interviews and performances necessary to complete my dissertation at the time.

My informal mentor, colleague, and friend Bakhytnur Otarbayeva, a professor of Kazakh history and the leader of an educational nongovernmental organization, helped to organize the students who would become my first work group for several months. Three highly motivated, insightful, and wonderful young women would arrive at my doorstep regularly each morning, ready to work as I was still waking up with a cup of strong coffee. They would spend several hours a day with me, in the little workroom I tried to set up in my small, one-room apartment. With multiple computers (one graciously donated by Bakhytnur) and earphones, pads of paper and dictionaries, we were ready to watch videos of poetry competitions, write down what was said, and translate from Kazakh to English (often with Russian conversation and explanation in between). This quickly became a collaborative process, as the young women shared funny or troublesome moments with one another and often talked through translations together. Over snacks of juice and cookies, we conferred about which performances seemed most interesting or important. When my apartment became too boring (and after we needed the computers less), we sometimes met at the local mall instead.

The poetry and other material translated from Kazakh to English that I present in this volume is the result not only of that work but of subsequent clarification and professional translation by native speakers, including Naubet Bissenov and former research assistant Bota Zhunussova.

The creation of a collaborative analysis process was a source of joy and helped to show that the power of aitys poetry is indeed in its capacity and potential for sharing and creating conversation. Given my theoretical focus on performance, voice and participant frameworks, and the inherently linguistic nature of my ethnography, after that wonderful summer's experience I began to wonder: shouldn't this dialogic process be more firmly at the center of all my research and analysis in the future?

DIALOGUE AS METHOD

In preparation for writing this book and for my most recent research on ancestral blessings (bata) and shrine pilgrimage (2012–13), I decided to do research itself differently. My primary research assistant (whose words precede the introduction to this volume), was the mother of one of my close friends, and it was their family with whom I lived for several months. We talked to people together about the themes of the project, and I paid careful attention to her own reactions and interpretations. We worked on translations together. We talked to other family members about the project. Our many forms of dialoguing were integral to the frame of analysis I present throughout this book: my "work" and "home" lives overlapped entirely, and the motivation and meaning of our efforts became the emergent quality of all our interactions and mutual analysis over time.

In the interests of protecting the rights and privacy of the people who so lovingly and generously shared their time and highly personal stories during those later years of research, I have decided not only to give them each a pseudonym but also to disguise the towns where they live and where I did my fieldwork. The private individuals whose words and experience structure the first two chapters of this volume—Saltanat, Meiramgul, Gaukhar, and Zhulduz (all pseudonyms)—bear certain clear similarities, though I did not intentionally select them as such: they are each professional women in their late fifties who identify as Kazakh (though at least two have only one Kazakh parent). They were educated in the Soviet system and tend to reference the social and moral values (as well as the films and music) of their younger days as something that has been lost or lessened. They have, in the post-Soviet period, unfortunately all experienced tragic life circumstances, emotional hardship, and financial uncertainty. They have all lost their first husband to death or divorce (only one is remarried), and they all have had at least two children (not all of whom, sadly, are living at the time of this writing). They are all very concerned with finding some comfort, stability, and certainty for themselves and others, and they are worried about the well-being and moral direction of the younger generation.

Each of the women with whom I worked also exhibited a pedagogical side; because I am approximately twenty years their junior on average, and because the fieldwork contexts created "learning" situations for me, my relationship to each of these women was similar to that of a student or beginning apprentice, and I was often treated in that manner. While this was at times frustrating, as I sometimes felt limited or quieted, I could ultimately see that this was the right approach; in our many conversations about bata, I was also receiving an education. My work on bata and shrine pilgrimage came later in my overall research career. I had already spent years working on aitys poetry, as described above, and was therefore in a good position to recognize the many ways in which these women's households mirrored the places, dynamics, and conversations or problems of those with whom I had lived and worked before, most notably the dynamics of a multigenerational family.

The woman with whom I lived and who directed my research, Saltanat, is a former teacher and currently works in her town's bazaar. With a beautiful wide smile and stylish glasses, she is ready to laugh and to instruct. She is highly perceptive, hard-working, and slightly nervous; there is often an urgency to her actions. She relaxes while drinking tea, which she likes to do with her husband and family several times a day. She and her husband share the external work of their homestead, which includes their private home, garage, large garden, and livestock. They live with her oldest son and his wife (a bride and daughter-in-law is a status conferring many responsibilities; Kaz: *kelin*) and their two young children. The daughter-in-law is in charge of her children, as well as cooking and cleaning within the house each day. As this kelin is as spirited as her mother-in-law, the two are often in conflict about how best to run the household. The conflict remains between the two women, as Saltanat's husband is relatively quiet and her son has a difficult job in law enforcement, so he is often stressed or tired.

While she would probably consider herself quite "traditional" about family values, Saltanat also has a global view of the world and has worked to provide opportunities for her children, who have all, somewhat unusually, had access to an international higher education. Over the years, she has opened her home to many international guests—her children's friends and others, such as Peace Corps volunteers. I came to live with this family for an extended period, because Saltanat is the mother of one of my close friends, a Kazakh woman I will call Dina, whom I originally met in the United States. When I arrived at Saltanat's home in Kazakhstan in the summer of 2012, Dina and her husband were also there. Together with Saltanat and Dina over the course of a few months, we had conversations with family and family friends, as well as connections through the work of Saltanat and her daughter. We came to meet Meiramgul, the second primary informant for my research, because she was the librarian at the vocational college where Saltanat's husband was a head administrator. I came to meet Gaukhar, my third primary interlocutor, because she was the aunt of Dina's friend.

CONVERSATIONS AND TRANSLATIONS

My presence as a friend and ethnographer motivated a particular general direction (such as the idea that I was interested in talking to people about bata, for example), but ultimately Saltanat was in charge of our further interaction. When she and I went to meet and talk with Meiramgul and Gaukhar, we did so in the sense of having a conversation or cultural encounter, rather than any kind of formal interview process (compare Briggs 1986). During these conversations, Saltanat was concerned that I remain relatively quiet and not "overplay my hand" as an experienced ethnographer. Rather, she believed it was important that the women with whom we spoke felt that they were telling me new things, rather than reacting to my previous knowledge (such as of places, terms, or social dynamics). Saltanat's strong opinion on this matter heavily informed the interaction dynamic, which should be apparent in the transcripts I present throughout the first chapter of this book: they consist of short collaborative dialogues in which she and her counterpart tend to build a description together; one woman takes a lead narrative or explanatory role, and the second woman tends to affirm, repeat, or explain her words. In our conversations Saltanat sometimes tells me what to write down (I was always also taking notes during our conversations). Thus, my own contributions tend to be minimal back-channeling, such as affirmation, a questioning tone, or mild exclamation. Sometimes Saltanat takes over from her conversational counterpart, in order to mark what she feels is particularly important for me to understand.[2]

I have transcribed participants' speech from our interactions in the excerpts I present in this volume, and the translation to English is my own. I have excerpted from longer interviews that material that is directly relevant to the point at hand, as well as that material which exemplifies the multiplicity of participant frameworks in conversation; every story, poem, and prayer is ultimately a dialogue between two or more participants, present or absent in time and space. While I tend to interact primarily in Russian, using Kazakh to interject or to clarify, only two of the informants I present here were also dominant Russian speakers (Gaukhar and Zhulduz). In general, the people with whom I lived and worked were either bilingual Kazakh-Russian or dominant Kazakh speakers. The topics of bata, shrine pilgrimage, relationships with ancestors, poetry, and nationalism, for reasons equally political, historical, and cultural, all tend to be what I might call "Kazakh-language" topics—subjects overwhelmingly discussed or debated in the Kazakh language among Kazakh people themselves. In presenting their ideas to me, they often employed a process of internal translation to Russian, which is perhaps most evident in the speech of the librarian Meiramgul, whose narratives and reflections I share in chapter one and in the conclusion to this volume.

The very issue of field language is indicative of the broader sociopolitical context in which these encounters must be understood: in Kazakhstan today, there is a discrepancy between Kazakhs who speak primarily Russian (who tend to live in urban areas and/or the north) and Kazakhs who speak primarily Kazakh (who tend to live in the south and west and/or in more rural areas). In my experience, the distinction between Kazakh and Russian is an ideologically salient one, but in everyday speech the boundaries between languages are very much blurred. A high degree of admixture in terminology and even grammar is quite common; directly reflecting this reality is my own speech in the field, which is a mixed usage that many people take as matter-of-fact. I found that if people commented on it at all, it was to laugh and say, "Now *that* is really Kazakh!"

However, in the linguistic contexts that overlap with ethnic nationalism in Kazakhstan, what is funny to some is potentially injurious to others. What is perhaps most important to recognize is that language becomes a metaphor for the valuing of culture and the protection of people, a point I emphasize repeatedly throughout this volume. Working collaboratively in a variety of regions and contexts forces to the fore the multiplicity of experience and linguistic reality among those who would identify as Kazakh, even within one country. The differences and discrepancies in understanding and explanation that emerge in dialogue between myself and others in the field actually dissemble and decentralize the very premise of ethnic nationalism. In the blessings, poems, and conversations I present here, the claim to be "Kazakh" goes beyond the temporal and political constraints of a strictly national ideology. Instead, the dialogues that I have experienced and that I have tried to share in writing allow access to a different kind of cultural worldview—that of ancestral belonging and a more fundamental loyalty, which may be described in multiple languages and experienced in multiple cultural and regional environments across Inner Asia.

LIVING LANGUAGE IN KAZAKHSTAN

INTRODUCTION
AN ANCESTRAL WORLDVIEW

SALTANAT: Well, for every person, in the family, in every family, there are relatives who have passed [away] . . . well . . . to the other world. And sometimes on the anniversary of this deceased person, the day of his/her death . . . um . . . Thursday, or on Friday, we welcome them [to our] home with fresh bread, and read the Koran.

THE DIALOGIC EMERGENCE OF ANCESTRY

Throughout Inner Asia, the relationship between the living and their ancestors, those who have come before, is a critical component of both structuring a cultural worldview and imagining a social future.[1] Heroic ancestors, such as Manas in Kyrgyzstan and Chinggis Khan in Mongolia, are a fundamental component of nation-building and national identity today; they are considered to be the spiritual forefathers of modern states. These epic figures and the mythic narratives of their lives and power set an example for their "descendants"—contemporary populations and their governments. At times, such a powerful legacy can undergird national leaders exhibiting increasingly autocratic and charismatic domination, as has been the case in Turkmenistan or Uzbekistan. But the state does not hold a monopoly on the symbolic importance of genealogy or history. In postsocialist environments of political repression and economic uncertainty during recent decades, many individuals, families, and communities are turning to their forebears—both personal and national—to develop mechanisms of care for people and for their ancestral land, beyond the bounds of any nation. From blessing and prayer to oral poetic traditions, the conversations between ancestors and the living constitute a basic aspect of many different discursive traditions.

Attending to the performative dimensions of language in *all* encounters allows linguistic anthropologists to describe the social roles, relationships, and negotiations emerging in the heteroglossia of everyday life. Who can speak to whom, and how?[2] Studies in linguistic anthropology have long demonstrated oral tradition and verbal art to be particularly charged and concentrated sites of ideology and social authority within communities (Briggs and Bauman 1990; Hymes 1981; Tedlock 1983). Abu-Lughod (1986) and Caton (1990) have argued powerfully for an analysis of the social production and the political consequences of particular poetic genres in Egypt and Yemen to emphasize poetry's centrality as a mode of action or a cultural practice, as an emergent space for the negotiation of values. The efficacy of poetry or other forms of verbal art lies precisely in their performative capacity, to transcend the frame of the everyday (see Bauman [1977] 1984). Performance blurs the boundaries of accountability in language: who is responsible for what is said?

Specific attention has been paid in linguistic anthropological studies to the social contexts and realities created by talk in interaction (Duranti and Goodwin 1992) and to the assumption (or attribution) of accountability in narrative and dialogue (Hill and Irvine 1993). A focus on words spoken in the world (Tedlock 1983) can also illuminate the metaphoric conversations between cultures and ecologies or landscapes (Basso 1996; Uzendoski and Calapucha-Tapuy 2012). My focus on the performative qualities of language in contexts ranging from poetry to pilgrimage is not just a descriptive exercise. Rather, this approach is an argument: that even under a regime characterized as "authoritarian," alternate forms of authority can and do exist, and they emerge in dialogue.[3] Ancestors are not just part of the realm of history or "cultural heritage" but rather an active part of conversations in performance and daily life.[4] In his ethnographic assessment of the political categories of time and space in social memory, the cultural anthropologist Jonathan Boyarin (1994, 27) asks, "Is it possible to conceive of a 'coalition' or 'dialogue' between the claims of dead ancestors and the claims of distant contemporaries?" This book answers with a resounding *yes!*[5]

As I elaborate in this volume, the concept of ancestry in Inner Asia has the specific connotations of mutual concern and leadership: if ancestral leaders are properly recognized and respected, then they may come to watch over and guide the living in turn. Ancestors' advice and blessing (collectively known as *bata*) together become a moral guidepost for contemporary families and communities. Such cycles of care, for many Kazakhs and other Central Asians, are also forms of interconnection and respect in the difficult and shifting political economy of the present. Here I take seriously the idea that any cultural imaginary is not a top-down project but rather the emerging product of interaction and contestation. All the conversations, prayers, and disagreements around and in an ancestral cultural imaginary—all of that talk is itself a politics of belonging. In the material I present here, I ask how forms of language and ancestry actually become a means of coping with and solving—as well as criticizing and changing—ongoing social and political problems in Kazakhstan today.

In answering these questions, I turn specifically to the spaces in which ancestors can communicate with the living and where a mutual relationship of care and guidance is actively enacted in the world. As described in the epigraph quote for this introduction, the family's deceased are welcomed weekly into the home with the aroma of bread, freshly baked or fried, and the short prayers of their relatives. Many families and pilgrims also go to visit the lands, tombs, and monuments of ancestors more distant, famous, and widely shared. Such sites are places where their caretakers can interact with visitors, who learn about the lives of the ancestors and receive their blessing. In their contemporary performances of oral epic traditions, Kazakh poets regularly intone the words and wisdom of these ancestors, thus presenting current generations with a moral guidepost. Great ancestors like khans and *batyr*s (warriors) serve rhetorically as an exemplar of great leadership for their descendants in the present.

The ancestors come to be involved in many different contexts, in spaces of social interaction where their wishes and intentions are expressed and where they can "watch over" their living families. I do not take their care as predetermined or absolute but rather as something that emerges in the world only when and if the living allow channels of communication that transcend the conventions of conversation, such as space and time. The forms of language and interaction I present in these chapters—blessing and prayer, storytelling and conversation, and poetic tradition—are each conventions and moments of dialogue, moments of understanding or contestation, within which an ancestral worldview is negotiated. This is an ethnography of the dialogic emergence of an ancestral cultural worldview (see Tedlock and Mannheim 1995).

By characterizing an ancestral worldview as dialogic, I also intentionally include the multiple layers of voice and experience brought into any given interactive exchange by social relationships and roles compounded through history. Building upon the insight of Mikhail Bakhtin that text and social life alike are heteroglossic, Mannheim and Tedlock (1995) argue that dialogue (rather than structure or individuality) is the fundamental premise of language and culture and that every interaction must always be understood in the contexts of social history. The ways in which language is imbricated in social processes are semiotic (indexical) and performative: linguistic forms invoke and enact dimensions of some shared, lived reality as they come into being, an emergence that is negotiated by participants through talk in interaction. If we take the specific concept of "voice," we can think about the ways in which the content and style of any given utterance may carry—in content and style—the perspective of a particular social and historical position, and we must also acknowledge that voices are not individual but multiple, carrying their previous contexts and forms of usage into the present (Bakhtin 1981, 262–66).[6] Such a Bakhtinian approach to the understanding of language and culture allows us to take very seriously the "world-making" of speakers as emergent and plural (Mannheim and Tedlock 1995, 12; see Behar 1995), and it becomes analytically imperative to pay attention to dialogism at multiple levels of language and social life.

In the use or application of Bakhtin's principle of "dialogic emergence" to the realm of oral expressive culture, we move from text to talk, and here Erving Goffman's classic model of "participant frameworks" in social interaction becomes a helpful rubric. Participants are those social figures, physically present or absent, who actively and passively contribute to the framework of interaction and therefore to its social meaning. While Bakhtin's discursive world is populated with a diversity of speakers and speech types, Goffman's interactive world is also populated by "observers"—those who function consciously or not as some kind of audience for what is spoken and therefore necessarily structure the relational and perspectival impact or implicature of what is said. Just as Bakhtin's (1981, 263) characters speak across categories of person, genre, and history, so too does Goffman's framework allow us to take the concepts of speaking and listening beyond the constraints of the present and to explore the "conversations" that take place across multiple dimensions of social space and time. If, for example, we expand the classic conversation framework to include ancestors as both active participants and witnesses, we can see the performative implications of their involvement, such as evaluation, reassurance, or protection: ancestors are guiding both families and nations.

Interaction with ancestors has become more salient and prominent across Inner Asia in recent decades, in part a result of strong nationalizing campaigns that have stressed genealogy and a connection to heroes of the past as a basis for the legitimacy of new states. It is quite true that, as C. M. Hann (2002, 8) has explained, "many postsocialist elites have drawn . . . on ideas of culture as an integrated whole to create boundaries of exclusion." But a connection to genealogy as both ideology and oral tradition is also a highly personalized cultural strategy for individuals and families, as well as for nations in the post-Soviet period (Jacquesson 2016; Yessenova 2005a, b). Genealogy provides a source of grounding, orientation, and purpose in the shifting tides of postsocialist life (Gullette 2010). Indeed, forming a solid and conscious connection with familial and cultural ancestors has been a basic strategy for many Inner Asians coping with social and economic uncertainty and exclusion in the decades since the dissolution of socialist communism (Buyandelger 2007). In this introduction I identify not only particular forms of language and interaction with ancestors but also the general social, political, and economic contexts during which such interactions have become increasingly meaningful as a form of guidance and care.

LEVELS OF INTERACTION AND CARE

As I describe in chapter one, bata is a short blessing given by an elder within the family on a specific occasion. Bata is a blessing given and received, a dialogic marker of a personal relationship between generations, a form of cultural education. I present these blessings as words that act in the world, that "do" something (see Austin [1962] 1975). The wishes of ancestors enact particular social conventions and commitments, specifically, the care and guidance of elders for the younger generations. The gifts of bata touch and hold the persons who receive them, gently shaping those persons to achieve a shared cultural future. Bata takes place in various contexts within the family, ranging from a small daily prayer over a shared meal to a special gift shared ritually at life-cycle events such as first steps, departures, anniversaries, or weddings. These blessings are at once commonplace and essential in the life course. My informants describe the deep sense of comfort they derive from bata, as well as their fear that if the tradition of blessing is diffused or lost, families and communities will fracture as a result.

Typically bata is given by living relatives, but many people also seek blessings from respected elders who are not kin. Within every community there are various individuals known for their ability to give bata, and people visit them in times of trouble. Bata is also tied up with the world of dreams and with memories of those relatives who have passed and whose relationship with the living is still unfinished. The deceased must be cared for properly by the living, problems must be resolved, and love and support must be conveyed before the living can carry on in peace. These complex relationships, as they transcend time and worlds, also often merge easily into a very general mythic history: everyone with whom I spoke referenced a cultural history of great Kazakh leaders from whom it was important to ask for bata. It is as if the quality of a respected elder or leader can be transmuted into the blessing itself, imbued with a special quality or virtue. The moral ground of this practice stems from the basic cultural belief that elders are to be respected. But this principle is not absolute. Rather, a respected elder is someone who *earns* that position over time, by being a good son or daughter, spouse, parent, and family/community leader (see Beyer 2010; Ismailbekova 2014b).

Many people have actively taken on genealogical narrative traditions as a source of personal and cultural-historical pride, within and beyond the nation itself. It is important that these heroic traditions tend to re-create the deep past as glorious, a source of pride at the same time that the past is evoked directly into the present. Genealogically focused narratives typically bypass a Russian and Soviet history, which becomes an interruption in the Inner Asian (Turkic-Mongol, Islamic) history of much longer duration (see DeWeese 1994). Connecting to ancestors becomes not only the rebuilding of a cultural landscape across geography and history but also a personal or rhetorical strategy.

A reciprocal relationship between the ancestors and the living means that both must become guardians of people and land—custodians of a Kazakh cultural worldview. This worldview is encapsulated in spaces around the country's many sacred shrines or sites where caretakers live and greet pilgrims, who come to receive the blessings of those buried at the sites. Caretakers are able to pray with pilgrims, to tell them the "miracle stories" of their ancestors, and to offer bata on behalf of the ancestors. The bata tradition has become a controversial social movement in some areas of the country, where trained practitioners channel extended bata as a form of diagnosis and healing for groups of pilgrims who travel together. Here the performative power of bata is elaborated and mediated as an active form of awareness and care, part of a sacred ancestral landscape. As caretakers describe it, ancestors protect their burial sites and the people who travel there, just as their personal stories may serve as inspiration or example for visitors. Bata has not only a moral basis but also a potency or real efficacy, and this is because once ancestors (or elders) have gained the status of being respected, their lives become exemplars, their experiences models to replicate, their advice sought after, and their words endowed with a spiritual quality or force. Their blessings are part of their stewardship of younger generations.

It is impossible to generalize life experience for all those who consider themselves to be Kazakh. More than 60 percent of approximately seventeen million Kazakhs identified themselves in the 2009 national census as ethnically Kazakh, reflecting a continued increase in total numbers of Kazakhs in that state since independence.[7] Millions of Kazakhs also live in western Mongolia and China. There are today broad and obvious distinctions in levels of education, wealth, urbanity, and worldview among these populations. Just as there is certainly a plurality *within* Kazakh culture, it is also true that Kazakhs hold much in common with *other* Inner Asian cultures, in various locales from Bishkek to Urumqi. With Kyrgyz and Uighurs, for example, Kazakhs share regional history, language, culture, and religious traditions. The very idea that Kazakh culture is distinct from that of other peoples stems from a complicated regional history and colonial past(s), as well as the nationalizing projects of the Soviet and post-Soviet periods. This book is concerned with the ways in which conceptions of a unified Kazakh culture are harnessed as a means of contending with a postsocialist environment in which the Kazakhstani state is a relevant but not a primary determiner of identity or opportunity, personhood or possibility. In the following section I give a brief overview of post-Soviet political and cultural history and describe the ways that local communities, families, and genealogical connections come to the fore as strategies of economic and moral survival and "well-being."[8]

STATE PATERNALISM

The former Soviet republics were semi-autonomous but absolutely dependent on the vast "centralized allocative power" (Verdery in Hann, Humphrey, and Verdery 2002, 16) of the Russia-centered political and economic system, led by communist elites, or *nomenklatura*. With the Soviet Union disbanded and the Central Asian states forced toward independence (see Jones Luong 2004), nationalization and privatization became among the basic functional and ideological tools of political and economic reorganization. These mechanisms benefited those already entrenched in power, along with their inner circles and children—groups that in the years since independence have grown and solidified into an elite class (see Cummings 2005; Dave 2007). Throughout the former Soviet Union, the presidents of the new nations and their immediate families figure prominently at the very center of the elite cadres of emergent national political economies. The presidential parties control appointment to parliament, while ministry members as well as city and regional mayors are often hand-selected by the president, though there are regular replacements put into office, to discourage competing local loyalties. Political opposition of any kind is low, and any activity seen as dissent is typically met with disproportionate punishment.

Such leadership has created a general atmosphere of repression and censorship in the former Soviet Central Asian republics, along with some fear or distrust of seated government officials, who are often perceived to be acting out of self-interest rather than the interests of those they purport to represent. I would stress, however, that the strongly personal and dominant nature of presidential power is not in and of itself perceived as necessarily problematic by Kazakhs. In fact, in traditionally paternal environments across Inner Asia such traits harmonize well with the figures of the great judges, warriors, and khans of the past. Rather, for average citizens it is the lack of moral and social welfare that is perceived as most hurtful. Strong leaders are good, as long as strength is defined as providing for those under one's care.

As Liu (2002, 2005, 2012) has described so well in the case of his ethnographic research on political authority and urban social life in Osh, Kyrgyzstan, what citizens tended to expect from their state was "a moral relation of stewardship with respect to the republic's productive resources and to its people. What they advocated is more accurately termed *state paternalism*, rather than 'authoritarianism.' State paternalism means that the state reserves for itself the nearly exclusive prerogative for directing the economic, political, and social course of a country. It involves more than central control, however, but the moral notion that the nation properly falls under the care and guidance of a state that knows what is good for it" (2005, 229, original emphasis). Liu's informants identified the state closely with the personality of its leader: if the leader was moral, the state was, too. They expected *boqmoq*, or stewardship and routine care, from the state as part of its provision of economic opportunity and social welfare. Liu's informants also believed that the state (and its figurehead, the president) should guide the "moral transformation of the people": "the relation of state to citizen is analogous to how Uzbek parents and elders are supposed to raise children in *mahallas*" (230–31). Family, neighborhood, and country function ideologically as varying levels of a single authority structure.

In my own experience, these ideals are widely held throughout Inner Asia and certainly resonate clearly with the material I present here from Kazakhstan. This general vision of some idealized form of leadership does exist in many ways; one need look no further than the culture of respect toward the authority of elders in communities (Liu 2005; Beyer 2010), the intergenerational cycles of caregiving and economy structuring most households (Werner 1998; Ismailbekova 2014a), the spiritual leadership of ancestors, religious leadership (Rasanayagam 2012; Louw 2007), or even at the many local business and political leaders, chosen by and involved with their constituents at a regional or local level, who *are* giving back (Ismailbekova 2014b). Strong (male) leadership is desirable for many in Central Asian postsocialist spaces, where paternalism and social welfare are seen to go hand in hand. Such leadership may even reconcile with local understandings and forms of democracy (Ismailbekova 2014b; Sabloff [2013] 2016).

However, these ideals tend to become more performative for seated government officials, that is, a network of favors rather than the moral prerogative of care. I have seen that for my own informants, families, and friends in Central Asia, judiciary and policing systems, as well as government bureaucracy, are widely perceived as corrupt—full of individuals acting for bribes or powerful interests, rather than in accordance with any rule of law. There is a painful gap between ideal leadership and the everyday reality with which most citizens have to cope.

ECONOMIC UNCERTAINTY

The largest and wealthiest among the post-Soviet Central Asian republics, Kazakhstan has seen immense growth and has maintained a crucial strategic position due to its vast reserves of oil and location at the junction of the Eurasian pipeline system linking China, Russia, and Europe. Kazakhstan is certainly far richer than its Central Asian neighbors, and the billions of dollars generated by the sale of its natural resources have created an emergent and quickly growing elite class. While the president's inner circle has controlled a highly centralized political economy in the decades since independence, it is also important to note that Kazakhstan's government has pursued a multipronged international economic strategy, including resource cooperation and the pursuit of foreign investment. Within the country, the government has simultaneously undertaken a domestic financial strategy, including multiple phases of privatization and neoliberal economic reforms such as shock therapy, with varying degrees of success.[9] Despite these efforts, however, there continues to be wide economic disparity. The visibility of economic growth and an aspirational middle or upper class in urban areas like Astana and Almaty might suggest more widespread wealth, but wide swaths of the population are still far less well off. As the socialist systems of social and economic security (ranging from jobs and housing to education, health care, and social security) have weakened in the post-Soviet period, Kazakhstan's national government has tried but not yet been able to develop systematic alternatives or replacements for social welfare to serve its population, particularly for those in more rural village (Kaz: *aul*) areas.[10]

Individual communities were left to deal with the local reorganization of Soviet industrial and agricultural collective infrastructure, at times without government help, while social support for children and families disappeared and pensions and state salaries dried up for long periods of time.[11] Many institutional jobs disappeared, leaving teachers and engineers alike to search for alternative employment. Many in the former Central Asian republics, including nearly all of the families with whom I lived in different regions of Kazakhstan, turned to informal trade in the period after independence as their only sustainable livelihood. While cross-border trade proved to be a phase of transformation during the 1990s in Kazakhstan, in other Central Asian former Soviet republics, notably Kyrgyzstan and Tajikistan, labor remittance economies continue to structure national economies, with regional and transnational networks and goods—from Turkey to Russia to China—providing income for millions of families.[12] Within Central Asia, Kazakhstan figures prominently as a host country for regional labor migrants (Marat 2009). The Kazakhstani state grew wealthy due to resource extraction and has therefore functioned as a labor importer, rather than exporter, and thus fostered a growing elite and supported an urban middle class. However, millions of Kazakhstanis (particularly in rural areas and villages) are still living in relative poverty.

Those with whom I lived and worked during nearly a decade of research (2004–13) in four different regions across Kazakhstan certainly represent another "new normal"—those who have relatively little access to resources and possess little specific knowledge about government programs. People see an increase in wealth among the wealthy but no significant improvement in their own circumstances, and they thus view government "reform" (such as liberalism or privatization) as highly corrupt. In the political and economic transformations taking place in recent decades,

> the relation between macro structures and everyday practices is that the collapse of party states and administered economies broke down macro structures, thereby creating space for microworlds to produce autonomous effects that may have unexpected influence over the structures that have been emerging. . . . This presents an opportunity for local improvisations that may press either in novel directions toward a "return" to socialism, [but] the innovation and reversion are responses to unstable environments, at least as much as they are evidence of socialism's legacies or its culture. Postsocialism has represented a period of constant change, so actors [have tended] to strategize within time horizons that are short. (Burawoy and Verdery 1999, 2)

Sustainability and social security have become an intense focus for many families and communities across Central and Inner Asia.

In the post-Soviet period, as socialist infrastructures and securities unraveled and as the demand for cash and goods increased, those without a strong social network or family structure were left highly vulnerable—the elderly, single mothers, young urban workers. Despite impressive and highly visible growth in urban capitals and areas of resource extraction, un(der)employment has persisted elsewhere, particularly in rural areas.[13] Substance abuse and male violence have also been widespread sources of stress for many in Central Asia, as has been the case elsewhere in postsocialist spaces.[14] The fracturing of families due to urban and international labor migration, as well as the stress of what is often semi- or extra-legal labor in bazaars or abroad, also cannot always be solved by the household, but family structure remains ideologically central. In the absence of steady state support (or *boqmoq*) to resolve these dynamics and problems, families and communities must act on a local level to encourage ideologies and practices that provide alternative narratives and trajectories to post-Soviet "chaos" or "abandonment" by the state.[15]

This approach resonates with an ethnographic focus on what anthropologists have termed "well-being," as well as local sense-making in the Central Asian post-Soviet republics. "Well-being" refers not to happiness but to "both the sufferings and the joys of life in relation to the social transactions necessary to be at peace with one's surroundings and the quality of striving for a better future" (Montgomery 2013, 424) and is a category of both meaning and physical, socioeconomic, and spiritual health. Till Mostowlansky has described in the eastern Pamir region of Tajikistan a strong parallel of paternalism undergirding the family and the state; in the absence of strong state support, it is the male head of the family who must step forward to assert a patriarchal "ideology of harmony" (2013, 472). Strategies of well-being range widely—from entrepreneurship and development projects, to negotiations over ethnic and religious identity, to simply sharing food and hospitality.[16] Analyses of these strategies emphasize the ways in which local communities and even the homestead can become the center of an economic and moral order.

In the post-Soviet era the household economy has functioned as a basic form of social security for families (see Werner 1998). But it is not easy. The domestic household economy requires constant labor inputs from all its members to grow and prepare food, care for children, maintain the house, share a car for necessary errands, obtain enough cash for needed goods and services, and to hold regular life-cycle celebrations for family and friends (see Ismailbekova 2014a; Roche and Hohmann 2012). This model exists in smaller towns and villages throughout the region, but it is more difficult to maintain in larger cities, where people are living in smaller apartments or where there are disparities in the income and priorities of family members (e.g., urban relatives who cannot or do not wish to contribute to a household economy but prefer to focus on their nuclear families). Those who have a household group are very fortunate because it can function as a safety net, but many people do not have such support. The strength and legitimacy of the household typically reside at the center of a patriarchal family and its extended relatives, both living and deceased.

As leaders and providers of care for both households and communities, ancestors can occupy a more permanent or reliable position in such a challenging political and economic context, and thus they become critical in the context and ideology of well-being, even when families are fractured by political or economic circumstances. Saulesh Yessenova (2005a, b) describes how the recitation of family genealogy (Kaz: *shezhire*) can become a coping mechanism for urban labor migrants in Kazakhstan, offering a source of legitimacy, pride, and purpose. An appeal to ancestral authority has had a heightened value in the postsocialist era particularly because of the conditions of state control, social and economic exclusion, and the cultural or ethnic nationalism characteristic of newly formed nations, which must also be read in turn as the legacy of Soviet rule.

CULTURAL NATIONALISM

There is no question that the territories and peoples of the former Central Asian republics occupied a very particular space in Russian and Soviet colonial imagination—the exotic (Islamic) "other" in need of modern education and liberation (Brower and Lazzerini 1997; Khalid 1998; Northrop 2004), as well as a vast expanse of land instrumental to the agricultural, industrial, and nuclear infrastructure of the Soviet Union. As Katherine Verdery has urged, "just as postcolonial studies examines the colonial pasts that shaped societies in present-day Africa, Latin America, and Asia, so we might now explore these same processes for Soviet imperialism" (in Hann, Humphrey, and Verdery 2002, 16). In Central Asia, as elsewhere throughout the former Soviet Union, people's contemporary understandings of everything from ethnic identity to political power are undergirded by the legacy of Russian ideological imperialism and the inequitable reformation of Soviet economic structure.

In the early Soviet system, communist leaders and activists were tasked with an ideological and practical mandate: from the existing structure of the former Russian Empire, they were to create a new multinational state. That project contained many fundamental contradictions and impossibilities. "Nations" or "peoples" were to be identified and celebrated but also taught to speak Russian and to read Russian literature (see İğmen 2012). The nations were to be semi-autonomous but also to operate firmly within the centralized communist hierarchy, with its pinnacle in Moscow. All the "peoples" were also to be liberated from any "traditional" systems of oppression, to be educated in "Soviet culture" (see Grant 1995), and to participate in the state redistributive economy (within which no single nation except perhaps Russia was individually sustainable). From an ideological, economic, and political perspective, Soviet intervention in Central Asia was statist but also colonial. While national cultures were celebrated, they were made functionally dependent on the broader Soviet system, what Francine Hirsch (2005, 14) has called "double assimilation." Each new Soviet republic became a container for its titular nationality, and all were ultimately to be "national in form, socialist in content."[17]

Soviet nationalities policies had obvious and major ramifications in the areas of religion and culture. In Central Asia, the policies meant that, despite early cooperation with modernist Islamic leaders (Khalid 1998), by the time of the purges Soviet Central Asian officials were actively targeting religious leaders and places of worship and implementing the *hujum* (the antiveiling campaign targeting women).[18] By the 1960s, the Central Asian nations also included an institutionalized state Islam, in order to promote a "soft Sunnism" as normative (Khalid 2007). The Soviet culture ministry helped develop and promote "national" styles of music, song, and poetry (see Hirsch 2005) that celebrated local "cultural folklore" while at the same time promoting a modernist Russian-language education and academies of arts, literature, and sciences.[19] Genealogy itself became a tool of nationality creation and politics, in Turkmenistan, for example (Edgar 2004). All of these phenomena helped to shape (and maintain) conceptions of cultural and ethnic identity in the broader context of Russian cultural hegemony; in Kazakhstan, this hegemony also flew in the face of what was in fact a highly pluralistic, multiethnic state. But by the end of the Soviet period, ideologies of "nationality" were contributing to the performative and political dimensions of ethnic nationalism, and they have been actively reclaimed in the post-Soviet period as the cultural face of new nations.[20]

Soviet Russian incursion to Central Asia was multilayered and caused extreme damage to the steppe environment. A number of projects caused particularly egregious damage, including the early Soviet collectivization of nomadic Kazakh and Kyrgyz peoples onto farms. Irrigation projects designed to grow crops in the steppe environment (as opposed to using the steppe for grazing and herding activities) created a water crisis and drained the Aral Sea, resulting in ecological disaster in that region. Northern Kazakhstan housed the Soviet nuclear testing zone (known as the Polygon in Russian), irradiating a massive area; to this day many people in the region suffer from cancer and other related illnesses. Compounding these issues is the lingering sadness over lives lost during the Stalinist purges as well as in the Great War (World War II). Today Kazakhstan has a narrative of tragedy and depression surrounding Soviet history, and this narrative emerged as one of the early faces of ecological ethnic nationalism in the post-Soviet period, under well-known leaders such as Olzhas Suleimenov (see Laitin 1998; Olcott 1995).

In Kazakhstan, in addition to general resentment over the fate of millions of Kazakh lives lost to famine, exile, and war over a century, there is also a clear contemporary moment in the "awakening" of a *Kazakh* identity as read against Soviet Russia: the events of December 1986. Those events, known simply as Zheltoksan (December), also clearly marked the beginning of the end of the Soviet Union in Kazakhstan. Then–Soviet general secretary Mikhail Gorbachev replaced Dinmukhamed Kunayev, who was First Secretary of Kazakhstan's Communist Party, with a Russian, Gennady Kolbin. This move represented a direct break with Soviet policy and tradition, specifically, the idea that the head of each republic should be of that republic's titular nationality. Kazakhs were outraged, and thousands joined a large student protest in the central squares in the cities of Almaty, Taldykorgan, Shimkent, and Karaganda. For three days (16–19 December), protesters clashed with police special forces. In addition to immediately arresting and jailing hundreds of citizens, police continued to hunt, interrogate, and imprison people for months after the protest had ended, as the police had filmed all those present at the demonstrations.[21]

The events unleashed waves of bad sentiment between ethnic Kazakhs and Russian leadership (which of course translated to interethnic conflict on the ground). The Kazakhstani government was trapped somewhere in between, wishing to ameliorate Kazakh concerns but reluctant to move toward complete autonomy. Kolbin was eventually replaced as First Secretary by Nursultan Nazarbayev, who assumed the presidency after independence on 16 December 1991, in a blatantly symbolic move meant to link Zheltoksan directly to national independence. Zheltoksan, not surprisingly, is an episode consistently invoked in popular nationalist discourse as the last egregious act of the Soviet Union against the Kazakh people. In the years following the December events, active efforts among poets, artists, musicians, and supportive cultural producers began to revamp traditions seen as particularly "Kazakh," to reclaim their pre-Soviet (and even pre-Russian) glory. Government, too, began to propel that activity in its promotion of pro-Kazakh natalist policies and a massive Kazakh repatriation program.[22]

However, Kazakh nationalism has run counter to competing internationalist visions and realities for the country over recent decades. Despite extensive pageantry at the national level, the state has provided little sustained or systemic support for Kazakh language and culture, leaving its citizens with a certain paradox: at the state level, Kazakh culture is celebrated in theory but not always in practice. Thus, when one looks at forms of culture and historical imagination that have been "nationalized" (such as ancestral figures, narratives, poets, music, and dance), it might seem that these forms are largely the products of state retraditionalization projects (as well as Soviet ideological projects). However, the argument of this book is that these cultural strategies are necessary and successful at the state level because they call upon and resonate with forms of pride and belonging that already exist in many different ways for people and communities struggling to make sense of political change and identity in the present.

Since Kazakhstan achieved independence in 1991, its state government has not been consistently providing for its citizens in terms of political integration, economic opportunity, or social welfare. As a result, people are increasingly turning to broader alternative cultural geographies and conceptions of leadership and care. In particular, ancestors have emerged as a powerful dialogic trope serving to unify and orient families and communities, as well as nations. At regional and local levels, many leaders are very actively involved in building, promoting, and inhabiting a new nationalized ancestral landscape that state funds have also sometimes helped to build and sponsor. The spiritual guidance of ancestors in the physical geography of the steppe, together with the practical and legal guidance of community elders (see Beyer 2010) fashions a cultural, historical, and political world that overlaps—but is not coterminous—with the nation-state of Kazakhstan.

THE STORY OF ONE FAMILY

Throughout my years of research in Kazakhstan, I was privileged to live with several Kazakh families in different areas across the country. For those families, as well as for most of my friends and colleagues, it was more comfortable for them to think of me doing research about Kazakh "culture," rather than "politics." While the category of "culture" is an enduring one and a source of pride, in general "politics" was perceived by all those around me as dirty—corrupt, shifting, and unstable. Without exception, my Kazakhstani families, friends, and colleagues tried to limit their interaction with and exposure to government offices and to organize their household economies and personal security through a network of social ties instead. While all citizens have to interact with bureaucratic offices at some stages of life, particularly for employment or travel, most people try diligently to avoid other spheres of governance perceived as the most dangerous: police and the judicial system.

I should note that of the four families with whom I lived for the longest periods of time in completely different regions of the country, *all* of them contained one (young, male) officer of the law, but nonetheless all of them were quite nervous about police, border customs, and the legal system in general, as they saw these realms as highly corrupt. These families were low- to middle-income multigenerational households in which grandparents, their children, and their sons' wives, as well as grandchildren, lived together and in which grown children had jobs. If the grandparents were still young enough, they worked as well. Families shared responsibility for the household and for child care. I was staying with one of these families during a politically contentious period of national elections, one in which an opposition leader was murdered in a large city far away from our small town.[23] Because the incident was highly relevant to my work at the time, I wanted to stay in touch with my friends in the city, to find out what was happening day to day. I had limited cell-phone reception and so at night would stand outside on tiptoe by the backyard fence, in the one spot where there was enough coverage to make a call.

Several of my friends and colleagues had personally known the murdered opposition leader, so the period following his death was intense in that way, as well as being a national tragedy. One friend in particular was very upset, so I suggested that she leave the city and come out to our smaller town to stay with my host family for a while, until things calmed down. She agreed that it might be best, so I went to check with my hosts. In general, it is both a great stereotype and a great truth that Kazakhs and other Inner Asians are incredibly hospitable, and they welcome guests. In this case, however, when I explained the circumstances, my family became very quiet. The kind grandfather, who had never really said much in my presence to this point, finally leaned forward over the living room table to tell me that this was not a good idea. He was adamant that we could not bring politics into their safe homestead, explaining that outsiders do not always understand how things work. He gave me several examples, including that of a man at his work who had apparently written an editorial piece for the newspaper that was critical of a local politician and had subsequently disappeared. "We still don't know what happened to him," said Grandpa. My friend would definitely not be allowed to visit.

I realized that there were other signs of my hosts' suspicion and discomfort, to which I should previously have paid more attention because those signs would have led me to understand the family's perspective. That family, who lived in a multiethnic residential area of private homes (rather than block apartments), also worried sometimes about their neighbors, in particular one woman who watched her neighbors for extra economic activity and reported them to the local tax police. For that reason, I was never allowed to mention that I contributed financially to my family's household economy—it was very important to them that I was seen only as a guest. They had saved up enough money to buy their youngest son a car, so that he could help the family with transportation, but were often too nervous that he would be stopped by the local police to let him drive anywhere at all (they considered traffic cops to be tied to organized crime syndicates). I knew all of this but had nonetheless acted in a selfish and cavalier manner. I was completely ashamed. I had not considered their sensitivities and had invited a guest without their approval, putting them in the incredibly awkward position of having to refuse hospitality they might otherwise have been willing to give. I felt horrible and apologized at length, but the incident introduced a slight tension in our household that did not go away.

In order to help make up for my mistake, I tried to support my family in other ways. The daughter of the family was my own age, in her late twenties—as yet unmarried but hoping to wed her boyfriend for love, though he was not in a strong financial position and had an estranged first wife. The youngest son had gotten into trouble with his parents for sneaking out, hanging around with a girl they did not approve of, and even sometimes having beer (the family were nondrinkers). When the grandparents decided it was best for their children to go participate in a local healing group to help solve (or prevent) problems, I went with them as well. The leaders of this group, which was called Ak Zhol (White Way), were mostly women, and they ran their organization out of a house in my family's neighborhood. The point of the group was to encourage active adherence to Kazakh ancestors as part of being a good Muslim, to encourage respect for male leaders within families, and to discourage the use of alcohol and drugs. I went with my family's daughter and youngest son to meet the group on a day they were receiving new visitors for introductory sessions.

When we arrived at the crowded house, we removed our shoes and entered a large interior room, joining a line of people moving forward to pray at a low shrine, which housed a Koran, a small dish for coins, and a colorful laminated sheet of instructions in Kazakh telling us to bow three times, hold a wish in our heart, say a short prayer (words provided), and if desired, put a few coins as alms in the dish. I did all this, then sat with my family against the back wall of the room, eyes carefully lowered. We were waiting to have our fortunes told through the channeling of the ancestors. On the other side of the room, there were active healing sessions happening with a healer, who symbolically used the Kazakh *kamcha* (horse whip) to beat evil spirits and sickness out of his patient's body.[24]

When one of the group leaders came in to greet us, my host sister explained that I was an anthropologist and that I had come to study the Kazakh poetry tradition *aitys* (described at length in chapter four). She replied in Russian, "Klassno!" (cool). She was younger than I but very clearly in complete control of the situation. She explained that she would take the first step of the center with me, telling me my diagnostic fortune through bata, to see what areas of my body or life needed further attention and care. As she was going to be channeling the words of the ancestors (Kaz: *ata-babalar*) in a semitrance state, there was a scribe—another woman, who sat to the side against the wall with large journal and a pen, ready to record. They would then together read and interpret what had been said. Here the term "ancestors" refers to a cultural amalgam, a general category. I personally cannot claim any Kazakh genealogy, but here the point was that I was being addressed by *those Kazakhs who have come before* and who embody the wisdom of Kazakh "family" in its broadest historical sense, even for a stranger.

The channeled bata, the words coming through the body of this female leader, came out loud and intense. The blessing lasted many minutes, blowing forth in a heavily cadenced stream of rhyming lines. Because of the heavy repetition and volume, and because as a listener you are required to kneel, to cast your eyes down, and to hold your hands up in prayer, the experience is like being pushed by words—it is a bodily listening. When she finished, the two women read back through what had been said and interpreted it to me. I was welcomed by the ancestors, they said, who were pleased by my interest in Kazakh poetry and who would facilitate my research. They noted several dates and numbers that were significant for me, as well as a few past life events that were somewhat accurate or relatable. My channeler said that I understand people well, that it is a gift. Whether this was flattery or commentary about my being an ethnographer, she decided that I was ready for the next stage of center activity: pilgrimage.

The following week, my host family helped with the necessary preparations for me, my sister, and younger brother; we were all going to travel together with a large group from the center. We were each to take seven loaves of baked bread to eat and share, seven white cloths (each a square meter) to lay atop burial sites at mausoleums, and to wash in the Muslim fashion in the early morning before leaving home on the day of the pilgrimage. We were all required to cover our heads (scarves for women, hats for men). We returned to the center, where five old sky-blue school buses were waiting for us, a group of some 140 pilgrims. Two or three group leaders came on each bus to act as our chaperones and guides.

On the ride to the first shrine site, after a brief welcome, a male channeler standing in the center of the rocking bus began to deliver a lecture about the best way to comport oneself in this lifetime. Some lessons were straightforward: he urged the group not to drink alcohol, because it sets a terrible example for the younger generation and because it makes it impossible to hold a family together. He then noted that people who drink can't be good citizens. He reminded our group of the great leaders (Kaz: *biler*) of Kazakh history—Aiteke Bi, Tole Bi, Kazibek Bi—the ancestors who were able to form a good government for their people. A *bi* is a judge, a position of judicial authority in society (see V. Martin 2001). Historical bi figures are widely incorporated in the new "national" history, considered to be cultural heroes, and featured in the new nationalizing canon of historical identity: for example, streets have been renamed after them in many cities, and anniversaries of their passing are celebrated. In the context of pilgrimage, the bis were invoked in order to establish a sense of cultural rules or norms created by a Kazakh authority. (I think here "citizen" is a good metaphor for proper cultural and moral comportment, as well as for Kazakh sovereignty.) These realms—of political and cultural belonging—were very much conflated on our tour that day, during which we actively sought the ancestors' guidance and blessing.

On the pilgrimage tour we visited seven shrine mausoleums in and around town. At each, we circled the shrine and removed our shoes to enter and pray together with a shrine caretaker, who could recite a *sure* from the Koran. We left our white cloths at the shrine or tied them to trees around the sites. One site was next to a natural spring, where we filled plastic bottles with holy water to bring home to our families. At the three sites with an outdoor assembly space, we crowded together on benches to hear center leaders deliver the words of the ancestors to particular members of the group, called out by name. Each individual was called at least once over the course of the day. These bata were done one after the other, channelers taking turns and other center members monitoring our prayer stance to ensure that it was correct for receiving these words. During bata sessions we were supposed to keep our head bowed, hands up in prayer, arms away from body, and feet planted on the ground. I was reprimanded twice, for letting my arms fall and for crossing my ankles. By the end of the day, my back and shoulders ached.

Pilgrimage is one step or stage in a process of commitment and transformation at the center; after this, people continue to come to weekly healing sessions, during which problem regions of the body and psyche are identified and a corresponding cure is administered. A mantra of the center was that the totality of their message, about how to live and how to follow a righteous path in life, was simply too complicated to convey in less than several months.[25] Pilgrimage and healing were each essential aspects of the journey, each guided by the words of the ancestors, actively embodied in the present. At the center, prayer, bata, and conversation were all spaces in which ancestors are dialogically present. Ultimately, the goal is to attain a pure heart, in order to strengthen families and communities. Scared by the broader political environment but desiring a strong familial center and purpose, my own host family was very much attracted to this mode of interacting; the worldview espoused by the center made sense to them as a way to cope with their at times uncertain world. It was also something they could share and teach me, which sparked my own interest and commitment to the topics that have grown into this book.

In her study of the Naqshbandi Sufi shrine pilgrimage in Pakistan, Pnina Werbner (1996, 309) notes that "the mapping of differential 'knowledges' onto culturally constructed space is a commonsensical discursive tendency, deployed not only by anthropologists but by the people we study, to define topographies of good and evil, truth and falsity." In the case of Kazakhstan, the cultural topography must be made so as to claim Kazakh bodies as the most valuable—not only the living but also those who have passed, those quite literally interred in shrines everywhere, those metaphorical grandmothers and grandfathers whose invocation comes in words. Their words can make the present more possible for the living, for those trying to cope with a variety of political, economic, and new social realities from day to day. Ancestors are guides and exemplars, moral pillars—different from the "corrupt" officials and forms of governance people experience from the state. An ancestral worldview becomes not only alternative to the state but actually a dialogic ground of criticism and confrontation: what would the heroic leaders of times past think of leaders today?

DIALOGIC LEADERSHIP

In the second half of this book I analyze extended examples from aitys, the oral performative tradition in Kazakhstan (or *aitysh*, in Kyrgyzstan).[26] In aitys, certain ancestral figures are commonly referenced in verse. Coming from the verb *aitysu* (to speak to each other), aitys is a verbal duel between two poets performed live before an audience. In this performance, the poets accompany their song, ideally improvised, by playing the *dombyra*.[27] This tradition also exists among Kazakhs in Mongolia and China.[28] There have been efforts among high-level cultural organizers to encourage international meetings and performances incorporating the dombyra. Poets speak as and for their lineages of kinship and learning, as well as their regions of origin. Thus, many cultural and historical voices are layered within each performance; ultimately, poets within the tradition of aitys speak as and for the "Kazakh people" (Kaz: *yel*) as a totality. More specifically, poets claim to voice the "truth of the people" to public audiences and to seated government leaders. This truth often takes the form of commentary and news sharing about national and regional events and ongoing problems in the country.

Aitys poets have powerful elite sponsors who tend to be Kazakh nationalists using the celebration of Kazakh language and culture as a platform from which to critique contemporary problems. Poets and sponsors alike consistently invoke a mythic Kazakh past in which deeply respected poets traveled widely, entertaining throughout the khanate, then returning to report to the khan, in poetry and song, about the condition of his people. While the poet's words might anger the khan, the poet was not directly responsible for what was said, as the messenger simply voices the sentiments of other Kazakhs. Most poets consider their membership in this oral tradition today to be a gift of God and of the ancestors, and they believe that their talent is embodied in their genealogy. Talking to me about their experiences as contemporary poets, many explain that they feel compelled to perform, feel a duty to help educate Kazakhs about their language, culture, and history, and have a duty to provide sociopolitical commentary about present conditions.

The aitys tradition presents an alternative model of leadership to the uncaring and autocratic state government. Poets' performances and their more successful relationships with sponsors invoke and enact a dialogic leadership in which the people can voice their concerns and in which leaders are present and responsive. In this sphere, "the people" are Goffman's (1981, 144) principal figure, a unified "someone whose position is established by the words that are spoken, someone whose beliefs have been told, someone who is committed to what the words say." The principal figure cannot be reduced to any one set of participants in the tradition (ancestors, poets, audiences, cultural organizers, sponsors); rather, all these together contribute continually toward the figure. The principal is someone who is always coming into being. Over time, the principal figure of aitys is engaged with government officials as an "addressed recipient" (1981, 133) in a conversation that thousands of people can be verified to have heard, a conversation with a thousand "shadows" (Irvine 1996).

One consistent trope of performances is the invocation of both mythic history and famous Kazakh ancestors. In this performative context, the mythic ground of just and sovereign rule lies in the great khanates of the past. The warriors and leaders most strongly associated with Kazakh self-determination are described and celebrated, often within the broader context of nationalist holidays and anniversaries. But at the same time, the greatness of those heroes' achievements and leadership becomes the standard by which contemporary leaders—at the local, regional, and national level—are negatively judged, for their failure to live up to the legacy of the past. Aitys poetry is a prominent public space in which a conversation with the ancestors performatively becomes a vehicle of cultural expression and sociopolitical critique (see Dubuisson 2009, 2010). In this genre of performance, forms of dialoguing with ancestors become a mode of reflecting on the patriotism of the present: what can and should be the nature of communication and accountability between leaders and their people?

Cultural performance is one way in which expression organizes experience, how we come to see and know ourselves; it is an "explanation of life itself" (Turner 1982). In their study of cultural performances (like the oral tradition of aitys) anthropologists have emphasized the spaces of exception that these "framed" encounters necessarily create, where social mores are revealed, held suspended, and either reinvigorated or challenged (see Conquergood 1998).[29] These spaces allow flexibility and change in the social order and become vehicles for the emergence of new or alternate critical "voices" in culture (see Fabian 1990). Culture itself is dialogic, requiring continual collusion in social interaction (Tedlock and Mannheim 1995). Thus, even in routinized traditions, cultural performances are emergent and therefore unpredictable: there is always both a powerful potential and the threat of complete failure. Cultural performance becomes an opening and a center for conversation and negotiation over moral understanding (and in turn for ethnography itself; see Conquergood 1982, quoted in Madison 2012).

In the sphere of aitys, a dialogue over legitimate governance is threatened within a complicated political economy of sponsorship; powerful and wealthy patrons may overpower (or literally "buy") the voice of poets for their own interests. A successful aitys is therefore one in which poets and patrons have mutual and balanced concerns and in which a dialogue is not foreclosed (Dubuisson 2014).

What is also clearly demonstrated not only in poets' performances but also in their lived relationship with their sponsors is that dialogue itself in turn becomes a basic model for leadership and good governance. In chapter four I examine three different sponsorship stories: three different politicians negotiate a relationship with aitys poets and cultural organizers in order to enhance their own prestige and leadership with the historical authority of oral tradition. Their sponsorship, in turn, provides a backbone and political legitimacy to the aitys tradition and its contemporary communities. These relationships constitute a form of dialogic authority and are an example of the patronage politics highly characteristic of Inner Asia, a politics of mutual accountability, cooperation, and respect.[30]

Qualities of care and leadership are paramount in a mythic retelling of the past, specifically, the great and lawful rule of khans, the sage advice of judges (Kaz: *biler*), and the heroism of warriors (Kaz: *batyrlar*) in the steppe. Rhetorically, that great past becomes a legitimate ground from which to judge the present and to condemn modern leaders for their failure to live up to the glorious precedent of their genealogical forebears. The uncertainty, precariousness, or perceived "corruptness" of the present is often contrasted negatively to an idealized cultural past where law was strong, leaders were caring, and the blessing of the elders was enough to help Kazakh warriors (Kaz: *batyr*) defeat their worst enemies. These stories tend also to be part of the state nationalizing narratives emerging through the Soviet and post-Soviet periods; part of my purpose is to understand why and how such a rhetorical strategy is so effective at both a personal and national level in a particular political, cultural, and historical environment.

I wish to underscore the performative potential of language and oral tradition in general—not only as my own topic or method but also as a political project in the world. This book is structured telescopically, describing the contexts in which conversations with ancestors occur: from the highly personal and immediate contexts of bata-giving within family relationships, to the more general forms of bata-giving and miracle-storytelling practices at shrines, to the very public performance of poetry and politics in a traditional sense. These are all moments in which ancestors dialogically come to be in the world in a "participatory politics" (Wedeen 2008) both within and beyond the boundaries of the nation-state in Kazakhstan.

ONE

BATA AND BLESSING

SALTANAT: It is said, "Without bata, the people cannot grow . . ." because in any case, you need [it]. Bata is the blessing of an older person, of a respected person—they give you their blessing. And I think [that] it is forbidden, [to be] without bata, it means you will not be fortunate. I consider this to be amazing! It is wonderful—this is the education of the young generation, the upbringing of a person.

"THIS IS THE EDUCATION, THE UPBRINGING OF A PERSON"

This chapter is based on a series of long conversations I had with my host family and friends in the field one summer late in my fieldwork and in preparation for writing this book. I had come to the point where I felt like I had many pieces of some kind of puzzle but lacked some kind of key to truly understand it all, a key that I sensed, based on years of previous fieldwork, might be *bata*. The word *bata* refers to a wish-blessing, which is ideally given by an older respected family member to a younger one. It is received by the "washing" of the hands over the face, as in the *aumin* of a Muslim prayer. As I will describe here, bata is a small act-in-the-world, a ritual that occurs at every major life-cycle event and ceremony for most Kazakh and Kyrghyz people.[1] It is also an ordinary and extraordinary occurrence in many other frameworks and contexts. Bata, which can range from a wish of a few words to an extended, poemlike version, is so ubiquitous that it acquires a mild invisibility, a subconscious and natural presence in the routines of life and family. It is so commonplace, in fact, that when I began my last period of fieldwork specifically on this topic, the people with whom I lived and worked initially had some trouble isolating a definition of what bata *is*. "It is a wish, a blessing." These words were repeated again and again. In the end, it was much easier for people to simply narrate meaningful family events from real life, because there was sure to be a bata in the story.

Older generations are responsible for the moral upbringing of younger generations. Each bata, each wish, is about the past and the future: each bata is about not only the life of an individual person but also the cultural connections many people share together over time. Receiving the blessing of bata in different contexts is highly desirable because doing so is an honor both for a person and for his or her whole family. Bata saturates the texture of family life and ritual, and going through the life cycle without bata is somewhat unthinkable. Certain individuals become known for their ability to say bata particularly well, and others may make a special request that they give their blessing on particular occasions. It is considered good luck to receive the bata of a respected elder or community leader.

From a linguistic perspective, bata in the grammar of Turkic languages takes the third-person imperative, roughly equivalent to "Let it be," or "May it be so." There are many sources or examples of bata in daily life; one may remember the phrasing of an older relative, one may compose bata extemporaneously in a particular circumstance, and/or one may rely on formulaic bata found in a multitude of publications on Kazakh "custom and tradition," ranging from academic encyclopedias to small booklets for sale at the book kiosks often located near sacred sites such as mosques and shrines in various cities and towns around Central Asia. Over the course of this research I compiled a small collection of these booklets, which are called Holy Bata (Kaz: *ak bata*).[2] These booklets each begin with a brief definition of bata as ancestors' wishes, and some explain how bata should be uttered and received, somewhat like a prayer. All of these little guides give sample texts of bata that should be said for specific situations, events, or purposes, ranging from the daily blessing of a meal (Kaz: *askha bata*) to large, shared life-cycle celebrations (Kaz: *toi*). For example,

Уа, Жаратқан, жарылқа,	O Creator, benefaction,
Бақ-дәулетін аумас қыл	Make their happiness [and] wealth never-decreasing
Жарылқағанмен жалғас қыл!	Make their benefaction never-ending
Ала ауызды алыс қыл,	Take foes far away
Қор қалғаннан алыс қыл!	Take unhappy ones far away
Ниеттері ақ болсын,	May [their] wishes be white [blessed]
Бейнеттері пәк болсын,	May [their] labor be honorable,
Мұраттарын асыл қыл!	Make their goals most valuable!
Қолқасын шаң қаррасын,	May their requests be heard,
Жүрген жерін жасыл қыл!	Make the earth [they] walk be green!
Аумин.	Amen.[3]

Most simple bata consist of good wishes for family members and wishes for health and happiness and a life without poverty or enemies. During my fieldwork collecting this material, I lived with a Kazakh family, and my stay coincided with the holy period of Ramadan. During that time, children from around our neighborhood would come as "carolers" in the evenings as it turned dark outside, to sing the song "Zhai Ramazan" in exchange for candies. One evening our family was sitting outside, and when the carolers came I was ushered over to listen to them. "Say it again, say it again so she can hear, say it well!" the grandmother of our family urged the kids. "Let's go, let's go!" said her husband, who was cradling their baby grandson. Three small boys stood outside our door, shuffling their feet. One by one, encouraged by Grandma and Grandpa, they rushed through their words—each of them had memorized a short bata, which they offered after their song:

Бата бата батасы	Bata bata bata
Осы үйдің атасы	The grandfather of this house
Кораннының құтты болсын	May your Koran be fulfilled[4]
Шараңыз иманды болсын	May your efforts be successful
Бүгүн дана балаңыз	Today your ingenious child
Жүзге толған шал болсын	May he live to be a hundred years old
Аумин.	Amen.

The last boy to speak was the eldest, but he became a bit nervous in the middle of his bata. He stopped abruptly and said a rather elaborate "Amen," washing his face with grave seriousness. Grandma and Grandpa and I laughed and congratulated them. We watched the boys walk off in the dusk before we reentered the homestead.[5] The daughter of the family, sitting with her husband in the cool evening, smilingly explained to me that after they sang, the kids in their neighborhood didn't expect just sweets but also coins from their audiences. After receiving this small payment, they also offered bata. My host family enjoyed this tradition, joking that if the same kids came every night, perhaps it wasn't right to give them coins *every* time.

As was impressed upon me at length over the course of my research and learning about bata, while these wishes may sometimes seem general in their wording, each of them is actually given within a specific context or occasion and is addressed to a set of listeners, some or all of whom must then receive bata. Bata is something spoken but also something given (Kaz: *bata beru*); it is both heard and taken in as a gift or blessing by its recipient.[6] The most simple example is perhaps in the wishes given to someone who is about to take a trip or journey, which may be just two words, "Жолың болсын," meaning, "May your road be" (open, free of trouble). In the academic and popular collections and guidebooks about bata available in Kazakhstan today (as well as a wealth of samples and instructions available online) there are examples of longer wishes given on specific occasions or circumstances, such as the various celebrations marking the cultural life cycle of a person.

From birth to first steps, to school, army service, and marriage, every change in a young person's growth and social status will be marked by bata. Wishes may also be offered to their parents and grandparents on these occasions, to emphasize the familial nature of a person's growth and to congratulate older relatives for teaching their children correctly. One schoolbook reference called these "words to encourage and caution."⁷ Each bata represents not only a wish but also an instruction or guidepost for those who hear it, a reminder of what a person and family should be considering at certain times of life. It is in this sense, then, that the grandmother of our family, Saltanat, offered her opinion of bata, the words that open this chapter. The bata tradition is a mechanism whereby respected family elders can train younger generations how to become a proper cultural person; it is a moment to teach, protect, and wish well.

In a conversation Saltanat and I had with another friend of the family, Meiramgul, the two women together emphasize this point:

> SALTANAT: Then any bata goes in parallel with the upbringing of a person.
> MEIRAMGUL: Exactly, exactly.
> SALTANAT: It brings a person up. Education begins with the young ones; they are waiting for someone to tell them [to author]: You see? This goes parallel . . .
> MEIRAMGUL: This bata, it is connected—it acts as the first key, with education.
> AUTHOR: Mm!
> MEIRAMGUL: You could say that education, it is the truest key, uh-huh. But in order for any step, to advance without stepping wrongly, it won't be expressed like that. Express it: "you should do it like this," so that each person [becomes] a little more conscious, a little more understanding. He's already *listening*. From this, he should walk with a different step.⁸

Here the women explain to me the concept of upbringing (*tærbiye*), which refers to the life lessons given within and by one's family. In the cyclical celebration of the life cycle of individuals and families, bata is a regular feature whereby elders can impart wisdom and thereby bless younger persons, who are still coming-into-being in a social sense. All three women featured in this chapter (Saltanat, Meiramgul, and Gaukhar) consider that bata is critical in order for a person (as Meiramgul says above) to take the "right steps" in life in a metaphoric sense. Bata is a part of life-training.

CONTEXTS OF BATA

Early in my fieldwork period, I sat down with my friend Dina and her mother, Saltanat, at the kitchen table to talk about my project. Dina had told me that her mom was quite knowledgeable and had her own ideas about bata and its significance, so we began with an informal conversation about that. Normally confident and assertive, Saltanat quickly disclaimed any expertise, and so the interaction became a three-way one, as Dina gently prompted and encouraged her mother to take charge. Dina was chopping vegetables, helping her sister-in-law with the day's cooking. Beyond the fact that Saltanat for the duration of our talk was not doing some kind of domestic task, the scenario was a typical scene at home—women together in the living space working, while the baby son of Saltanat's daughter-in-law played in his chair. Every baby is wonderful, but this baby was particularly wonderful: a plump, happy being whose smile lit his entire face on a regular basis. In this household with its normal share of familial tension, the baby was a constant peacemaker, and everyone loved to be around him. His gurgles and coos punctuated our conversations, as Dina and Saltanat explained to me how one elder can give bata to an assembled group of family and guests, a very common context.

It is one of the greatest stereotypes and truths that Inner Asian societies are extremely hospitable and that the hosting of regular and lavish life-cycle events and feasts is one fundamental way in which each family performs, maintains, and expands its reputation and social standing and those of its immediate community. The figure of the "guest" is a deep-seated cultural value, and in keeping with the traditions of a nomadic ancestry and heritage, the most sacred place in the family home is the innermost one reserved for guests (Kaz: *tør*). Families keep careful track of their hosting and guesting responsibilities, and indeed much of the shared household's resources will be put toward the neverending cycle of feasting, life-cycle events, and hospitality (Werner 1998; see also Ismailbekova 2014a; and Roche and Hohmann 2012). The family's table, whether at home or at a more elaborate celebration held elsewhere, should be filled to overflowing with foods (breads, fruit, candies, salads) and especially meat that has been prepared specifically for that event. This is how a family demonstrates its generosity and good intentions. This table is the *dastarhan*, which should be blessed.

> SALTANAT: It's wonderful—like all people have for example . . . when at home, you invite guests over, these kinds of events happen . . .
> AUTHOR: Mm?
> SALTANAT: And the most elderly, the most respected person there, they've eaten *beshbarmak*, they've drunk their tea.
> AUTHOR: Yes, <laughs> yes.
> SALTANAT: And then having said "Amen," [they say,] "Give your bata."
> AUTHOR: Mm-hmm?
> SALTANAT: This person spoke, bata.
> AUTHOR: Mm, to everyone.
> SALTANAT: And the whole company.
> AUTHOR: In general.
> SALTANAT: In general, an awful lot of people, not five or six people, but—
> AUTHOR: For the whole company, not to each one.
> SALTANAT: Yes, there were many, a whole company—one bata for everyone.

The many bata a family shares with their relatives and guests is, in my mind, a part of the intense nature of that hospitality. To share time, food, and company together—this social experience should rightly be blessed. In this context, which recurs so many times (at least monthly, to mark some life-cycle celebrations of one's family members), the bata is given by one respected individual and received

FIGURE 1.1. Dastarhan is the special table of foods set for guests and celebrations.

by all together. It is a memory and wish they will all then share. Saltanat and her daughter also explained to me that spirit ancestors are aware of the cooking and baking within a home and are attracted to the smell of freshly baked or fried bread, which is usually prepared in accordance with the Muslim holy week on either Thursday evening or Friday morning, depending on the family. And so by Friday, the Muslim holy day, ancestor spirits will be welcomed and will enter the homes of their living family to help protect and care for them, receiving continued respect and hospitality in the afterlife.

Saltanat and her daughter explain to me that bata must be given within a particular *context* or frame of reference. The giving of bata must be anticipated in some way. There are appropriate phrases offered during particular ritual life-cycle events and ceremonies; bata will be directed toward a particular relational and familial context, such as the birth or first steps of a child. Saltanat and her daughter also give examples of good wishes given when relatives gather to celebrate a child who has graduated from an institute or university or when a family member undertakes an important journey. But bata may also be expropriated from the immediate family, a literal kinship context, and placed in the more general framework of elders giving good wishes within the community. Dina explains that as the figurative grandparents within or of a community, elders can provide a blessing in a more general sense. Depending on the context, elders will alter or change the kind of blessing they give. Thus, bata given within a specific participant framework in one context may be addressed toward—and become part of—the future unfolding of events and relationships created in that original context.

Bata becomes a part of an ongoing future, something embodied as transformative potential. For example, if a person begins a new project, then elders' wishes would be directed toward the success and future growth of that endeavor. As Meiramgul explained at length during her interview, before one takes any "beginning action" in the world, it is necessary to ask for bata:

> MEIRAMGUL: There's this, for example. My sister, they were doing a bit of this, of this trading, and she says, "Before I start off," and she says, "I ask from your ancestor spirit, 'O dear one, like a grandfather, in this way today open the road,' such things . . . I ask several times," she says, "and that day, that day things go well."
>
> SALTANAT: Mmm.
>
> MEIRAMGUL: "Our ancestor spirit, your dear one," like that. And now the oldest brother's wife also trades from home, they hung up these [goods] . . . and before, as if, going somewhere or something, she says, well she bows and asks him, God's helper, so that his guarded way, as they say, was made open.
>
> AUTHOR: Mmm?
>
> MEIRAMGUL: Well, belief, probably. Yes, we, this is probably belief. Like for example now we say everything, when we pray to God, for us this is all connected with the cosmos, this helps us. Probably you just need to *believe*, and everything will succeed.
>
> AUTHOR: Mmm. But bata helps to fulfill [wishes] with the help of God?
>
> MEIRAMGUL: A spirit, a spirit, mm-hmm. With the help of this God.
>
> AUTHOR: Mmm.
>
> MEIRAMGUL: This opens your *eyes*, this already cleans your chest. It clears you.

Meiramgul gave the example of relatives who were beginning new ventures in business and trade and sought out the bata of their elders before they began. Meiramgul and her relatives think that the ventures are much more likely to succeed with the blessing, and just as likely to fail without it, and that receiving bata is a way to open and clean your heart, to be ready for a new beginning. The family and its social community itself could be considered in this sense as a neverending and cyclical "beginning action"; relationships, for example, could be considered a metaphoric journey or project, each of which needs good wishes in order to be strong and successful.

BATA, *NAMAS*, AND TOASTS

In my initial conversation with Saltanat and her daughter, my friend Dina, I asked them specifically about marriages and wedding contexts and about the family's and guests' wishes for young couples being married. I was having trouble distinguishing the notion of bata from other similar forms, such as prayers, or even from the traditional toasts given by guests at most celebrations.

AUTHOR: But for example at a wedding, everyone stands and says a toast, right?
DINA: No. It's different. When a wedding is starting . . .
AUTHOR: It's different. You need to—
SALTANAT: And there, Eva, listen: when [the wedding] is beginning, bata will absolutely be given, but this is when it's *beginning,* opening—
AUTHOR: Which part?
SALTANAT: [When] *zhar,*[9] all of that has happened.
AUTHOR: First.
DINA: The first. There when it *opens.* And before eating, [before] heading to the tables. Before the wedding begins, they say, "Give your [formal] bata."
AUTHOR: And who will give it?
DINA: They want [it] from elders, the eldest. For example, a grandfather or a grandmother. Well, they're the most—
AUTHOR: Mm, most respected, ah.
SALTANAT: Of course if there is a grandmother and a grandfather, then the grandfather gives it. If not—
DINA: If not then the grandmother gives it.
SALTANAT: There. The eldest gives it, or . . . uncle . . . [people like that] give it.
DINA: And they, they go out and say there, they say these wishes there, so that it was like that for you. And after that amen.
AUTHOR: Mm-hmm. Everyone?
DINA and SALTANAT: Everyone says amen.
SALTANAT: And so it will be bata, this part is [bata's] role. This is completely different from prayers in Arabic, and it's different from just good wishes, when they say—
AUTHOR: When they say toasts, mm-hmm.
SALTANAT: Mm-hmm.

Dina and her mother explain that ideally, a grandfather would give bata; in his absence his wife might take over his role, or his eldest son. A bata is not part of the general wedding celebration; rather, it is important to consider that bata *opens* the entire event. A bata is blessing the couple as well as their families, in the very beginning steps of their new relationships.

It is important to clarify that the wedding dinner I mentioned is actually only one event (usually the last) to mark a new marriage. Most Kazakhs (like other Central Asians) wish to symbolically mark the departure of a girl from her natal home (Kaz: *kyz uzatu*), as well as her arrival at her new home and meeting her husband's relatives (Kaz: *betashar*). Depending on family wishes, timing, and financial ability, couples will also create an event out of the official court signing of a marriage document and may also have a religious marriage ceremony. Couples will often do some local sightseeing (monuments and sacred sites) together with their friends on the day before the last wedding dinner and also take photographs or make a wedding video.[10] A wedding can take up to a week, with numerous celebrations, gatherings, events, and rituals. Thus, by the time the extended in-laws and friends have gathered for a final dinner celebration, they have reached the last event, the one marking the end of the wedding and the beginning of a marriage. At this elaborate dinner, the master of ceremonies (Kaz: *tamada*) will ask honored guests to stand and wish the young couple well. The speeches and wishes delivered over the course of the evening are not bata (they do not open the wedding and they take a different linguistic form), although many relatives may embed a short bata in their speeches as well, for example, to conclude their remarks to the couple.

Saltanat actually draws a distinction between bata and other forms of wishes or prayers, like toasts or speeches given at celebrations, or Muslim prayers (*namas*). While I had previously stressed the similarity of the *intent* in these forms, Saltanat emphasized the broader *contexts* in which these traditions take place as being quite distinct. Toasting, for example, most often goes together with contexts in which alcohol is served and is a common practice for many post-Soviet citizens; it could be considered a Russian or Soviet tradition, rather than an indigenous cultural tradition.[11] While many Kazakhs do drink alcohol, the conjunction of celebratory inebriation with bata could be considered uncomfortable, inappropriate, or even wrong. Muslim prayers, on the other hand, being associated with Islamic traditions and contexts, religious teachers, and elders, are considered to be more strictly formal or rule bound. In a nonorthodox Muslim context, namas is offered by someone who "reads the Koran," such as a mullah or religious elder; someone who "says namas" can also be a gloss for an observant Muslim who prays five times daily. While namas prayers can certainly be offered as a form of guidance, they generally appear within a greater panoply of Muslim contexts, an overlapping but different sort of religious geography.

In this sense, the "contexts" of bata are different—seen as something cultural, life-cycle oriented, and communal. But while they are often offered in the way that someone might offer a wise proverb at the right moment, they are also *received* as a prayer, with a Muslim "Aumin" and washing of the face.[12] (Indeed, even when Saltanat quotes bata, she and her daughter also receive the reported bata in this way.) But Saltanat also points out a basic linguistic distinction among these traditions: she notes that namas will be said in Arabic, while bata will always be in Kazakh (or any other indigenous language). Toasts can theoretically be offered in any language, but for Saltanat and her family, in the many celebrations I shared with them, toasts were almost exclusively in Russian. Here, language itself is seen to index one set of cultural associations, particularly between older and younger generations, and to emphasize one possible referential world apart from other possibilities simultaneously existing in a multilingual and multicultural environment.

In Saltanat's opinion, bata is best understood not as a Muslim prayer but rather as a cultural wish, supported by God, for the younger generation. She gives several examples to strengthen her point:

SALTANAT: That is, so this bata, it's totally different.
AUTHOR: Mmm.
SALTANAT: Well, you see, he—Allah—said, "May the life of a two-year-old be long."
AUTHOR: Mm-hmm?
SALTANAT: To a grandchild, so that [he or she] becomes a masterful leader. "May there be many children, may there not be enemies, may you have much strength"—well, there is just so much like this, and afterward they say, "Amen."
DINA: Everybody listens.
SALTANAT: Everyone listens and says "Amen."
AUTHOR: Mm-hmm.

In these examples, Saltanat characterizes bata as God's wish, imparted by elders, to ensure the safety and prosperity of their family. There should be many children in a family, they should grow to become leaders, they should be strong and not face enemies. In listening to her mother explain to me, Dina also emphasizes the reception of the wish: it is not enough that these words are uttered; what is most important is that they be *heard*. In that sense, the physical action of aumin (which was described and enacted over and over again in our conversation) is the bodily recognition of listening and *having heard*. If bata is not taken in by its recipient(s), then the good wish will not come to fruition in the future.

BATA AS COMFORT IN TIMES OF DISTRESS

Bata is given and received, held and embodied. There are several performative aspects or dimensions to its transmission: the enacted relationship between elders and the younger generation, the unity of family in celebration, the transmuted wish oriented toward a clean and successful future. But as a genre, bata also has for many individuals the performative capacity to provide reassurance in times of distress, sadness, or uncertainty. Bata can be experienced in dreams or be recorded and remembered, and in these ways it becomes part of a broader kind of conversation between not only the young and old but the living and those who have passed away. Bata is the discursive connection, a diagnostic tool and memory path essential for coping with the sometimes tragic circumstances of life. In our kitchen conversation about bata, Dina urged her mother to explain this concept to me—that bata wasn't just a symbolic act and that it has functions in life beyond explicit instruction. Dina asked her mother to think of times when bata was given in difficult moments as an active way of wishing in the world and as a source of comfort.

DINA: Mom, also say now, you've talked about the symbolism of bata, the historical symbolism. But now you [should] tell about—
SALTANAT: Mm-hmm.

DINA: For example, take some kind of bata—any, so that, well, like I [told you] that time, when [my husband] came, what kind of bata was given?
SALTANAT: Well now, I don't remember all the details. For example, I, uh
<clears throat>
<long pause>
SALTANAT (to AUTHOR): Such a thing, between us, such a thing happened when Dina was left without a father, he died. At that time, every Thursday, mm-hmm, I baked specially, fried breads. I waited for this mullah, so that he would come and read us namas, so that all, all the neighbors would come, and then after she gave bata—
DINA: Namas separately?
SALTANAT: Yes, yes, yes, yes, yes. There was [something] from the Koran, she read the Koran, read *sure*, and bata, she was already speaking Kazakh. She read Koran in Arabic, the Koran. And . . . these words, for me? For a person. It was *very* good for me.[13]

During the course of our work and relationship, Saltanat mentioned the death of her first husband several times. He was a precocious young man whose intelligence and character were noted by Communist Party leaders in his village. He applied for a job as a mechanic at the regional *sovkhoz* (Soviet state farm); after talking to him for half an hour, the boss decided to put him in charge of the whole place instead. He was hard working and creative. Saltanat, herself a very smart and stubborn character, sometimes mused about their passionate and volatile relationship. He died as a relatively young man, leaving her alone with three young children. His passing unfortunately coincided with the end of the Soviet Union and the socioeconomic upheaval of the early post-Soviet period. Unable to support her children with her job as a teacher and unwilling to ask for financial help from her family, Saltanat began to engage in cross-border trade, and her life changed fundamentally. Her children went to live with her sisters for a period of time, and she worked and traveled regularly; she still trades in the local bazaar.

Saltanat is strong and hard working; she is also highly sensitive. The passing of her first husband marks not only the loss of a man she had once loved, the father of her children, but also the first time that she suddenly faced the future alone. Although she is now happily remarried to a man who is devoted to her well-being, the theme of "being left" is a frequent one for her. She worries about being older and alone, she has general worries about children who abandon their elderly parents, and she bemoans the weakening of intergenerational family ties. She has a particularly difficult relationship with her daughter-in-law, an equally strong and stubborn young woman, which adds to her despair. The research theme of bata was an emotional one for her, because in her own life she experienced these wishes as one way to "warm her heart" or to help heal from difficult times and relationships.

On one occasion, after we had spent about an hour talking about bata, Saltanat went into the kitchen and rummaged about. She came back to the dining room table with a stack of old papers in a plastic bag; it was a bunch of old magazine clippings and recipes, together with Saltanat's mother's own small notebooks containing jotted notes about cooking and making medicinal household remedies. Saltanat flipped to the back of one of the notebooks, where her mother had written a bata:

Аумин деп көтердім	At the word "Amen"
Білегімді	I raised my arms [to receive bata]
Құдай берсын тілегімді	May God grant my wish
Нәсібің зор болсын	May your fate be great
Душпаның жоқ болсын	May you not have enemies
Дастарханың тоқ болсын	May your table be full
һалекеті[14] жоқ болсын	May you not have troubles
Аумин ел тілегің	Amen is wished to your hands
тілегің қабыл болсын	May your wish be fulfilled

Saltanat read this to Dina and me several times, smiling and touching the paper gently. She showed us other things in the box—recipes and magazine clippings—reading us the contents and telling us stories. This activity I likened to looking over a photograph album together, something one does when visiting a family (or joining them as an ethnographer); every family has, usually in their living room armoire, at least a few albums of family photographs. Sharing those images and naming the people in them together is very much part of learning about the family. Touching the pictures, touching the bata, reading and sharing the words and relatives aloud is a way to invoke them in the present, to reconnect. In this way, her mother's blessing became part of our present.

Saltanat found a kindred spirit in our second primary interlocutor—the character or teacher I present here as "Meiramgul," a gentle soul who currently works as a librarian in a local vocational college where Saltanat's husband is an administrator. She has been good friends and colleagues with Saltanat's husband for many years. While Saltanat and I were working on this bata project, it occurred to her husband that Meiramgul could be an excellent source of knowledge, so he set up a semiformal meeting for us in the library at the school and chauffeured us there on the appointed day. We took a small tour of the college grounds, where a team of gardeners was hard at work on the landscaping outside and where small clusters of young students would step forward shyly to greet their head administrator.

We met with Meiramgul in the library, a bright, open space with large windows looking out onto the college's garden, where groundskeeping staff were busy watering. One large part of the room was dominated by rows of metal bookshelves, each of which was decorated with the portrait of a Kazakh hero (one of the poets, writers, or philosophers touted in the Soviet cultural project and/or in the

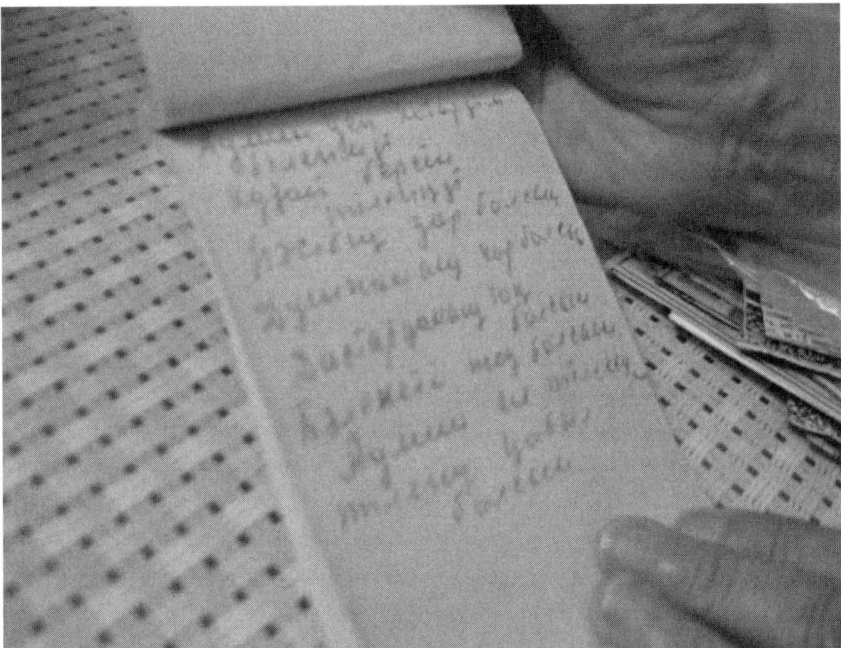

Figure 1.2. Saltanat reads her mother's bata.

post-Soviet project of nationalism) and an inspirational quote from his writings. (Interestingly, there had been a similar project on the small public buses in the town, many of which now also displayed pictures and quotes of Kazakh cultural figures, alongside the many talismans and decorations that bus drivers typically have in their vehicles.) The other side of the room was filled with wooden tables and chairs, and Meiramgul's two young student assistants (both Russian) were energetically cleaning the floor. Toward the far side of the room, behind the card catalog and a wall of metal cabinets, was a space for Meiramgul herself, so that she could have some privacy and drink tea.

Meiramgul looks something like a caricature of a lovely, grandmotherly librarian. Dressed casually in a large purple shirt, leggings, and white wedge sandals, she had her black hair done up in a large neat bun and was wearing glasses on a cord and silver Kazakh-style earrings. She has dark bright eyes and a photogenic smile. Like Saltanat initially, when we began our conversation she expressed some concern over being considered an "expert" about bata, and she encouraged us to look at books and encyclopedias instead, where we could find classifications of bata by occasion, as well as written examples. She mentioned that great warriors (Kaz: *batyrlar*) were given bata by elders before going into battle, and she gave an example from the well-known film *Kyz Zhibek*, in which the hero must receive his father's blessing in order to succeed in love and war. She also told some of the stories of well-known cultural-historical figures of the region where we were living.

But as Dina had encouraged Saltanat, Saltanat now also encouraged Meiramgul, telling her that we were really more interested in her own ideas and experiences. And so she began to talk about her own family.

As Meiramgul talked, Saltanat and I soon realized that Meiramgul's nuclear family story was unfortunately a very sad, heavy one of loss. Her husband had not been a part of the picture in some time, and she had raised their three children on her own. Saltanat's own story obviously converged in these details. Although she said nothing explicitly, she conveyed her sympathy and understanding by listening closely to Meiramgul and touching her hand when the narrative became too difficult. She and I both also responded with reactions of disbelief and grief. When her youngest son was eighteen, he was murdered by other young men involved in street crime. Meiramgul was particularly aggrieved that they had attacked him when he was leaving the mosque after reading namas on a Friday afternoon.

> MEIRAMGUL: And after that. . . . as they say, we had here . . . [my] head was just in shock, it can't be, it can't be.
> SALTANAT: <exhales loudly>
> AUTHOR: Mmm (sadly).

Meiramgul then suffered further when, after his death, her son appeared to her in her dreams, asking for her help to take away the strength of his killers. The Russian word she used, *snit'sia*, does not refer to the agency of the dream toward the dreamer; rather, a dream *is dreamed*. In this particular story, the relationships among the living and the deceased were complicated, because *prior* to her son's death, she had actually gone together with him to a community healer for guidance, to an older man who helped them to read the Koran. Meiramgul explains that she went to see him because she was having hard times and difficulty finding the will to keep going. She blamed her troubles—and her lack of will to carry on—on the presence of an evil or dark ancestor spirit, whom she called Nefrit Ata:

> MEIRAMGUL: Nefrit Ata. He holds [me] like this <demonstrates his grip on her arm>, and yes, when he holds me sometimes I want for some reason, I want to surrender my hand. In life there is all of this, you know? Everybody comes and says, "I can't do it," like that—practically any person. In life I have "black stripes" [dark periods] if it's like that. I want my road—
> AUTHOR: To open the road?
> SALTANAT: To open, uh-huh. I believe them, I want . . . but everybody goes—who hasn't gone! It's like they can reach each other, and to you they say, "You should ask God, but . . . and then everything will be all right." And so we went . . .

Meiramgul and her son had begun to visit the healer to find a way to deal with the negative energy (the "black stripes") Nefrit Ata was bringing to her, challenging her will to carry on. They had been told to visit him seven times, most likely because seven is seen to be a holy number in Islamic theology and therefore seems most significant to those who are culturally Muslim. Meiramgul explains that, on their fifth visit, something strange happened. While they waited for the client before them to finish talking to the elder/healer (she overheard that his family was having financial troubles), her son turned to her and said he'd had a dream (or, a dream was dreamed to him). Nefrit Ata was calling *him*, urging him to follow.

> MEIRAMGUL: [The previous] séance ended, and I told [the healer] about the dream.
> SALTANAT: Mm-hmm.
> MEIRAMGUL: I was scared! This dead man is calling to him and begging, saying, "I want you," now what the heck is this?
> SALTANAT: Mm-hmm.
> MEIRAMGUL: So we, "Come on," [the healer] says, and we go to the living room. A pure open bata. <pauses> There, you see? Already there is bata going on, already.
> AUTHOR: Bata, mm-hmm.

Just as Saltanat had tried to explain to me how she saw the linguistic and contextual differences between bata and other forms similar to prayers, here Meiramgul makes the same clarification, indicating that though they go to pray with the male healer, actually it is also very common to bring gifts of food and candy so as to receive in return the bata blessing of the healer's wife. Saltanat and Meiramgul then together explained to me what it means to seek out someone's fortune-telling or healing bata in this way, that it is given in exchange for gifts of food or candy (preferably handmade), as this exchange marks a new social relationship; it is like a performative miniature of the ultimate sign of hospitality, the full dastarhan as described earlier.

> SALTANAT: They bring there the sweets, cookies, meat, fried breads, you can [bring]—
> MEIRAMGUL: Yes, like that, that kind of thing.
> SALTANAT (to AUTHOR): You can prepare anything. For example, [Meiramgul] cooked and then [she] went to this house and they read Koran there, . . . so it's as if she gave bata, not something else.
> MEIRAMGUL: Mm-hmm.
> SALTANAT: They're gathering for bata.
> AUTHOR (to MEIRAMGUL): This, you gave him? Or the other way around?
> SALTANAT and MEIRAMGUL: No.
> MEIRAMGUL: The host of this house reads prayers and gives us, as they say, [he] asks also for bata, for these good, these good wishes.
> AUTHOR: Mm-hmm. So they went with gifts.
> SALTANAT: Went to pay respect.
> AUTHOR: And then he gave you bata?
> SALTANAT: [When] they got there, a different person read bata, a mullah.

AUTHOR: Aah?

MEIRAMGUL: He gave good wishes for us, so our dreams would be fulfilled.

SALTANAT: The mullah was different, right? The mullah?

MEIRAMGUL: Well, where we went there was no kind of *molda*. An old woman sat—

SALTANAT: Over there, uh-huh.

AUTHOR: Uh-huh.

MEIRAMGUL: A grandmother, his wife sat, she sat and began to speak. And so it began like that, this event.

In this extended conversation, Meiramgul is explaining in some detail what she and her son did in order to understand and possibly counter the negative figure who had entered his dreams, a spirit who had taken a liking to her son and wanted him to follow (into the land of the dead). While "reading the Koran" (saying prayers) together with a mullah would be one normal avenue of recourse, in this case the healer/leader was not a Muslim elder; it was an older woman (his wife) who would read their fortunes using small bones. This fortune-teller warned them that while a man could do this once, a woman would have to do it seven times in order to be equivalent to a male reader. While neither Saltanat nor Meiramgul dispute the potential efficacy of reading the Koran, receiving (or "kneeling") for bata, or even consulting a fortune-teller, in this case the negative energy of the dead man chasing her son prevailed, as he was later actually killed. Meiramgul, in telling her story, and Saltanat, in listening, do not interpret the boy's death as a sign that prayers, bata, or fortunes are ineffective. Rather, they focus on the power of the boy's dream itself, as a vehicle of agency and warning:

MEIRAMGUL: The child had a dream; he asked his mother to share it.

AUTHOR: Mmm, mm.

MEIRAMGUL: And this grandfather is asking him, . . . they asked this old man, turns out he was alive, "Go to him," ah—

SALTANAT: In a dream, this was dreamed.

MEIRAMGUL: In a dream, this was dreamed. Well. And not long after I also learned that, how it turns out he probably wanted to take [the boy] with him.

SALTANAT: To take the boy with him, yes. How many years did he survive?

MEIRAMGUL: I can't . . . a year . . . but not more than a year—

AUTHOR: <whispers> Wow.

MEIRAMGUL: In a year he himself, this person died.

AUTHOR: And this is called revelation?

MEIRAMGUL: Revelation. And we, what is it, we thought this [was], you see, revelation. But in general, that kind of person, it seems he spotted the boy probably, or something, he wanted to bring [the boy] closer to himself.

SALTANAT: How to understand this, Eva?

AUTHOR: Yes, how to understand it.

SALTANAT: First he saw him, this kid, and he . . . uh, to himself—
MEIRAMGUL: He liked him.
SALTANAT: He had a grip on [the boy's] soul.
AUTHOR: Mm.
SALTANAT: You see? It's just like some kind of mysticism! It's on the level of mysticism.
AUTHOR: Mmm.
MEIRAMGUL: I don't know. Sometimes I . . . maybe it really truly is this. My friends also believe that.

In sharing this conversation and story, what I wish to convey is that in the relationship between the worlds of the living and the deceased, dreams become a part of the terrain, and intermediaries may be consulted to change or influence these relationships across spheres. People understand that their good or poor fortune is directly related to particular relationships with the deceased, particularly members of their own family or lineage. This conversation highlights the multiple possible participant frameworks common for people in this community today, what sorts of spiritual elders are sought out, how they operate, and for what purposes. At the same time, understanding and interpreting these visits and experiences become a dialogic process: Meiramgul has spoken about it with her friends, trying to negotiate the meaning of what occurred, the series of events and the loss of her son. Consultation itself becomes an ongoing cycle by which people and families can weigh their status and progress in spiritual worlds, and it serves a fundamental practical and emotional function as a coping strategy in times of uncertainty, loss, and misfortune: it establishes strong positive connections with the living and with the world of the ancestors alike.[15]

Saltanat becomes an active part of Meiramgul's narrative process, reinforcing certain ideas through suggestion and repetition; I did this as well, by characterizing what I was hearing as an example of *ayan* (revelation)—what I understood to be the appearance of an ancestor in a dream. I had heard of this phenomenon only in a positive sense, however, so I was somewhat surprised when Meiramgul readily confirmed it.[16] I understood that, in these dreams, ancestors can come and give some kind of advice or direction to a person, who then is responsible for a certain new course of action to change their state of affairs, as with a job or family. A revelation can thus sometimes be understood as finding one's calling, with the enlightenment delivered by their deceased relative or another popular ancestor. Meiramgul responded more reluctantly to Saltanat's suggestion of "mysticism," however, attributing that belief to her friends, whom she sees as being more observant Muslims than she is. Her Muslim friends get mad at her for not "reading the Koran" (praying) more regularly. But when she is depressed about her son, missing him as she sets the dinner table, daydreaming about having another son, she says that she will always pray:

MEIRAMGUL: [When] I really can't do *any*thing, then three of these lines [that] I learned from the Koran—
SALTANAT: From the Koran.

What Meiramgul refers to here are lines from sure she has memorized; the lines of prayer act for Meiramgul much in the way that bata might: these short phrases are a great source of reassurance for her. Toward the end of our conversation, Saltanat asked if she could see Meiramgul's own collection of bata, contained in a small bag of clippings from the local Kazakh-language newspapers, some of which publish a bata or proverb (like those in a fortune cookie) with each edition. The two women sat at a small wooden student desk there in the library, holding and reading the small pieces of paper. I could not help but be reminded of Saltanat at her own kitchen table, looking over the small papers inscribed with the words her mother had written for her (see fig. 1.2). Just as she kept her mother's bata together with pages from magazines and recipes and the like, Meiramgul also clips pieces from articles she likes and keeps them together with her bata and proverbs; she notes that sometimes journalists too have "special wishes" for their readers. As she combed through the clippings, she talked softly about each one in the collection, even finding some quotes from President Nazarbayev she had liked. Meiramgul was happy to share, as well as to point out which ones she liked best. She repeated her favorite proverbs several times; I asked if she would also write them down for me:

Асыл туған жақсынын	The noble-born good person
Ақыл-ойы кен балан,	[whose] wise thoughts [would be[17]] wide,
Атадан жаман тұғаннын	The person born evil from his grandfather
Ақыл-ойы кем болар.	[whose] wise thoughts [would be] narrow.
Жылы-жылы сөйлесен	If you say [it] warmly-warmly
Жылан ініінен шығады.	A snake comes out from its lair.

Meiramgul explained the meaning of the first proverb: if someone appears on this earth with a good familial core or center, that person's thoughts are then wise, far-reaching. If someone was born from evil, then his or her thoughts would be equally narrow. The second proverb also goes to demonstrate the power of words, the connection between language and the human psyche in the form of moral guidance. As evidenced by the narrative excerpts of our conversation given here, Meiramgul's worldview is one in which the family and ancestors play an active role in the shaping of a person's intellectual and moral consciousness, for better or for worse. Thus, the behavior of a person reflects family and ancestry, and words have a real power in the world. Meiramgul gives the example of negative words, which can wound or hurt; by contrast, bata is her favorite form of positivity, because its words, she says, act more like medicine, to heal. In order to fully explain her point, she quickly finishes narrating the story of her son's death and its aftermath for her family.

Meiramgul's daughter (her son's younger sister) was about to graduate high school and get married at the time of her brother's death, but she could not survive the grief. She also passed away some months later, leaving Meiramgul with only one last son, who lives far away from her. Meiramgul explained that before her children's death, she had worked for a dairy company as a product checker; her job was to check all the company's products for sale at the local bazaar to make sure they were fresh. She said that she and the small team she worked with would put on their uniforms and approach the bazaar with a small amount of dread, because they were regularly harassed and verbally abused by sellers at the bazaar, who were irritated at their meddling. She characterized some of the bazaar workers as an uneducated bunch of people who behaved like animals. Saltanat, a former teacher now working in the bazaar, nodded slowly in acknowledgment and agreed a bit reluctantly, as she has also witnessed unpleasant dynamics in bazaar interactions, and they have caused stress. Once, Meiramgul said, a man threw a bucket of yogurt drink all over her, yelling at her as he did so. She left that job but was fortunate to have found this position in the vocational college library, where she is surrounded by books instead. She says that most of her coworkers here don't really know her background story and that when some of them learn of it they are always shocked and saddened (as were both Saltanat and I).

Meiramgul tried to focus quietly on her job, working in order to cope. She considers herself extremely lucky to have found such a rewarding and peaceful workplace, and she shudders to think what might have happened if she had tried to return to the bazaar after her children's deaths. She worries that she herself would have turned into some kind of angry animal. She considers that God saved her from such a fate and brought her to the library instead, so that she would survive:

> MEIRAMGUL: Just this was the most difficult moment. It seems to me that I, well only these *words*, there, these keys saved me. God probably specially made this protection, brought me [to the library], so that I *lived*.
> AUTHOR: Ye-es, yes, probably.
> MEIRAMGUL: <quietly> So that I lived.
> AUTHOR: Not for nothing.
> MEIRAMGUL: Huh?
> AUTHOR: Not for nothing.
> MEIRAMGUL: Well! This is all fate! All of these—
> AUTHOR: Yes, it is fate.
> SALTANAT: All of it.
> MEIRAMGUL: The fact is that everything gets better.
> AUTHOR: Mm-hmm.
> MEIRAMGUL: So that's what I'm saying. There's strength in these <gestures to her

bata clippings>, strength. I always said, "What difficult days . . ." And after these difficulties, after about six months I came here, I just dried my tears with these . . . what words!

SALTANAT: Mm-hmm.

AUTHOR: Mmm . . .

MEIRAMGUL: And God, this is life.

SALTANAT: Yes, this was strongly said.

AUTHOR: How strongly you said it.

Meiramgul's son was called by a bad ancestor spirit in the world of dreams; in the physical world he was an innocent victim of criminal violence and the everyday reality of the streets. His killers were never brought to justice. As a result of his death, she lost not one but two children. When we met her, it was years after these events, and she told her story somewhat matter-of-factly; Saltanat and I both were deeply impressed by her resilience in the face of such a huge tragedy. She attributes her healing to the fact that she is surrounded by the "words" she loves (books, bata, proverbs, etc.), and she says that she draws strength from these things. She uses the metaphors of medicine that heals or a handkerchief with which she can dry her tears. These metaphors are evidence of the sense of embodiment that bata is meant to impart; just as it is something *given* (as described above), it is also something that is *taken in* and becomes part of the heart and mind of the recipient. Words like these are not only instructional or proverbial; there is a more active relationship between the words and their recipient. Meiramgul talks also about their capacity to soothe and heal.

In her narrative, Meiramgul puts bata together with several other types of "words in the world," which can be in conversations, dreams, or even the local newspaper. These words are part of metaphoric dialogues in which elders or community leaders (living or deceased) are trying to help the living to learn, to cope, and to structure a moral and cultural path (Kaz: *zhol*). These words are part of relationships at many levels: for a person, within a family, or circulating within a community. Kazakhs most often use the metaphor of a path to mean a lifeway or upbringing, the lived result of a proper cultural education.

MORAL COMMUNITY

In their conversations about bata, the women with whom I spoke during my research tend to move fluidly between specific personal experiences and expositions on the poor moral climate of the community or country. That is because the "moral upbringing" at stake is at once individual and cultural. They share a general worry: if younger people are not educated properly about social life, then criminality and disrespect for human life (and the moral authority of the family) will just get worse. For example, respect for elders within a family unit is at once a token of and an analogy for respect for elders in society generally. If individ-

Figure 1.3. Meiramgul's collection of bata, shown here in the library where she works.

uals lose their way, it is because they have not had the proper type of education, of which bata is a necessary part. If a community suffers from a wide range of indignities—from disrespect, drug abuse, and crime, to prostitution and pregnancy out of wedlock—the issues can all be traced to the more fundamental problem: a lack of education about social life, an education that should take place within each family.

Meiramgul compared the cycle of family life to the seasons of the year, saying that there are no "bad" seasons in nature, just different ones; the same goes for Kazakh families. Sometimes there are difficult periods. Saltanat, who herself was having ongoing troubles with her son and daughter-in-law, was quick to laugh and agree:

> MEIRAMGUL: We have a kind of family "winter"—
> SALTANAT: <laughs> Yes!
> MEIRAMGUL: It gets cold.
> SALTANAT: Winter!
> MEIRAMGUL: And then spring enters—there can be bountiful dastarhan in the autumn, right?
> SALTANAT: Yes, [to author] you see? Already such a good example!
> MEIRAMGUL: I'm also happy. This is the nature of life, if you look at it logically, philosophically.

In a strong household, Meiramgul felt, there should be an older person who can lead with bata, inform young members about this kind of emotional cycle, and reassure everyone that "spring" will really return—that if a family is experiencing some kind of trouble or drama, eventually it will pass. As a counterexample, Saltanat gave the example of divorce; she worries that more young people are divorcing now than ever before, because it is seen as an "easy exit" when things in the family become difficult. Rather than expecting perfection, she felt, young people should be warned that things are *not* always easy when living together and that no one should expect family life to be without problems. If young people were prepared (for example, by elders, with bata) for this reality, they could survive it, rather than breaking up the family. Meiramgul agreed that elders can give advice or guidance not by force, but rather with words and by example.

Both Saltanat and Meiramgul, as well as the third woman in this chapter, Gaukhar, whom I introduce below, stressed the importance of bata in the beginning of a relationship between a new mother-in-law and daughter-in-law. This is because the young bride (*kelin*) moves ritually toward her husband's household, leaving behind her natal household. Ideally, a kelin would come to live with her husband's family and take care of her parents-in-law.[18] In all our conversations, the women I talked with mentioned the loss of the "kelin" values for the younger generation, who, in their opinion, no longer respected (patriarchal) traditions. In particular, young kelin were not adjusting to the subordinate position they occupied within their husband's parents' household but were instead trying to do things in their own way. If young brides would just *really listen* to the messages of the bata they receive at the time of marriage, they would realize that they need to accept this new family's style as their own and to learn within that family, doing so more quietly and respectfully. In the words of Saltanat and Meiramgul in the first example of this chapter, young women who did so would take the "new footsteps" of an obedient daughter-in-law.

Listening to the narratives and examples of these three women, and getting to know their own personal stories better, I was struck by the notion that while their *own* marital history certainly did not match these ideals—they had lost husbands to death or divorce and did not stay with their husbands' families nor receive any help from them—they mourned the disaffection of younger kelin.[19] I think this stems equally from a tendency to emphasize or romanticize certain cultural values in the face of change and uncertainty, as well as the recognition that a good relationship with a son and daughter-in-law ensures that parents will be cared for properly in their old age. A bad in-law relationship (among many other possible factors, such as migration or social or legal trouble) directly jeopardizes that possibility. The loss of "proper" relationships within the family or household is seen to correspond directly with the loss of culture in a national sense, the loss of something Kazakh.[20] Saltanat responded in an impassioned way to Meiramgul's list of the traditional family and life-cycle bata:

SALTANAT: You're telling it right, there. In Kazakhstan, at the time of independence, a lot of people said, "If we lived seventy more years like that, we would become *mankurts*."[21]

MEIRAMGUL: Or, a year!

SALTANAT: Because—again I'm repeating—upbringing! Already for Kazakhs and Muslims—a son? He should be, well, respect elders, father and mother. He shouldn't abandon them in their old age, but again already, for example—

MEIRAMGUL: A responsibility.

SALTANAT: Relatives should help each other, although [that does happen] everywhere, of course. But anyway, those sorts of examples. Or for example . . . mm, mm . . .

MEIRAMGUL: Well, there a *lot* of those examples!

SALTANAT: For us, little by little, little by little . . . children have stopped respecting elders. They're not thinking about elders, they're only thinking about themselves or, for example, about their own . . . everyday life. They're not thinking from their soul, well, like that. And step by step, step by step . . . we're losing our own national object. We're losing exactly as Kazakhs.

Both women agreed that, from their perspective, as the sense of obligation between family generations decreases, the very social fabric of Kazakh society begins to unravel. There is a saying for Kazakhs, as the women told me: if you don't support your own mother, it doesn't matter if you go to Mecca ten times, you won't end up in heaven. In this worldview, having a proper sense of respect and responsibility is a cultural duty—it is at once both Kazakh and Muslim.[22] For example, it is considered the duty of a son and his wife to take care of the man's parents in their old age (or more generally, for children to take care of their parents and grandparents). The abandonment of the older generation is described in the women's conversation excerpted here as a disgraceful example of the predicament of the mankurt.[23]

In using this metaphor of the mankurt, a person who has lost his own culture under conditions of cultural colonialism, the women are talking about the breakdown of the cultural unit of the Kazakh family as an outcome of Soviet socialization. However, while they are using the metaphor of cultural forgetting from that explicit historical context, I think the figure of the mankurt in their conversation is not located in any one particular political geography but has become instead a generalized fear that the loss of culture is actually happening on a national scale and that the immediate effect can be seen in soured (or terminated) relationships within each family.

PATH OF THE ANCESTORS

The third woman whose words and ideas I present here, Gaukhar, is a retired teacher and self-styled spiritual healer in the community. She is involved with a movement called Ancestors' Path (Kaz: Ata Zhol), which is active at both the national and community levels in Kazakhstan. Those in the movement are proactively promoting a return to ancestral support and values, as well as urging contemporary Kazakhs to reconnect with their cultural predecessors in order to overcome difficulties in the present. This connective process combines bata with pilgrimage to ancestral shrines; newcomers are given a series of lengthy bata delivered through a channeler, a member of the Ata Zhol group who voices the spirit of some ancestor. Through bata, a person hears about his or her past misfortunes, future potential, and connection to a particular ancestor or group of ancestors who can help someone turn away from a problematic past toward a more fulfilling future. With these practices, those individuals associated with Ata Zhol and its subgroups aim to repair communities and families through the healing of individuals. The movement is widespread but highly controversial in Kazakhstan and was in fact banned by the Kazakhstani government, as officially announced on a website listing "occult and mystical organizations": "By the judgment of the Specialized Inter-District Economic Court of Almaty from 5 February 2009, the activities of the LLP [Ata Zholy] and the movement [Ata Zhol] are banned, including through the media regarding the diffusion and propaganda of such an activity, which undermines the security of the state by posing a threat to health of the population of Kazakhstan."[24]

The controversy surrounding the movement is twofold. First, Ata Zhol has a nontransparent business dimension. In fact, many of the groups associated with Ata Zhol are organized in a pyramid scheme, where new inductees pay fees to access services, contacts, and care. Second, the various groups claim to heal in a medical sense; among the three groups with whom I've interacted at various points in my research in Kazakhstan, leaders actively target drug and alcohol addiction but also circulate miracle stories about adherents recovering sight, hearing, or even the ability to walk or to conceive. Ailments are diagnosed and targeted in localized areas of the body, such as the heart, stomach, other internal organs, the head, or the limbs. A wide range of other social conditions, such as joblessness or bad family relations, are similarly classed as "spiritual sickness," and to address those problems the groups urge similar courses of healing.

In the town where I did my bata research specifically, a group of women healers had been the target of a class-action lawsuit, on behalf of people who were promised but did not ultimately achieve physical recovery from some ailment. The medical capacity and legitimacy of the group were called directly into question. This background is personally relevant to my research, because Saltanat's two sisters were both medical practitioners trained during the Soviet period. She respected them, and they very much influenced her opinions and perspective. One of her sisters in fact had recently published in a local newspaper an article in which she suggested that large numbers of people were seeking alternative healers because medical professionals were not providing the psychological support their patients also needed. Saltanat herself agreed with her sister, and she discussed the article with Meiramgul, who said that people going on pilgrimages and listening to bata in that context were obviously seeking the spiritual or emotional support they wouldn't get from a doctor. The women drew a certain line, however, at the idea that bata could be used to heal in a medical sense. Throughout our time working and living together, Saltanat was somewhat curious or fearful about alternative healers, and she tended to prevent our research efforts from heading in the direction of what she deemed some kind of dark magic.

We met with Gaukhar knowing only that she was the aunt of Saltanat's daughter's work colleague. Her niece met me and had heard about my research, and she suggested immediately that we meet her aunt. She did not introduce us personally but instead set up a phone introduction, during which Saltanat and I agreed to meet Gaukhar in the popular park near where we all lived. We met her at a bus stop just outside the park, so that we could walk together; Saltanat and I were a bit late arriving and rushed to find her. We had no trouble identifying Gaukhar, however; she definitely stood out. A very tall, older woman, with her hair caught up in a sparkly purple headscarf and wearing a blouse and business-apparel-type skirt hitting just below the knee, Gaukhar sported bright red lipstick and a huge smile. She began talking immediately upon meeting us. We walked to find some park benches together, and Saltanat introduced the subject of my research, bata. Before she answered, Gaukhar quizzed me: did I know about Kazakh poets? Yes. "She did a whole project on aitys. Of course she knows the poets!" Saltanat interjected. Did I know the concept of the seven forefathers (Kaz: *zheti ata*)? Yes. Recitation of genealogy (Kaz: *shezhire*)? Yes.[25]

The questions kept coming, now with terms I didn't immediately recognize. *Tuzkhan?* No. I asked her to repeat them several times, so that I could write them down. "Fatiha," I said. "Suresi!" they replied in unison. Gaukhar and Saltanat responded as if to a child, while I fumbled with understanding. Even things I knew did not come quickly, so I felt like a student failing an exam. Who are a person's closest relatives? "Mothers?" I finally ventured. Saltanat pointed to my notepad: "Just write down 'mother's relatives'" (Kaz: *naghashy*). Gaukhar threw her arms up in mock frustration. "How are you going to write a book then, when you don't know anything?" she exclaimed. She asks me if I've heard of Ata Zhol; I have indeed. "The road of the ancestors, do you know why it's called that?" Gaukhar answers her own question: this is a movement predicated upon following the traditions and customs of Kazakh forebears. It's not a sect or a cult, but just general cultural knowledge that everyone shares.[26] Kazakhs can always turn to their ancestors for help and guidance; these "grandfathers" are always watching.

Gaukhar described why and how she became involved with this group. Hers was a story both practical and mystical, delivered with a matter-of-fact tone. At a point in her life when she was going through a difficult time, she met a woman who offered to read her bata. Gaukhar agreed, and she joined a small pilgrimage tour during which her bata was read by this woman, whose heart was able to channel the ancestor Toktybai. "Who is that?" Saltanat wanted to know. "It's a relative of Nazarbayev!" Gaukhar exclaimed, "one of the five grandfathers: Toktybai Ata, Suinbai Ata, Saribai Ata, Zhambyl, and Kainazar Ata." I recognized these names immediately, having been on the very same pilgrimage route many times: it is the main pilgrimage route outside the large city Almaty, where the Soviet-era poet Zhambyl Zhabaev is buried.[27]

> GAUKHAR: It's just that these grandfathers open the road. This Allah, how much he sees, how much it means for us to have his fairness on the earth. There is a war between good and evil. And [he] began to convince our ancestors, to help, to raise children, girls, boys . . . and these, thanks to this, bata? We are cleaning people.

Here Gaukhar is telling both her own experience and the general experience of those who join this group. Each of them has a specific ancestor, one who has spoken to them in a dream or through their heart, to ask them to help channel his or her words into the contemporary world. That channeling takes the form of an extended bata, which pilgrims receive on the tours they take together and which become part of their physical healing process. Gaukhar asks us to imagine that a person is hurt somewhere but doesn't know it. She then performatively enacts the loud "sssuuuuuttttt!" sound I had heard previously only in the company of a shamanic healer in a center for traditional medicine—the sound of the shaman removing the negative energy or "blackness" from a patient's body. In that context, it happened after the patient had been ritually cleansed with the burning of sage and short prayers from the Koran. Gaukhar explains that she personally experienced this healing, when she first joined the bata group. Her knees had been aching, but after she went on one of these pilgrimages, her pain disappeared.

The form of bata as both a channel to ancestors and as a form of healing made sense to Gaukhar, because like both Saltanat and Meiramgul in the examples above, she has derived a great deal of comfort from bata in difficult times in her own life. She shared at length a story about her niece Aliya, through whom we had met her and with whom she is very close, because she is like a second mother to her brother's daughter. Aliya's own parents passed away within six months of each other during the same year, when she and her two siblings were still children. As some time passed and more children were born in the extended family, Gaukhar had the sense that Aliya's parents were watching them from the other world. When Aliya's mother wanted to give her daughter a bata, she channeled it through the heart of Gaukhar, and Gaukhar spoke her sister-in-law's words: "You think that we do not see [our children], but we see them every day." This bata experience was a comfort to Gaukhar herself, as well as to Aliya, because they were reassured that the family connection does not end with death.

When she joined the bata group associated with Ata Zhol, she received the sign of another (nongenealogical) ancestor, one whose voice she was destined to channel. The purpose of this channeling (which I also describe in the introduction to this volume) is to teach and guide others that they must take care of ancestors in order to live well today:

> GAUKHAR: If the ancestor spirits aren't satisfied, the living will never improve. Blessing, this isn't in the sense of [material] wealth!
> AUTHOR: Yes, yes, yes, I understand.
> GAUKHAR: Ancestor spirits, they—
> SALTANAT: Spiritual wealth.
> GAUKHAR: There are many rich people, for whom there is jealousy. But this all passes on to their children, to their children and grandchildren.
> SALTANAT: *Yes. Yes.* It can [pass] to them.
> GAUKHAR: Yes, and maybe there won't be grandchildren, and—
> SALTANAT: In the next generation—
> GAUKHAR: The family line won't continue. God can punish them [for] this.

Gaukhar understands that ancestors channel using bata (through the hearts and minds of Ata Zhol healers) in order to actively intervene in the lives and spiritual health of their "descendants" so that the next generation can prosper. Here she extends the concept of genealogy from family to community in the concept of "generations." In this example, she explains that the bad energy of jealousy, if left unresolved, can become something like a genealogical residue, a social debt for which subsequent generations must pay. Resolution or "payment," then, would be the correct reformation of social ties, reconnection with the family's ancestors, and goodwill during this life. In order to avoid jealousy or the "evil eye," for example, a family could practice sharing and giving back to their kin and community. The idea that the bad energy directed at one generation could carry through to the next is important, because (as described above), many people feel that the multitude of mistakes made by those now living will be amplified in deleterious effects on future generations. Gaukhar listed at length during our conversation the many social ills that have been occurring in Kazakh communities—alcoholism, prostitution, families abandoning one another. For each of these ills, the absence of a properly functioning kin network in the face of joblessness and poverty becomes a recipe for disaster, even a reason to face the wrath of God if one has ignored the help and warnings he sent through the ancestors.

Because Gaukhar had been participating with the Ata Zhol–related bata group for a number of years, and probably because she was also a former teacher and a slightly theatrical personality herself, she had the manner of an experienced orator who has processed through certain narrative strategies many times over. Her speaking style included ever-shifting tone, volume, and speed. She introduced new topics of conversation with a rhetorical question and ended her statements with tags such as "right?" and "isn't that so?" Her interaction style allowed for only minimal feedback from myself and Saltanat; if we actually started to answer at any length, she simply interrupted us and kept talking. If we became too silent or unresponsive, she would include our names loudly in the ending tags: "right, *Saltanat?*"

> GAUKHAR: Vodka. Smoking. Prostitution. Nothing good will come of this. And for that, for all of it, Allah can . . . the ancestors a little bit. <nudging motion> The ancestor spirits wake up. They begin . . . they begin to help the living.
> AUTHOR: Mmm.
> GAUKHAR: Don't they come to you, in revelations?
> AUTHOR: Mm-hmm, mm-hmm.
> GAUKHAR: Don't you—
> AUTHOR: They are dreamed?
> GAUKHAR: Yeeesss, they are dreamed. They begin to warn <lowers voice confidentially>. They even put signs here and there <mumbling>. They gather here. *Saltanat!* <clear, loud>
> SALTANAT: Mm.
> GAUKHAR: Patience.
> SALTANAT: Hmm. Mm-hmm.
> GAUKHAR: Patience.
> SALTANAT: Yes.
> GAUKHAR: From here they support <inhales loudly>, this is a *feeling*, it happens there, you're starting something, worrying, yes? Your will isn't enough <exhales "Huh!">. [Your] hands can't <demonstrates frozen hands> . . . But if someone else, atheists who don't understand, "Oi! <inhales, high breathy voice> My hands hurt, oi!" But [a] grandfather is holding on, there. "Eh! Put up with it!" and we put up with it. And then after a while they let go.
> SALTANAT: Mm-hmm.
> GAUKHAR: Everything passes. When you already understand and begin, really.

After enumerating various social ills at some length, Gaukhar moves on to describe how ancestors effectively intervene. Prompted or "woken up" by God, ancestors come to the living in dreams or in spirit, to hold their hands in times of trouble. Those who don't understand the signs don't recognize that they have help, that someone is there with them, telling them to hold on. Different characters are enacted in different voices by Gaukhar; ancestors have a low, solemn voice, making them seem serious. "Those who don't understand" (or don't believe in God or religion) have a high, breathy voice, making them seem silly. In this small (slightly forced) dialogue, Gaukhar demands Saltanat's attention for the important point: in the face of social problems, the first thing that ancestor spirits demand of the living is patience, a word she repeated in both Russian and Kazakh. Her point is that they can help the living to get through something new or something difficult. The example recalls the point made by Meiramgul and quoted earlier, that the wishes of the ancestors (in bata) are very important for any beginning action and that their support or connection has palpable effects for the bodies of the living: ancestors not only can help the living but they can also "touch" them somehow.

Ancestors may help allay the misfortunes of the living, but, by the same token, if they themselves are not taken care of, the living will suffer. One way to take care, Gaukhar explained, is to always remember them when you pass their graves, to always be quiet and respectful, to say a Koranic prayer for them, and perhaps even to ask for God's bata:

Аллаһ, атабабалар жатқан жай болсын	May the way be easy for those lying here,
көп рахмет, аман болсын,	many thanks, may they be healthy/well,
бастан нұр болсын, Аумін.	may light come from their head, Amen.

(GAUKHAR to AUTHOR): There, "bismillah rahxman rahim," write it down?
AUTHOR: Mm-hmm?
GAUKHAR: This . . . clean Kazakh words.
SALTANAT: Mm-hmm.

Saltanat also urged me to write down this phrase—the first lines of the Al Fatiha sure that opens the Koran (Kaz: *Fatiha Suresi*), although I found it to be simple and ubiquitous. She was concerned that I notice the words used in Gaukhar's description, the bata and prayer, the words that Gaukhar described as "clean," and "Kazakh." These terms relate to the concept of the ancestors' path itself, that language is part of the relationships between the living and deceased on this journey together through the trials and tribulations of life, and it thus can be evidence of a "pure" culture (Kaz: *akh*), the right way of doing things. Here the Koran itself is reclaimed from within an ancestral worldview. Looking back on this conversation, it is striking that the "words" capturing Saltanat's attention were so similar to those that Meiramgul described as comforting when we talked in her library: a brief Koranic prayer and short bata, the kind that explicitly seeks guidance, linking the minds (thoughts, imagination, ideas) of ancestors to the moral possibilities of the present. She was right to make me notice, as I would have overlooked this as a routine or pedestrian cultural Islam, rather than seeing these words as being authored by ancestors, and therefore a source of comfort and care.

Going into this interaction with Gaukhar, Saltanat was highly skeptical, because she (like Meiramgul) did not believe in bata as a form of medical healing. Gaukhar's domineering and semirehearsed interaction style did not help matters. However, as our conversation went on (we talked for nearly two hours, as we had with Meiramgul), Saltanat became visibly more relaxed and invested in talking to Gaukhar. Although Gaukhar was still the primary speaker, Saltanat began to talk and respond more, and to explain things to me together with Gaukhar. The subjects we covered were all familiar ground for her—Kazakh customs and traditions, the heroes and famous personages of times past, the sharing of stories about the breakup of families, child care, the need for good daughters-in-law, and crime in the community. The two laughed together when remembering movies from their youth. Just as Saltanat had told me many times in the kitchen at home, Gaukhar told me now: Soviet films were a morale booster, happy stories about living a good life. They worried about morale today.

Gaukhar began to talk about herself a bit more, noting that she herself babysits her granddaughter so that her daughter can work. She is reluctant to give her to any kind of daycare, because she worries that her granddaughter would not be properly brought up in that type of setting. Saltanat readily agreed, saying that it is important to see to this personally.

GAUKHAR: This is upbringing [for] my child.
SALTANAT: Ye-es!
GAUKHAR: Because tomorrow, this child will grow up. <pauses> And how will she grow up? It depends on the future—
SALTANAT: Yes.
GAUKHAR: If she grows up to be good, you'll be happy. If not . . .
SALTANAT: Yes, the whole government situation depends on it, what kind of kids.
GAUKHAR: Absolutely. Kids, what kind of kids. What are you planting? Even for flowers, you take care of them.
SALTANAT: Yes.
GAUKHAR: And this is a *child!* This is a *person!*
SALTANAT (to AUTHOR): You see, *again*, it's talking about re*li*gion. This is our upbringing, *everything* is parallel with pedagogy.
AUTHOR: Mm-hmm.
SALTANAT: Everything, everything [depends] on the right upbringing,
AUTHOR: Mm.
SALTANAT: On the upbringing of *children*, on the upbringing of society.
AUTHOR: Mm-hmm, mm-hmm.
GAUKHAR: You plant a tree crooked, it grows crooked.
SALTANAT: Yes.
GAUKHAR: You plant it *evenly*, it will be straight, and it will even give you its seeds tomorrow. <pause> You bring a kid up evenly? Tomorrow he will be kind to you, gentle, and he will never hurt you.

Here the women again repeat the themes that emerged as the most significant over the course of my fieldwork with Saltanat about bata. Bata is part of the life lessons or training within the family. But raising children well is critical to the success not only of the family but all of society, culture, and good governance. Furthermore, the family is related analogously to the community. If there are failings in tradition or upbringing within the family—the lack of a figurative bata-giver—other spiritual authority figures may compensate for those failings. Really listening to, or receiving, bata means that a person may walk on the "good path"—the path of elders and ancestors.

Receiving the bata of ancestors (through channelers or spirit guides) is one way a growing number of people feel that they can begin to heal their families and communities. These activities draw on the cultural resources of elders: words, prayer, the presence of ancestors in spirits and dreams. I asked Gaukhar how she would want me to present her point of view when I wrote about it. She was surprised at the question, and both she and Saltanat shook their heads. They told me that what Gaukhar had to say was nothing secret, special, or overly controversial—just general knowledge, just a matter of "custom and tradition" for Kazakhs. As our conversation with Gaukhar drew to a close, we sat on the benches of the town's lively central park, watching children and families play and a small amusement ride—a train—pass by. We made plans for the upcoming weekend, to join Gaukhar for a group pilgrimage to receive our own bata with her group and other travelers, and then we said goodbye.

TWO
GUARDIANS OF THE ANCESTORS

> ZHULDUZ: At sacred sites we ask the ancestors to help as intercessors in our prayers to God, because they themselves were people who lived a holy life guided by God. During their own lives, these ancestors . . . gave bata to their own protégés, to help guide them along the right path. We always have to think positively, because words and prayers at sacred sites act on our bodies and have a positive effect from within.

NATIONAL ANCESTORS

In this chapter I discuss how the wishes, prayers, and intentions of a variety of ancestors are conveyed to living "descendants" through the mediation of caretakers at sacred sites around the country. These graves and shrines where ancestors are buried become part of an affective landscape, one that is visible throughout Inner Asia at sacred sites.[1] With the passing of time and centuries, some shrines become relevant for a wide variety of generalized "descendants" (see Dubuisson and Genina 2012), whereby Central Asian ancestors join the Sufi saints as the recipients of pilgrimage in a broader Muslim sacred world. Pilgrims come to receive a blessing at those sacred places, the largest of which have also been absorbed, together with geological, historical, and archaeologically significant sites, by nationalist cultural history projects in different countries.

The nature of pilgrimage to sacred sites tends to be described in local or national contexts more narrowly, as part of ethnic religious tradition, as something "Kazakh" (Dubuisson and Genina 2012), "Uzbek" (Louw 2007; Rasanayagam 2012), or "Kyrgyz" (Aitpaeva 2009; Feaux de la Croix 2011), because this research reflects the viewpoint of those undertaking pilgrimage in different countries —pilgrims for whom ethnic (national) identity is central and differentiable. As described in the introduction, these distinctions among nationalities became more salient due in part to Soviet nationalities policies, and later, in the post-Soviet period, they began taking the form of strong ethnic nationalism supported by state governments. While the history of identity formation in Central Asia is a complicated one stretching back centuries, today categories such as "Kazakhness" or "Kyrgyzness" are very apparent and seen as natural and somewhat distinct by most despite heavy overlap in cultural worldviews and practices.[2] Another layer of belief and belonging undergirds sacred site visitation: pilgrimage is seen to be something inherently Muslim, as ethnicity and Muslim identity are often conflated in Central Asia (see Privratsky 2001). Culture and religion thus overlap as categories and identities; a pilgrim can, for example, be at once both Kazakh and Muslim. These realities are reflected dialogically at sites, where both Koranic prayers and ancestral *bata* are offered.

These questions about the relationship among ethnicity, religion, and culture are also very much part of changing discourses related to an upsurge in Islamic education in the region in the post-Soviet period and to the fundamental question of whether Central Asian nations will or should identify as Islamic in the near future. To date, the former republics have maintained a secular political stance, rhetorically distancing themselves from the external threat of "Wahhabi terrorism" but at the same time creating a "state Islam" with appointed imams (see Khalid 2007).[3] Among my Kazakh families, friends, and those I worked and traveled with over the years, most of those who were raised in the Soviet period are familiar with a "cultural" Islam, while more orthodox forms of Islam are seen as something external to Central Asia and disseminated more recently by youth traveling from other countries and by other sources, such as social media. The idea that reconnecting with ancestors might coincide with forms of state or global Islam has been an increasingly salient one in the post-Soviet period, in part a reaction to perceptions of new religious freedom. Shrine sites such as Turkestan, as part of a historical landscape, are often places where discourses of ancestry and religious identity converge.

While nationalism and Islamic teaching or propaganda are aspects of these shrine sites and pilgrimage practices, the sites are ultimately spaces of discussion and exploration where a variety of ideologies, beliefs, and practices merge into localized conversations with on-site caretakers, who help to mediate visitors' understanding. Writing about sacred site visitation in Uzbekistan, the anthropologist Maria Elisabeth Louw (2007, 169) explicitly rejects any notion that these practices should be judged "relative to Islamic orthodoxy" or that they represent "some kind of quasi-objective social amnesia" resulting from Russian and Soviet rule. Rather, she focuses on the "experiential reality" of people: what they actually go through, as well as the social and historical contexts in which they make sense of the world around them:

> Experiencing their lifeworlds as fragmented and insecure, Bukhara Muslims pursued what they were missing, and the knowledge to put it into perspective, at sacred places which they saw as manifestations of the divine in the world which

> had somehow escaped the corrosion of time. Their pilgrimages took them to the shrines that were visible in the physical landscape and which were found all around the city; to sacred space temporarily created during rituals . . . to dream-encounters with saints of past times, or to the innermost corners of their very being. Sacred places were thresholds or doorways to the divine, to what lies beyond ordinary human experience. (Louw 2007, 171)

Louw also emphasizes temporal transcendence and problem solving, in the form of incorporating saints' blessings and pilgrimage experiences into lives back home. Upon their return, those who have undertaken pilgrimage share their experiences, as well as any holy objects they have found or purchased along the way, such as water or pamphlets (Feaux de la Croix 2010), with family and friends.

Similarly, I found that while shrine visitation is perhaps by definition out of the ordinary, talk *about* these visits is enfolded into the discursive fabric of the everyday. Tagging along with my research partner Saltanat to her work at the local bazaar, I would sit with her and have tea with other women working in the neighboring bazaar, and we would chat about their experiences with bata and pilgrimage. These women described their troubles at home—ranging from marriage and children to health and finances—and explained how they had been compelled to pilgrimage as a means of problem solving. They talked about their experiences of the sites visited, as well as the dreams and relationships that keep them connected to that experience, and the wish to return one day. In this way, narratives of shrine experiences also continue to circulate beyond the initial day(s) of actual travel, in the form of camaraderie and advice. This speaks to the general purpose of pilgrimage for many Central Asians: occupying a sacralized geography of the past, in order to cope with—or even to reimagine—the precariousness of the present.

I would emphasize that the landscape and spiritual dimensions of sacred sites are best understood as part of a vast, interconnected Inner Asian landscape extending from Turkey to China (see Grant 2011). Ultimately, I think we must focus on *why* people visit these sites, what they do there, how they interact, and what they hope to find or discover through these journeys. People visit these sites for a wide variety of reasons, ranging from faith and illness to tourism, and there simply is not any single ideological way of understanding those activities. Visitors' interests or needs may vary significantly, and their understanding of sacred sites and what may happen there also varies. Some pilgrims may identify as Muslim, following tour guides known to be knowledgeable in Hanafi Sunnism or Naqshbandi Sufism, while others travel in caravans with versions of the Ata Zhol healers' movement that combine Muslim and ancestral worldviews, as described in chapter one.[4] Some (international) groups come to sacred sites in connection with cultural and historical nationalism. Still others travel independently with family and friends out of curiosity or to seek care from the ancestors. Many if not most pilgrims are hoping to find some kind of spiritual or even physical healing

(Aitpaeva 2009). In any case, visitors' experiences are conditioned by those with whom they travel and by their own expectations (Bellér-Hann 2005), but they are also actively managed by the men whose job it is to manage the sites—the caretakers (Kaz: *shyrakhshylar*).

The fundamental unifying principle behind a variety of local sites and practices is that ancestors' burial sites are merged into a sacred ecology that also includes mountains, water, trees, animals, and the steppe itself, as well as Islamic history and the heritage, beliefs, and practices from a wide variety of Inner Asian belief systems, such as Tengrism or Buddhism. If one were to reimagine Inner Asia without any national borders at all, sacred sites would come to the fore as constituting different forms of geography and of historical or spiritual belonging. On this natural and ancestral landscape, ecology and culture are sacralized and given agency to heal in the present. Pilgrimage becomes a way to seek this care, to establish meaning, and to cope with forms of social and economic uncertainty, as well as to heal the body and spirit. The anthropologist Jeanne Feaux de la Croix (2010, 100) considers that visiting burial sites (*mazar*) as a part of the broader land and natural world is constitutive of what she calls a "moral geography," an exercise in seeking out a "good life." As with bata, such learning comes from connecting with and learning from generations past. Moving across an ancestral landscape, establishing connections with ancestors, and receiving their blessings and prayers is a way of sense-making. This argument is directly comparable to the case of shamanism and ancestry as mobilized problem-solving in postsocialist Mongolia (Bernstein 2006). Burial sites and ancestors are also involved in the embodied practices of dreaming and prescience for many Central Asians. From within this multidimensional geography, ancestors can act to protect the land and the living.

SACRED GEOGRAPHY

Central Asia's own rich and multilayered history itself becomes part of an ancestral landscape and a sacred geography in the present. The great cities of the erstwhile Central Asian khanates, such as Khiva, Samarkhand, and Bukhara in Uzbekistan, have all become pilgrimage sites. Within Kazakhstan, pilgrims come to the small town of Turkestan, which, according to longtime researcher Bruce Privratsky (2000, 53) sees approximately two hundred thousand visitors a year, or about seven hundred a day, making this "the dominant center of a vast periphery" and a place considered by Kazakhs to be a second Mecca. "Second Mecca," a term also applied to Solomon's Mountain in Osh, Kyrgyzstan (Montgomery 2007, 362), has related but shifting meanings. Many people believe that two trips to Turkestan are equivalent to taking one trip to Mecca, Saudi Arabia. Others believe that Turkestan must be visited before one is considered holy enough to visit Mecca. There are many important sacred sites across the territory of Kazakhstan, but Turkestan is arguably the country's spiritual center. For many of my Kazakh friends and families, a trip to Turkestan was a major life-goal. I have visited the site twice, once with a colleague, Margarita Madanova, as part of an archaeological tour of southern Kazakhstan, and once as a tourist.

The site at Turkestan is the shrine of Khoja Ahmed Yasawi.[5] He was a poet and mystic often credited with bringing Sufi Islam to Kazakhs across the Syr Darya river valley in the twelfth century. Yasawi founded the Yasawi *tariqah* (order) in Central Asia and lived the last years of his life in a group of underground rooms at the site in Turkestan, devoting himself to God. Visitors to the site can explore these rooms, but it is the enormous shrine built for Yasawi by the Uzbek leader Timur (Tamerlane) in the fourteenth century that utterly dominates the physical landscape of the place. The sacred site of Turkestan blends the authority and legitimacy of both the Yasawi and Timurid legacies, a feature capitalized upon by Kazakh khans who, in their occupation of the site, could "claim Islamic political authority in the same way" (DeWeese 1994, 633). A pilgrimage to Turkestan also includes a visit to the shrine of Yasawi's teacher, Arstan Bab. In both places, pilgrims first circle the buildings, praying and seeking the blessing (*baraka*) of the place itself. Privratsky (2001) also notes the common practice of circumambulation at sacred shrine sites like Turkestan and how this "going around" at tomb sites further sacralizes the interred saint there; the act of circling indexically creates a metaphysical "center" or place through the interaction of living pilgrims with the memory of the saint.

I agree with Privratsky (2001, 49) that belief and activity at sacred sites in Kazakhstan are best seen as part of an "affective image schema" in which dreams, premonitions, and feelings serve to unite language, landscape, and embodiment: "The collective memory both spatializes the sanctity of the saint and sacralizes the land which the people have claimed for themselves." I would consider this to be a "place-world," in the sense described by the anthropologist Keith Basso (1996, 6; original emphasis); a place exists in a sense as the ideas *of* that place: "Every place-world manifests itself as a possible state of affairs, and whenever these constructions are accepted by other people as credible and convincing—or plausible and provocative, or arresting and intriguing—they enrich the common stock on which everyone can draw to muse on past events, interpret their significance, and imagine them anew. Building place-worlds . . . is not only a means of reviving former times but also *revising* them." Today, the site at Turkestan and the ways in which it is conceptualized and inhabited by pilgrims combine the legitimacy of an Islamic legacy with the totality of contemporary spiritual life, including the revering of ancestors and the natural world.

An Inner Asian spiritual landscape merges historically Sufi shrine pilgrimage practices with the natural world itself, such as mountains, springs, and trees, as well as with the sacred ground around burial sites and tombs. As David Abramson and Elyor Karimov (2007, 321) note, "a sacred site can consist of anything from a natural site, such as a water source, to an extensive complex including mosque, religious school, tomb, cemetery, and additional buildings for administration, artisanship, and even tourist facilities. [However,] most sites consist of at least a tree, a water source, and a tomb, all of which are considered sacred because of their affiliation with the site and miracle stories about the interred saint." These all become holy because they "touch" ancestors. From major sites like Turkestan to local pilgrimage sites, visitors travel to receive the blessing of their predecessors and from the place itself. The ubiquity of this worldview and sacred site visitation throughout Inner Asia as a whole is sometimes masked by the pointedly national character of the sites themselves, as well as the discourses associated with them, such as the prominent example of Turkestan being holy for Kazakhs in particular because it is located on the territory of the modern state. Ultimately, however, the spiritual domain or ground of an ancestral world does not correspond to the geographic boundaries of nations or to the spiritual boundaries of any one religious tradition.

ZIYARET

Pilgrimage to sacred sites in Central Asia raises the obvious point that practices associated with Islam in a variety of locales are usually in harmony with other practices that could be considered nonorthodox, such as having minimal Koranic knowledge, believing in the granting of wishes, burning sage, interpreting dream prophecy, saint and ancestor worship, shamanism, Tengrism, fertility cults, and natural healing sites, as well as a "cult of the hearth" (see Privratsky 2001), which features a strong emphasis on the home and familial duty rather than attending a mosque.[6] This rich set of beliefs and practices is evidence of the complicated cultural and political history of the Inner Asian steppe and probably characterizes a broad majority of Central Asian Muslims, but it runs counter to more orthodox forms of Hanafi Sunnism. Researchers of Islam in Central Asia find themselves grappling with these realities—the legacies of the complicated religious history in the region. They must also address the role of imam-centered Sunni Islam, or state-controlled Islam, which seeks to control and centralize religious activity across the region. What then is the "real" Islam?[7]

Central Asians tend to merge shrine visitation with visitation to other sites considered sacred. Pilgrims typically visit multiple sites over the course of a day or week, on a route referred to either as a "tour" or by the Muslim term for pilgrimage (Kaz: *ziyarat*). In the case of Uzbekistan, where the government has explicitly adopted Sufi tombs as a part of "national" culture (Rasanayagam 2012; see also Louw 2007), pilgrimage itself becomes contentious for religious leaders, and the state apparatus seeks to micromanage the spiritual activities of followers. For example, researchers Abramson and Karimov (2006, 326) in Uzbekistan found that a printed list of rules now adorns the entrance to one *khoja*'s shrine in Samarkand, forbidding a long list of practices at the gravesite, including bowing, lighting candles, placing coins, tying cloth, or asking the saint for help to "resolve personal problems," as "these can be asked from Allah." In their description of the place, these researchers were quick to note that the shrine is still covered by white cloths and piles of ash.

The theological problem here is the relationship between God and the saints or ancestors: Who can actually intercede in the lives of the living and provide practical or spiritual help? To whom should prayers be addressed? Should Islam be considered completely separate from other spiritual or religious traditions such as shamanism, Tengrism, or Buddhism (evidenced by the practices listed above)? While strict interpretations of Islam might disallow these visitation practices altogether, Central Asian Muslim leaders have traditionally been more accommodating. However, the trouble for more orthodox Muslims is that, across sacred sites, "the local practice of *ziyorat* comes dangerously close to polytheism" (Rasanayagam 2012, 139). Whether or not pilgrimage to sacred sites in Central Asia should even be referred to as *ziyarat* is, in my experience visiting sites over a decade, a question that has become increasingly central for pilgrims and their guides in recent years.[8]

For example, during our research on bata, Saltanat and I decided to take a day trip to her town's central historical shrine site, hoping to meet and talk with the site's caretaker (whose role is described at length below). He had the reputation of being a more strict Muslim than others and of training Muslim students at the site compound. The day that we arrived, a bright, hot summer day, we were struck by the beauty of the place. Visitors came and went in a small but steady stream, some talking and laughing, some looking serious. The compound's brick walls enclosed gardens and pathways, three historic shrines, a closed archaeological dig, and a pump to access a water well, where visitors were supposed to drink and to wash their hands and faces. Off to one side stood some small buildings for the groundskeepers and a small kiosk where they sold small pamphlets and Kazakh cultural memorabilia. I saw in the kiosk a large selection of jewelry and wall hangings with the "evil eye" symbol (Trk: *nazar*).[9] The symbol was common in Turkey, where I lived. Saltanat was interested in looking through the books and I wanted to see the evil eye amulets, so after we had toured the grounds and prayed with a group of other visitors in the mausoleum, we headed to the kiosk.

We immediately found several books on bata, on the history of the town and region, and on the famous ancestors buried in the region. Soon a thin, smiling young man, his floppy brown hair covered by a traditional Uzbek hat embroidered with an Islamic quarter moon, came to see if we needed any help. He was an apprentice in training at the site and had thus come to get an Islamic education there. "Are you Turkish?" he asked me excitedly upon meeting us. I was startled and did not answer immediately, confused by the fact that though I am Canadian-American, I actually did live in Turkey, so I was wondering if that somehow counted for something. "I knew it!" he said, "I can tell just by looking at you." I commented about the large selection of Turkish nazar at the kiosk. "Yes," our young friend answered, "Turkish things. One day my dream is to go to Turkey, to Istanbul, to study Islam; there are good schools there. I can't afford it now, but I hope one day I will go." Looking at his bright, earnest face, I wished I could ignore the complexity of the matter and just hand him a plane ticket then and there.

We introduced ourselves by name, and Saltanat decided to ask this young man, Miras, some of the questions we had on our minds.[10] Who are we praying to at a sacred site, to God or the ancestors? What is the relationship between them? He quickly shifted into a recitational mode, speaking rhetorically at length with no hesitation:

> MIRAS: The ancestor of Mohammed, before his death, used to go to the grave of his mother Hadishe to read a prayer from Koran (Kaz: *Bagyshtau*)[11] for the spirit of his ancestors to be happy [Kaz: *riza boly*], and he told people, "You people should also go to your ancestors' graves and read prayers [Kaz: *ziyaret kabyrstanga*]." Spirits of the dead will also be grateful. With what goal, and what do people say at the tomb of a sacred site? What do they ask about? People say, "O Allah, we have come to this holy place/person and ask from you that you fulfill our wishes." In Arabic, this respect for holy people is called *tausil*. People come to these places and say, "O Allah, you gave so many people Islamic belief and gave them faith, Islam, please help us—the sick, etc.,—to get better." God can do anything, [he is] all powerful. God wants people to come to him, and helps, because there were people who began to go after these instructions, and people began to go heal.
>
> AUTHOR: What is the relationship between spirit ancestors and God?
>
> MIRAS: Spirit ancestors and God [Kaz: *Khydai*] . . . In the Koran or hadith, I don't remember where, when a person lives honestly and accomplishes things, and he knows that he will end up in heaven, and he wants to end up there and that's why he does good/right things. After his death, this person becomes a spirit [Kaz: *aruakh*]. Only his body dies, but his spirit remains. When we sleep, our souls leave our bodies and travel, the souls leave the grave. But people who end up in heaven, they leave their souls behind with the rest of us—they travel, go to their descendants, their relatives, they are happy that relatives are doing good things. We often say, like when we read *namas:* "Please protect the spirits of our ancestors."
>
> SALTANAT: Like you're praying for help for yourself, that the spirits of the dead ancestors will help you? People's souls who have become—
>
> MIRAS: God says, "I am merciful; if you ask me I can help you. I am generous, I can help."
>
> SALTANAT: <interrupts> That's why people go to God, people who are sick. You take care of your ancestor spirits after death by saying prayers and baking bread.
>
> MIRAS: Yes, that happens too.

Later in the day, when we were sitting at the kitchen table, listening to our recording of this conversation and transcribing it, Saltanat was frustrated by this last comment, which seemed too vague for her and therefore created uncertainty or doubt. Miras was both confirming what she understood to be true and telling her something different. Despite Miras's youth, Saltanat and I were impressed by his rhetorical skill, and Saltanat did not question that he had knowledge of Islam. Our transcription process was telling in this regard, as she was uncomfortable with many of the words he had used and made me look them up on the Internet one by one. "Grave" (Kaz: *kabyr*) was easy, but "kabyrstan"—what did that mean? Graveland? A cemetery? Life in the other world? But isn't that heaven (Kaz: *zhannat*), I wondered? Miras's small speech now seemed like a puzzle to us. But the word that caused Saltanat the most trouble was *ziyaret*; it was unfamiliar to her and seemed "Muslim." She was worried that these words and ideas had to be understood in terms of theology, and she, as a cultural Muslim raised in the Soviet Union, did not know them. She finally threw up her hands and joked that I should ask my Turkish husband what the words meant (because he should be Muslim—a joke because he is actually nonobservant). The Arabic terms we were going over are actually very ordinary elements of the Turkish vocabulary. For example, *ziyarat* is a very common term, meaning simply "visit," while *kabyrstan* is a slightly outdated word meaning "cemetery," the more common term being *mezar* (the same term, *mazar*, is used in Kazakh and Kyrgyz to mean burial site; see Feaux de la Croix 2010).

While we were talking with Miras that afternoon, a large tour bus had arrived at the front gates, and a stream of young to middle-aged women and men had made their way toward the mausoleum. "It's a national tour," Miras explained. "They're coming from Almaty. They'll visit sites all around the country for a week or two." "Isn't that a rough schedule?" I asked, exclaiming, "They must be exhausted!" "But look how fast they go," he answered. "They don't spend much time in any one place." Sure enough, after praying in the mausoleum, touching the building's sides, and drinking water from the spring, the group immediately left. Miras nodded knowingly toward the line filing back out the gate. "They have the sight [Kaz: *arkasi bar*]," he said simply. Saltanat raised her eyebrows in surprise, as we had just recently had a conversation with her daughter-in-law about the meaning of the term. Her daughter-in-law explained that it meant people who had visions. Even if they don't want to, they have the ability to see dead people; sometimes they can use this ability to help heal others, and they can talk to the ancestors. Saltanat was very uncomfortable with the idea, which seemed to her like black magic. She herself had actually seen a spirit take her father in a dream at the moment of his death, and the experience had frightened and troubled her very much. But Miras raised no question about the intentions or religiosity of the seers. He seemed to accept their presence as common and natural, also explaining to us that the visitors come to take power from the ancestors.

In this way Saltanat and I, together over the months of fieldwork at sacred sites and in conversations with friends and family, opened our own growing set of conversations over some central questions: Are ancestors "Islamic"? Does it matter? Why do tomb sites have a water spring, and why is it appropriate to come for healing there? When those gifted with the sight come to take power from the ancestors, what is the role of God? While I would argue that a majority of visitors have no trouble at all finding all of this to be perfectly commonsensical and coherent as a worldview, for more orthodox Muslims, especially those in the government ministry of religion and state-appointed imams, the practices enacted at sacred sites continue to be troubling. They are also outside the sphere of state control. As noted in chapter one, Kazakhstan's government went so far as to ban the pilgrimage- and ancestor-centered Ata Zhol movement for being a cult. As Rasanayagam (2012) describes in his ethnography of Islam and morality in everyday life in Uzbekistan,

> There are a large number of saintly shrines in and around Samarkand, and the head *imom khatib* [the officially appointed head of a registered mosque (122)] for the city complained that visitors were praying directly to the *avliyo* [Muslim saints], not to God. He did not consider visiting the tombs as in itself contrary to the *shari'a*. It is, he said, perfectly acceptable for Muslims to visit cemeteries to remind themselves of their final end, to address prayers to God and recite the Qur'an at the graves of *avliyo*, and even to dedicate these prayers in the name of the *avliyo* as a person who had been particularly close to God. He drew the line at the common practice of touching the physical structure of the tombs or taking water from the springs that are frequently in the vicinity of the tombs (this water is believed to have healing properties), as this smacks of idolatry. (139)

Across Central Asia, there is often competition between different communities and ideologies over sacred sites and pilgrimage routes. There are "big questions" circulating around sacred sites and the practice of pilgrimage: nationalism, religion, culture. In my view, these are all single aspects of one unified picture, which is the emergence of and contestation over potential natural and social orders—the organization of the harmony of being. In my attention to dialogue in this book as a whole, I hope to pay careful attention not to "what is true" but to the spaces of possibility opened within conversation. I attend to words in the world as a means of sense-making, exploration, discovery, and reassurance. Our experiences together with Saltanat during our period of research are quite telling in this regard—from initial encounters to the process of transcription, talking with other family members and friends about what we had seen and heard, and our own reflections about conversations—these were all small, dialogic acts-in-the-world, moments of learning and sharing something new together.

From a broader perspective, there are certain spaces of dialogue that provoke or allow communication specifically with ancestors, performatively creating a context and channel for it.[12] From the wishes of bata to the conversations at shrine sites, these moments of dialogue have a particular cultural context. While in the case of bata blessings the contexts are often family and community, at shrine sites the contexts become much broader, branching out from religion to nation. Ancestors can become a source of authority in and across any of these various frames.

The people who live and work at shrine sites are considered to be particularly knowledgeable about all these contexts and therefore can act to lead and mediate visitors' understanding of sites, their historical significance, and their efficacy in the present. An ancestral worldview is an ongoing communal project, one in which prayers and conversations in many different places together help to create an emergent sacred ancestral geography. Ancestors have the help of site caretakers, who serve to protect and guide.

CARETAKERS

Caretakers are ideally the descendants of the ancestor(s) buried at particular shrines or cemeteries. They are considered to be the most knowledgeable about the life story of that ancestor, and they are usually acquainted with the deceased person's immediate family living in proximity to the burial site.[13] In one of my early conversations with Saltanat and her daughter Dina, they had explained to me that caretakers can mediate in the realm of ancestors, God, and healing, because they themselves are "clean" people. This notion of cleanliness is very much related to the concept of purity.[14] When people encounter trouble or obstacles in their everyday lives, they can visit sacred sites as a way to pray and solve problems together with the caretaker, as Saltanat and her daughter explained to me.

> AUTHOR: What about when people have problems?
> DINA: They go to these holy places.
> SALTANAT: And they ask from these holy people, "Help me." Help me, so that my mother or my close relatives get better, recover, so that they were all healthy and alive. There, women ask for children: "Let there be a child," they say. This is already not bata, this is a request.
> AUTHOR: A request.
> DINA: No, but Mom, absolutely when you go—
> SALTANAT: Like a caretaker—
> DINA: The caretaker reads a prayer, and then you talk to him, right? And what he says there, "Let all your . . . let all the wishes of the person who came now, let them all be fulfilled," like that.
> SALTANAT: That's how [one] asks Allah.
> AUTHOR: Mm-hmm.
> DINA: Uh-huh.
> SALTANAT: Ask, so that . . . Allah has, "Let this light fall, let [good] light fall upon him, let all good things be," is said.
> DINA: This is also bata, right?
> SALTANAT: This is also bata! This is also bata.
> DINA: Mmm.
> AUTHOR: Mm-hmm. Can bata come from Allah?

SALTANAT: Well, this is all connected with Allah. With everything higher. Even the person who gives bata? He's also a *person*. He asks from God.
AUTHOR: Mm-hmm.
SALTANAT: It's considered that this person, he is a *clean* person. You understand? Not every respected person who, there . . . well, like this, he lived a good life—that kind of person asks.

What Saltanat means by "clean" in our conversation here is a person who prays and who avoids earthly temptations, who does not use any drugs or alcohol, never takes part in any crime, is either single or a faithful spouse and parent, a person who knows how to read the Koran, who helps other people, and who avoids the lure of money or profit. A good caretaker serves as an example to those who visit, an example of a life worthy of emulation. These individuals embody a connection to the deceased and to God; therefore, they should have relatively pure (Kaz: *akh*) intentions. Saltanat explained that the word *shyrakh* itself means a candle, one made of sheep fat and wound with cotton; a shyrakhshy metaphorically then is the person who lights the candle. As the caretaker of a holy person who reads prayers and offers bata, this person can "light the way" for others.

Caretakers play a pivotal role in narrating the "place" of a sacred site. They receive guests, read the Koran and pray together with all who travel there, and tell stories about the ancestor who is buried there or interred. They explain what practices are most beneficial at the site and how to understand this site as part of a broader worldview or cosmology (local, ancestral, national, Islamic, environmental, cultural). Caretakers may spend extra time and attention with particular visitors if they so desire, and they tend to be very familiar with the various tour guides who lead people to their sites. Together their narratives frame the experience of inhabiting a site, which is often very brief (typically multiple sites are visited over the course of one day). Caretakers also often talk to visitors about their own experiences of connecting with particular ancestors and overcoming troubles. Their stories are well rehearsed and to the point, repeated multiple times every single day. If guests have more time, it is considered most polite or natural to sit together with the caretaker and his family, to drink tea, break bread, and simply spend time together over a figurative "family" table.

Those visiting shrines and other sacred sites, even tourists, are encouraged to speak or think their own wishes toward God and the ancestor, who can then "reply" in some form mediated in part by caretakers. Guests can then receive the blessing of the ancestors whose stories, lives, and bodies are intertwined with the physical landscape of a place. Visitors often collect water from sacred springs to bring home, as the holy property of the place is transmutable. They will also read Koranic prayers together with the caretaker, and they will listen to his stories— condensed moral tales that are also part of what guests can take away from these places, either to be repeated in some form to friends and family as part of a continually shifting oral mythology of sacred sites and ancestors or to become part of a particular process of spiritual healing. Abramson and Karimov (2006, 321) note that "the telling and retelling of miracle stories by shrine caretakers and other devotees essentially reenact the miracles themselves and intensify the experience for audiences in search of a saint's good will, grace, or blessing ([Kaz:] *baraka*)." In other words, these are stories that act in the world. In the sections that follow I explore how caretakers' stories and personal biographies resonate within the geography of pilgrimage sites. How do the words, themes, voices, and relationships of those who lie beneath the earth become embodied by those who live at these sites, and how do stories become a form of mutual protection?

CARETAKERS CALLED TO DUTY

In the summer of 2013, I visited the well-known pilgrimage route of Bes Atalar (Five Forefathers) in the southern Zhambyl region, which I had first visited nearly a decade earlier with the ethnomusicologist Margarethe Adams. Adams has rightly explained that pilgrimages to these and other sacred sites should be understood as a form of "faith and imagination" in the face of uncertainty, a way to construct "actual futures."[15] I also think that the persistence (and even increase) in this type of pilgrimage is itself a reflection of such a worldview. I have taken the Bes Atalar tour several times since my first visit, in various capacities, but for part of my more recent research on bata I traveled to the sites on a daylong pilgrimage with a small group of women from Ata Zhol, because they channeled bata at these sites. We spoke together with caretakers because these women had visited often before; they also offered their opinions and descriptions of what takes place at sacred sites. After the caretakers offered typical prayers at the shrine site itself and presented a brief biography of the ancestor, we asked about how they themselves came to occupy their role and about their interactions with visitors.

The caretaker at one of the five sites, Kainazar Ata, is an older man with a face slightly leathered from the sun. He jokes that we must have come here because we missed him—his name, Saghynbek, comes from the word *saghynysh*, which means longing. He does not live at the site, but there is a small house with a kitchen and living room next to the gravesite where he can receive guests. When we arrived, two women were busy cooking, and there was a permanent rotating *dastarhan* set up in the living room: a low table, spread with bread, tea, and candies, where we sat and talked together. As we sipped tea, Saghynbek gave us a brief biography of Kainazar Ata, who was responsible for gathering the family of his leader, Tarbai Ata, and bringing them to live in one village, where Saghynbek himself lives and previously worked on a collective farm. He is very modest in dress and demeanor, welcoming each visitor with a smile and ushering them to his dastarhan, saying, "Kosh keldiniz, kelingizder!" (Welcome to you all, please come in!). Saghynbek was asked to become a shyrakhshy by people from his village specifically because he was known to be a good man, a nondrinker, and a pious person who could read the Koran.[16] Although he was initially uncertain about the role, he eventually accepted it as his fate (Kaz: *kyzmet*).[17] Now he spends all day at the site, receiving visitors, praying with them, and giving them bata on behalf of the ancestor Kainazar Ata, such as the one he gave to us:

Мал мыңдасын, мал алмасын	May your livestock number a thousand, may they not be taken away,
Қазар бабасын қолдасын	You are in the hand of your grandfather Kazar.
Жұрт қандай жолдарымыз болсын	May our path be like that of the people,
Алдағыңыздан ақ болсын	May our future be bright,
Тек қана жақсылық бақыт береке қуаныш	May [there be] only goodness, abundance, and happiness
Мерелеріңіз устем болсын	May your honor be elevated
Жұлдыздарыңыз жарық болсын	May your stars shine brightly
Еліміз адал жұртымыз тыныш болсын	May our people be honest, our country calm
Аллах аспаннан жайдыр жерде үйдіріп	Let God's sky fall upon the earth
Ел жұртымызға береке бер.	Give abundance to our country, our people.

Saghynbek explained that there are ancestors who can always hear our hopes and wishes when we come to pray at sites like these, but if you do not enunciate "Aumin" at the end of your prayer, then it will not reach God's ears. As explained in the previous chapter, bata must also be received by listeners saying "Amen." Because he is a good, "clean" person, Saghynbek was chosen to take care of the holy ancestor Kainazar and to convey his wishes and blessings; the site is inherently holy and it is where, again with the help of Saghynbek's prayers, visitors can also convey their needs to Allah.

Kainazar is perhaps a less well-known figure on the Five Forefathers tour. Two other shrines, however, are quite famous due to Kazakh nationalist activity in the post-Soviet period, during which particular cultural figures have been very actively promoted as the historical face of ethnic nations. Just as Chinggis Khan is Mongolia's most famous ancestor (Kaplonski 2004; Sabloff 2001), Manas is Kyrgyzstan's (Gullette 2010), and Tamerlane is invoked in Uzbekistan (Liu 2012), so too does Kazakhstan have its national ancestors. Among the most well known are the figures of the Kazakh poets Abai Kunanbaioly and Zhambyl Zhabaev, who were invoked as the literary or artistic "face" of Kazakh nationality during the Soviet period, ironically enough, for their praise of Russian rule (Abai 1845–1904) and then Soviet rule (Zhambyl 1846–1945).[18] In the post-Soviet period, their friendliness toward Russia is overlooked in favor of their status as exemplary Kazakh poet-ancestors, and the state has sponsored the building and restoration of elaborate museums and mausoleums in their hometowns, which have become major cultural tourism destinations.

Abai and Zhambyl, together with many other famous Kazakh ancestors, have been invoked as part of a very active nationalization campaign in the post-Soviet period, as street names have been changed from Russian to Kazakh, new statues of Kazakh heroes have replaced those of Lenin in republican spaces, and a host of new books, calendars, and posters celebrating Kazakh history fill bookstore shelves and local bazaars. In the new nation it is not only poets but also philosophers, judges, and, importantly, warriors (Kaz: *batyrlar*) who are celebrated as heroes in national monuments and statues, who are celebrated in national anniversaries, and whose gravesites are sacred in the new Kazakh nation (see Dubuisson 2009). Zhambyl's home, museum, and shrine therefore make up one site on the Bes Atalar pilgrimage, cared for by his (now elderly) granddaughter (and her granddaughter, in turn).[19]

Zhambyl's teacher, Suinbai Aronoly, who is another famous national poet, is enshrined nearby. Suinbai Ata is cared for by his great-great-grandson, Usen Sulbanalyoly. The Suinbai site was refurbished early in the 2000s, as part of the nationalization projects, and it is now an impressive small compound of beautiful red-brick buildings: the shrine monument, a small structure that contains a stone from Mecca, and a small house where Usen and his wife greet their guests at an ongoing dastarhan. They also have a small store outside the site, where they sell pictures, books, pamphlets, jewelry, amulets, and *kymyz* (fermented mare's milk). When our little group arrived, there was already another group at the table, so we had to crowd in a bit to drink our tea and break figurative bread. The conversation among the men and women was quite informal; they were on pilgrimage that day for spiritual and physical healing. One young couple had brought their small daughter, who was terribly shy and charmed everyone into giving her extra candies.

After Usen and his wife said goodbye to the previous group, we walked together to the shrine site and went in to pray. We sat on small wooden chairs around the periphery of the tall room; Usen stood and told us about the impressive architecture of the place. Because Suinbai, as a poet (Kaz: *akhyn*), played the *dombyra*, a wooden stringed instrument, the curve and style of the walls are meant to physically resemble that instrument. At the top there is a metal roof, domed like the inside of a yurt, with a metal *shangyrakh*, the wooden circle that holds the yurt structure together. A shangyrakh is one of the most spiritual and significant symbols for all former nomadic peoples: it represents the sacredness of home and family, as well as the protection those provide. Those living (and who have lived) under one shangyrakh are supposed to take care of one another; the physical object is often passed down through generations. Usen pointed out and read a quote engraved on the shrine's rear wall:

Арғы атам әруақты ер Қарасай	My farthest father-spirit, the man Karasai,
Теңселген дүбіріне тау менен сай	The mountain and ravine sway to his sound.

Пірім бар жыр несерін аспанға атқан	I have a patron saint, his epic song shot to the sky
Сұңқардай ер Сүінбай	Like a falcon, the man Suinbai.

He did not elaborate about the poem, but my companions (who had visited the shrine several times and had thus heard all of this before) explained to me as we drove away later that Kazakh Batyr Karasai (1589–1671) was Suinbai's spiritual leader or patron saint (Kaz: *pir*); in the story circulating from his shrine site, Suinbai prayed to Karasai for inspiration. In this way we see that sacred shrine sites are not necessarily originary points in Kazakh ancestry but are themselves imbricated in centuries of relationships and mutual awareness. It was impressive to my fellow travelers that day to think that the ancestor they came to for blessing had likewise turned to an ancestor for blessing and inspiration. I think the idea helps to naturalize their experience as "something Kazakhs do" in a general (cultural, historical) sense, and this is something they learn from caretakers like Usen.

I met and spoke with a variety of caretakers in different parts of the country.[20] Having done so, I began to notice certain commonalities in the stories they told about themselves. Many told me (and the various groups I was with) about being called in dreams to come to the site. The caretaker of a local cemetery in rural western Kazakhstan explained that he saw in a dream one of the ancestors buried there and so came to work there; that ancestor also helped him to quit smoking. Usen had a similar story, which he tells at the site and which my traveling companions also narrated to me on our drive. In the late 1990s, Suinbai came in a dream to a teacher living in the region where he is buried. In the dream, he spoke to this teacher, Kydyrali Ata, giving him instructions: "My grave needs a caretaker. Find my grandson of the fourth generation, to be my shyrakhshy." Kydyrali, together with his students, went to find the grandson, Usen, who at that time was a heavy drinker. Kydyrali helped him get sober; my traveling companions repeated the story later in the car: "they cleaned him up, healed him," so that he was able to come to his great-great-grandfather's grave with his family, to actively care for the site.

Visitation dreams like these are common among caretakers, as well as with others called to a particular vocation.[21] I view these dreams as culturally essential spaces for dialogue between the deceased and the living. The education and upbringing of a person take place over the course of a lifetime. But the relationship between generations and the cycles of visitation and care between them continue long after death. A family is responsible for the care of the spirits of the deceased (Kaz: *aruakhtar*), whom they must "feed" with bread cooked in warm oil and with prayers. This type of respect and active connection ensures that ancestors who have been given the proper attention can thereby come to protect and to aid the living. The dreams of the caretakers, which have an instructional or prophetic quality, influence the life course of individuals and families. In these stories, ancestors are also taking an active role, to intervene in the world of the living and to ensure their own proper care in turn. If properly cared for by his or her family, each individual who passes from this worldly life will become part of a much larger kin group, that of all Kazakhs: the ancestors (Kaz: *ata-babalar*), who will continue to educate and to raise the Kazakh people as a whole (Kaz: *yel*) through bata and prayer.

Caretakers' personal narratives, usually conditioned or influenced by the ancestors, become part of the conversation space for visitors and pilgrims at the sites. Caretakers provide a living human example of the ancestral care cycle, and, as noted above, they often tell "miracle stories" about the ancestor that are meant to educate and to inspire, because they are in a privileged position to talk to visitors about the special qualities and characteristics of the ancestor they serve. The special qualities of the ancestor (such as artistic talent, leadership skills, fairness, strength, and healing) can be conferred to believers on pilgrimage and embodied by a wide variety of "descendants."

TOKTYBAI ATA

One of my primary guides on the pilgrimage that day was herself a special example of how ancestors can interact over a landscape of dreams and waking to confer a special quality or gift to the living. Zhulduz, my main companion on the tour that day, was a spiritual descendant of one of the ancestors whose shrine we visited. Zhulduz, the aunt of Saltanat's second daughter-in-law, was a divorced woman in her fifties who lived with her elderly mother. For a period in her life she had been very active in the sacred sites/bata healers' pilgrimage community, traveling with them regularly. Her involvement there had helped her overcome a difficult period in her life, when her grown son passed away and she (amicably) divorced her husband in part because they could not handle the grief together. After she left him she quit drinking alcohol and began to devote herself more toward a lifelong interest in healing and bioenergy. At the time of my research, she was happy to teach me about religion, energy, and the sacred sites but noted that she was no longer actively involved in the community. In fact, when we traveled to the shrine, we spent the day with two women she had not seen in a long time.

Before we took the tour together, we met and talked at length.[22] Zhulduz had given a great deal of thought to the idea of cosmology, and she explained to me how she thought about things, which I quote here (her words also open this chapter):

> At sacred sites we ask the ancestors to help as intercessors in our prayers to God, because they themselves were people who lived a holy life guided by God. During their own lives, these ancestors like Zhambyl gave bata to their own protégés, to help guide them along the right path. We always have to try to think positively, because words and prayers at sacred sites act on our organisms and have a positive effect from within. Each word has its own vibrations; good words act on people in

a good way, bad words in a bad way—they make people react and become nervous. Indifference also works in the same way—caring must be mutual, as we are all just part of the natural world. Every natural site like a water spring or an underground cave has its own spirit that acts upon different visitors in different ways. God formed the world of the spirits first, after all, before the angels and then only lastly the material world.

Zhulduz has traveled many times to different sacred sites all over the country and has often interacted with the healers who travel there, who even told her that she herself has the gift (Kaz: *dar*) for healing. Like Saltanat, however, Zhulduz also worried that this gift might be related to dark or bad energy, and she prayed to Allah to help her stay away from such things. Unfortunately, she noted, among the healers and tour guides at sacred sites, some quickly become very proud and let their egos (or money) guide them, instead of healing from the heart, just for the sake of making people well or happy. She feels that among people there is a fundamental problem of the ego, paying too much attention to what other people think. (She did not say it explicitly, but I wondered if this was part of the reason she did not interact with the community as much anymore.)

In addition to its own spirit, each place has its own rightful caretaker; these individuals are chosen to come to these places and to live there. Zhulduz said that many caretakers told her stories of being called in a dream but resisting their fate. In their ordinary lives, however, other doors and opportunities closed, until they came to see that their true path was toward a particular shrine site. On the Bes Atalar tour that Zhulduz and I took together with her friends, the caretaker at one site was exceptional. The shrine of Toktybai Ata is cared for by his sixth-generation descendant, a young man living with his own family at the site. Ten years before, on my first visit to this place, the site was just a mound of earth on the steppe along with the caretaker's compound. But he has worked hard to build up a mausoleum, and now the large mound of earth is surrounded by a striking domed structure of metal and glass. He explained to us that many people come to this site for healing purposes, because Toktybai Ata healed by playing music on the *kobyz,* a stringed instrument made of wood. His great-great-great-grandson is now the guardian of that kobyz. When the caretaker greets guests, he leads them to an alcove where the instrument is kept in a case covered by cloth, and he tells the story:

> In front of us here in this case is the musical instrument kobyz. This instrument is more than three centuries old; it is the one that Toktybai himself played. When Toktybai was fourteen years old, he was compelled to journey to a particular tree. When he reached the tree, he found this kobyz on the ground by its trunk. He picked it up and found that he could play, and he understood he was to take the instrument and that it would become his guide. Sure enough, in the next years, this kobyz would pull Toktybai to certain places and people, and when he arrived,

he would find that someone was ill. He would play this kobyz and they would be better: this is how Toktybai became a healer.

At the conclusion of this short narrative, the caretaker ceremoniously removes the cloth covering the trunk, opens it, and takes out the magical kobyz for guests to see. But not only see—we were instructed to touch the instrument and take its healing power into our hands and, through the motion of prayer, into our souls. We did. Only one person, chosen by the caretaker, is allowed to photograph the kobyz; on the day I visited with Zhulduz, the honor went to her friend Ainura, who quickly snapped a picture on her cell phone. The ceremony of the kobyz reminded me of visiting the museum of national instruments in the city of Almaty and looking at displays of stringed instruments behind glass, presented to us as the musical heritage of the steppe. The kobyz in particular, in its sound but also as a symbol, figures in the cultural imagery of the nation, as well as being an agentive character in many legends and stories.[23]

While the idea of a kobyz as a sacred object seemed familiar or understandable, we were being further encouraged by the caretaker to understand the connection between the instrument and the land as the sacred source from which we could draw inspiration or strength. After a final prayer and bata in which the caretaker wished us well, we shuffled out of the house and over to the glass dome, to take more pictures outside. Guests who have come specifically for healing are encouraged to roll on the ground outside the monument, as the healing power of Toktybai is carried through the earth. The land is holy because Toktybai was holy.

Our visit to Toktybai was particularly important, because Zhulduz is his spiritual descendant. She is also connected genealogically, through various relatives on her mother's side of the family; she discovered this connection during a pilgrimage to the shrine of another ancestor, Baidibek Ata, many years ago. She also told me this personal story, which she considers to be one of the important legends of Toktybai, so that others could also know and tell: Normally the caretaker of Baidibek does not allow guests to stay overnight. But when she visited, he chose her and a few others in her group specifically and asked them to sleep at the site that night. She felt very scared to sleep near a grave and had trouble falling asleep, but eventually she closed her eyes. The following morning when they were gathering their things and preparing to leave, a strange, low sound came out from within her body. The caretaker pulled her aside and explained that this was the musical sound of the kobyz that had come to her, that this was its music. Indeed, when we drove through the nearby village (Kaz: *aul*) and approached Toktybai, Zhulduz began to make this sound again, performing her bodily connection to the ancestor. I was quite taken aback, as I did not immediately understand what was happening. It became clear only in our conversations later throughout the day.

Guided by the caretaker at Baidibek and sometimes her own dreams, Zhulduz began her pilgrimages across an ancestral landscape in Kazakhstan, a form of

FIGURE 2.1. The entrance to the Toktybai shrine.

movement and inhabitation in which time and space are collapsed into a different kind of present, in which different generations can actively "touch" and care for one another, through words and prayer. Over the next few years she received many bata and blessings at sacred sites, learning more about those buried there. By the time I met her, she could act as a guide for me, telling me stories and playing the kobyz of the ancestor Toktybai with her own vocal cords; she herself literally embodied the protective spirit of the ancestor, who helped to guide her new journey in the present. On pilgrimages Zhulduz travels together with other experienced women (such as those from Ata Zhol, who have had a heavy and active role in creating and propagating the shared mythology of sacred sites in recent years), and they compare stories and experiences, reaffirming this worldview to one another.

As noted in chapter one, this particular movement is somewhat controversial in Kazakhstan, not only for the government, which views it as a possible religious cult, but even for the people who join the pilgrimages or are more actively involved within the group. The story I presented in the introduction to this book, about a pilgrimage undertaken together with some family members in the early years of my research, was my first serious exposure to the group, and I have since gone on pilgrimage and talked with women involved in the movement on many occasions. I also had the opportunity to observe other new pilgrims who travel with them. In this environment, my own will to believe is combined with a sense of skepticism,

FIGURE 2.2. The architecturally dramatic exterior of the Toktybai memorial.

a contradiction I have seen and heard in the countenance of many companions on these journeys. Like others, I have waited impatiently and anxiously for bata, channeled by a group leader, both to affirm my participation or acceptance in the group and to portend what is to come in my life and experience. Like others, I have sometimes found the conditions and demands of pilgrimage—long bus rides, extended lectures—uncomfortable or overly controlled. Ultimately, however, I think that the success of any style of pilgrimage (be it Ata Zhol or something else, such as cultural or religious tourism) lies in the underlying supposition that the metaphysical quality of ancestors is transmutable and suffuses the earth. However individuals or groups may interact with the sites, what is important is the connection of these places across a broad spiritual geography.

ANCESTORS PROTECTING THE LAND

While ancestors can help to protect the living, they can also take an active role in protecting the land where they are buried (i.e., their kabyrstan, to quote the word used by young Miras earlier in this chapter). Around cemeteries and shrine sites, another kind of miracle story is circulated, in part propagated by caretakers: how those who tried to remove trees from the site or use the ground (e.g., as a building site) where Kazakh ancestors are buried fell victim to horrible accidents or even death or their projects faced catastrophic construction disaster. Zhulduz told me a legend about a large tree near a sacred site in southeastern Kazakhstan, a tree so large that "it took eight people to hold arms around it." Someone once tried to uproot the tree but ended up paralyzed from the waist down in a terrible accident instead. In the mythology stemming from sacred sites, ancestors are intransient.

There is a predictable antagonist in tales like these, often either a Soviet construction team or a modern developer. In rural western Kazakhstan, I went on a small informal pilgrimage to local sites with the poet Kenzhebai, who told me a story about how Soviets tried to build a railway across a cemetery there. They laid the wooden ties and metal frame, but when the workers came back the next morning, they found everything crunched and curled in an unusable mess, and they were defeated. Kenzhebai's further evidence is that even the river itself curves around the gravesite, and, on the other side, the water has moved. One obvious quality of stories and discourses in which Kazakh ancestors act to protect Kazakh peoples and land is that the Russian and Soviet past is seen as a short and painful episode in a longer—and greater—*Kazakh* history. The moral of this historical story is that Soviets wrongly invaded lands naturally belonging—by occupation and genealogy—to others and were therefore defeated.

While Zhulduz had a direct and individual connection, it is also very common that ancestors act generally, to protect all of their living "descendants." For example, if one enters the city of Almaty from the northwest, as from the nearby town of Kaskelen, one comes in on the crowded Tashkent highway. I took this trip once with a municipal officer, a tall man whose job for the city *akimat* (municipal authority) was doing road construction in the mountains south of the city. As we drove along, we chatted together, complaining about the heavy traffic around us and the high prices of everything in the city. Nearing Almaty, my companion "washed" his face with his hands, which I knew meant that we must have passed a gravesite or cemetery, which I had not noticed. He explained that the great Kazakh hero Raiymbek Batyr was buried here by the road, and he prayed for drivers who cross, to make their way easy (Kaz: *zhol ashu*) and safe.

In the city, the Tashkent highway ends and becomes a broad boulevard, leading toward a busy central part of town near the old bazaar and the city's oldest mosque. Watching over the broad intersection there is a huge statue of Raiymbek Batyr, an eighteenth-century warrior famous for fighting enemies of the Kazakhs.[24] The municipal officer, who also felt a personal connection to the hero because he comes from the same horde (Kaz: *zhuz*), explained that Raiymbek's power in the present is to protect drivers. In this crowded urban context, accidents are unfortunately common; particularly on the highways leading in and out of the city, drivers from other cities (or coming in from neighboring Kyrgyzstan) are tired at the end of long shifts behind the wheel. The heavy traffic aggravates everyone. The fact that a great hero takes a personal interest in watching over the living is a source of pride and comfort for many drivers. The specific history and accomplishments of Raiymbek are conflated into a general figure of strength and protection in this local geography.

Figure 2.3. Visiting the grounds of a sacred site with my host family (an ancestral burial site is on the hill at right).

I also learned in more dramatic fashion about the way in which ancestors are able to protect themselves and to give warnings to those trespassing. One hot summer day early in my bata research Saltanat and her husband, her daughter-in-law Aida, and Aida's second son (a very happy baby) decided to get away for the day to show me a natural spring site about an hour outside of town. We all bundled into the family car and set off. From the windows of the car we watched the town fade and then eventually we were on the empty steppe, with low hills shadowed black in the distance, and open, rolling land all around, with herds of sheep appearing every so often in the distance. We pulled off onto an unmarked dirt road to drive toward our destination; Saltanat's husband knew just where to go, joking that, in the past, "all the roads were like this!"

The site itself is an oasis, a small clearing where an active spring rushes through hillside rocks into a pool, half of which is filled with reeds. There is another small clay pond, and a hill behind, where two wooden prayer posts were covered by wishing cloths. A small stream of people made their way up and down the hill to visit them. The spring was crowded. We parked next to a group of Russian visitors who had set up two SUVs and a large tent between them so that they could camp at the site. Saltanat, Aida, and I walked to the spring while Grandpa took care of the baby. In our swimsuits we clambered carefully over the rocks and joined the line of people going down into the freezing water, shouting at each other where

FIGURE 2.4. Locals play and pay their respects at a water spring and wishing tree located at a sacred site.

to step and what to do. There was a particular decorum for those coming not just to swim but to observe the sacredness of the site—you had to touch certain rocks and plunge yourself under the water three times at various places. We held hands and went down in a circle.

Saltanat and Aida were laughing and swimming easily, and the water was incredibly refreshing. Aida said she wished she could stay there all day. The last thing we did before leaving the pool was to drink a little bit of water bubbling from the mouth of the spring. Then we wrapped ourselves in towels and, all together, went to see the caretaker Nurbek, who keeps a large yurt set up on the far side of the spring, where his family can receive guests. He is fifty years old and had moved here six years prior; his male relatives were at work building a large mud-brick house nearby. (He joked that the winds were so strong on the steppe, they kept knocking down his yurts.) The extended family keeps a horse ranch there as well, and they are known for their excellent kymyz. We entered the yurt and sat at a low platform table, drinking bowls of kymyz, which the caretaker's two teenage sons brought to us, while Saltanat and the caretaker made small talk; it turned out that Saltanat's first husband and the caretaker's brother had worked together at the same factory, which made everyone more comfortable, and he began to talk to us about the history of the place and his presence there.

Every place has its proper owner, he began, adding that the "owner" is the ancestor buried there. There had been some contention over the caretaker role at this spring site, however. Nurbek had felt a strong compulsion to come to the site, the home territory of his in-laws. When he arrived, he found that a developer on the other side of the hill had blocked off the spring, to redirect the water toward his own farm. But he had made some mistake and the farm was flooded, so the spring was reopened and Nurbek asserted his right to watch over it as part of a sacred site, because the water has healing properties. There is also a cemetery at the site, under the hill. Nurbek said that a taxi driver had once come out here, and not knowing the terrain, he drove too far up onto the hill, where he got into an accident and lost consciousness. While he was passed out an old woman came to yell at him, "You broke my arm!" which terrified him because he realized people were buried there. When he came to, he ran down to the caretaker, telling him, "You're crazy to live here next to the graves! You have to read the Koran, every Thursday!" Nurbek replied, "We already do. Every Thursday I invite a mullah to read prayers for the people who are buried here; we prepare *baursakh* [fried bread] and read the Koran." When Saltanat and I were listening to and transcribing this narrative, she stopped at this point, shook her head, and said to me, "How are you not going to believe?" As noted above, the "miracle stories" at sacred sites function like testimonies, to strengthen the belief in and power of those buried there.

At this site, there is no one famous person or saint; it is simply a small local community burial ground, with burials going back several generations. The families of those buried there have long since moved away, and during the Soviet period the director of the kolkhoz turned that area of the steppe into a feeding area for farmed pigs. At one point, kolkhoz workers riding horses noticed that the ground sounded hollow under the horses' hooves, and they began to speculate that there might be a cave or an archaeological site underground. So they began to do exploratory digging. But the person leading the team fell sick and became paralyzed, and the exploration stopped. Grandpa interrupted him here to tell the story of another (very famous) sacred shrine site in the region, where researchers had tried to investigate the site during the Soviet period but their helicopter crashed and they died. "Aruakhtar zhibermedi," he said. The ancestors didn't allow it.

Yes, agreed Nurbek. In their case, eventually people realized that there was an underwater spring, as well as a graveyard, which he and his family now try to protect. They also have a personal relationship with those buried there, who safeguard them in turn. Nurbek told the story that once his car started by itself while he was drinking tea with a group of visiting soldiers in his yurt; the car went rolling toward the parking lot where children were playing, and he had to race to chase it and turn it off. That night, his wife had a dream in which an old woman covered in blood rose from under the water and said, "You all owe me!" (Kaz: *sender maghan karyzsyndar*). There was no accident, because she had protected them. So the following morning Nurbek and his wife baked seven breads and gave them out to people. "You shouldn't eat those at home," Nurbek explained, "but give them out to strangers, and when you hand it to them you should say, "Kairyngyz

FIGURE 2.5. The interior of a local shrine site caretaker's yurt.

kabyl bolsyn." This is a small bata, words of condolence meaning "may your grief be fulfilled"; it is said in both positive and negative circumstances as a way of sharing the fortune of events in life.[25]

After drinking kymyz, Nurbek's wife came to join us and listen to our stories. Their youngest daughter, who was just five, sat next to me, tugging my hand and pointing to her coloring books while her father spoke. We played at making faces at one another and making each other laugh. "And that's how we live," Nurbek finished. "I have to bathe in the water here too, or else I would die. The water is really good for people, they need to come [here]—they're in such a rush that they jump in with all their clothes on! It's good for them, people are so anxious." His wife volunteered that she knew of a woman who drank water from the spring for two years and cured her kidney stones.

Our informal conversation was interrupted suddenly by the arrival of the mullah. He had gray hair covered by a cap and was wearing dark sunglasses and a linen shirt. Saltanat, Aida, and I, still wearing our bathing suits, scrambled to become as "covered" as possible with towels and scarves. As our conversation was already winding to a close, Saltanat took the opportunity to receive the mullah's blessing, so he joined our table and said a prayer, after which Nurbek himself offered us bata. Grandpa was the last to say a short blessing, and then we gathered our things to go outside and see how they made kymyz. After we said goodbye, we went to the spring one last time. Saltanat and her husband bathed in the clay pond, covering their bodies with wet, gray clay. The main spring was now crowded with people splashing and playing, as well as dipping three times for healing. Aida sat in the spring, a huge smile on her face, watching me shiver. We didn't want to leave. But the day was passing, and eventually Saltanat brought several empty plastic bottles so that we could fill them up with water and go home.

Aida loved the excursion so much, in fact, that she took her husband (Saltanat's son) on a date there the following evening. When they came home he commented that he was disappointed to see old alcohol bottles strewn about the place; he thought people should be more respectful of a sacred site. Aida had also noticed this the previous day and commented that perhaps if they built up a shrine at the site, the people who came for camping and pool parties would not come. Her husband responded that the entire place was actually still owned by a private entity—builders who planned to make a resort there. I wondered if Nurbek knew that, or if he was involved. Aida and her husband had been arguing recently at home, but the spring site brought them together, at least for a little while. He joked to the family, "Thanks for taking her [to the spring]; you saved our home life!"

THE PRAGMATICS OF PRESENCE

Ancestors and caretakers protect one another, and together they create not only a place where pilgrims can come to receive their blessings and bata but also a sacred space where they can commune with God on visitors' behalf. Time, space, and the divide between the natural and lived worlds collapse, to create a worldview of care, healing, and inclusion. Various activities—ranging from swimming to drinking kymyz to praying, to touching the earth at and around natural sites as well as shrine sites—are localized and embodied forms of this worldview. Those who come to be re-energized at such sites likely face forms of neglect and exclusion in their everyday lives. Conversations guided by caretakers allow visitors to enter into the emergent worldview of these places, to connect with the ancestors buried there, and to understand their stories. In contexts like these, people's relationships with God and ancestors alike are a mediated form of dialogue that can recirculate like the energy and clean water visitors take away from sites. The experience of spending time at a sacred site, because it is embodied in words and relationships, is something that pilgrims "take home" like bottles of spring water, much in the way that blessings like bata are also physically received.

To this point I have described moments of dialogue and the physical and/or spiritual co-presence of ancestors with the living, as well as the words, wishes, prayers, and stories they share together. Forms like bata and the miracle stories of shrine sites' caretakers, moreover, create meaningful moments when that intergenerational relationship of mutual support becomes dialogically present in the world. These words have a clearly pragmatic dimension, as direct or partially mediated forms of blessing and care, evincing a worldview wherein people look to the past within the present, in order to cope with the contemporary tribulations of family and community, in the precarious social environment so many in Kazakhstan and elsewhere in the former Soviet Union have experienced during decades of postsocialism. How can people and families connect with ancestors' wishes and inhabit their physical worlds? In the chapters that follow, I move from the performative dimensions of conversations in the everyday and at shrine sites to the public performance of ancestral dialogues. In order to understand how discourses of ancestors' legacy, protection, and care function rhetorically at the level of national governance, it is first imperative to understand how and why ancestors' words function in the geographies of mundane encounter and how the landscape is already sacred.

THREE

ANCESTRY IN *AITYS* POETRY

> Pray for liberty,
> Is there a demand from no one then?
> Sovereignty, my people waited for you,
> Please settle in my country for eternity.
> As goodness comes to your land,
> Ancestors' voices every day
> reached the ear [were heard].
>
> —Renat Akhyn

THE *AITYS* TRADITION AND A NEW NATIONAL NETWORK

In this chapter, I turn toward a performative tradition in which the relationship between people and their ancestors is performed and embodied in another kind of dialogue: a live verbal duel between two poets. This is the oral art of *aitys*, which comes from the verb *aitysu*, to talk to each other. The tradition is widespread across the Turkic-Mongol world, including Kazakh regions of China and Mongolia, as well as Kyrgyzstan.[1] In Kazakhstan aitys has been actively revived as a national tradition, and some one hundred poets—young men and women from all around the country—meet one another regularly for performances before live audiences, most often to celebrate a national holiday or the anniversary of a famous Kazakh hero. I analyze at length here transcripts of poetry from competitions in 2004, held as part of a large and active new national network. In these performances, poets specifically use the frame and trope of ancestry to enact a public conversation about contemporary affairs. Poets wonder what Kazakh leaders of the past would make of current situations and problems. I explore the connection between the words that poets (and pairs of poets) create and utter, as well as the voice of the oral tradition as a whole. How can a classic cultural form become a space of reflection and criticism on sociopolitical affairs? In this context, ancestors support, protect, and affirm the words and voice of aitys poets and audiences. That rhetorical system is in turn actively supported as a form of publicly accessible media and modern history by cultural organizers active in a new national network. The ideological frame is one of ethnic nationalism.

After Zheltoksan (the December 1986 riots often associated with Kazakh ethnic nationalism in the postsocialist period), a poet named Zhursin Yerman began traveling around the country to find practicing aitys poets and to bring them together in competition. He is the man directly responsible for linking many poets from across regions with elite sponsors in a new national performance network. As a result of his extensive efforts, Yerman has become one of the most well-known media figures in the Kazakh-speaking community stretching through Uzbekistan and Kyrghyzstan.[2] The influence of this network goes beyond Central Asia, as Yerman is also in a position to forge ties, via aitys, to poets and cultural organizers in Mongolia, China, and Russia. During the time of my research (2004–6), Kazakhstani poets in Yerman's national network traveled to all those regions to perform.

What Yerman has proven in his tenure as the self-established head of republican aitys is that "knowing" culture, or making culture intelligible, relies specifically on a peculiar sort of commoditization of culture—its creation and transmission within and along financial, political, and personal networks. His intellectual and business partnership with key sponsors has provided relative financial security and even success in this endeavor. Together these partners have a mission to revamp and repopularize aitys in Kazakhstan and to link Kazakh poets not only to each other and to audiences within the country but to Kazakh-speaking populations outside the country as well. Their success depends on their ability to maintain the form of an ethnic cultural ideal embodied in performance and poetry, which further enables an ethnic nationalist political content.

One of the most important figures within the sponsoring elite with whom Yerman has worked is Murzatai Zholdasbekov, a former Soviet dignitary and personal friend of the president. A former ambassador to Iran and minister of the Ideology Department of the Kazakh SSR, Zholdasbekov has interests that are many and varied. In 2004 he headed a new research center at the Eurasian University in Kazakhstan's capital city of Astana. The center housed the faculties of the Kazakh History and Kazakh Languages and Literatures Departments, where scholars researched topics ranging from archaeological reconstruction and historiography to China and Euro-America, the practice and theory of Eurasianism, and of course aitys.[3] In the new center, researchers of aitys work together with cultural historians to place poetry in the new history of a nation.[4]

Part of the massive project of Yerman and Zholdasbekov (over more than a decade of work together) was not only to establish and develop a national network of poets actively competing but also to televise their performances. This was tricky, as Yerman's poets performed in the genre of *zhek pe zhek* (one on one) specifically in order to encourage political content in performances. In Kazakhstan's climate of heavy media control and censorship, most television stations were not interested in a show with relatively open political content. Yerman's group switched stations regularly. Over recent decades most performances have been videotaped by regional representatives of a national television network, edited for public consumption, and circulated wherever videos and DVDs are sold (in stores, bazaars, etc.). In the years of my research (2004–6) aitys competitions were even being broadcast live on the national television station Khabar, part of a large media conglomerate then controlled by President Nazarbayev's daughter Dariga, who was also at that time a political party leader.[5] The state media channel very much wanted to broadcast shows on "national culture," but because the content of aitys verged on the political (and the critical), it presented a risk for the station. However, because both Yerman and his daughter had worked at the station by that time, they could take advantage of personal relationships and work to persuade from within.

In our conversations, one producer at the station emphasized to me the ubiquity of musical talent among Kazakhs: "It's not like in the US, where there can be 'professional' musicians—here everyone is a musician, it is in our blood. Kazakh music is genetic, it is the duty of children to carry on these traditions. Everything for nomads is connected with our genes, even research. Nomads research everything, everyone has his own opinion. A shepherd working on the steppe could go to the stage and have a high-quality aitys [replete with] complicated language and rich metaphors; if he knows seven ancestors, then he knows seven centuries of history."[6] Here the producer used the rhetorical frame of "seven ancestors" (Kaz: *zheti ata*) and pastoral nomadic history to justify his arguments. In my experience, such mythicization was characteristic of the cultural organizers, the academics and writers, and the sponsors who formed the national aitys network.

Ultimately, the goal of the national circuit is to create famous poets—poets whose personae and words will be known and remembered. Edited transcripts of performances are made from these recordings, and excerpts are regularly published in the Kazakh literature newspaper issued by the writers' union in Almaty.[7] Yerman and his sponsors worked together with the newspaper at the time of my research to publish those transcripts in a three-volume series, *Kazirgi Aitys* (Contemporary aitys). These forms of enscription serve both to publicize and to historicize the words and voices of contemporary poets as a tangible and recognizable source of modern cultural history.

AITYS AUDIENCES

Under the auspices of the nation's cultural affairs office, every region of the country holds at least one national aitys every single year, and they are generally well attended, with audiences ranging from three hundred to five hundred persons. Audience members included prominent figures in the local literary community, journalists from local newspapers, local academics, politicians, businessmen, distinguished senior citizens, and veterans—a sea of Kazakh-speaking persons of all ages from the city who purchased tickets for 500 tenge (roughly five US dollars). Many in the audience came as part of a multigenerational family group. For all the poets with whom I spoke, a sense of camaraderie, care, and mutual support with audience members in attendance is an absolutely essential aspect of an inspired, successful performance. As a poet sings his or her thoughts, the audience responds in real time by yelling, clapping, laughing—generally urging the poet on. If a poet's words are boring or uninspirational, it is immediately obvious because the audience sits quietly or even begins grumbling. Audience reaction can make or break a poet's aitys.

Traditionally, aitys poets would battle each other in a struggle of word and wit until one poet triumphed—that is, left his or her opponent with no way to respond, with no audible voice (either because the poet can't think of anything to say or because the audience is cheering so loudly that the poet's attempts to speak are drowned out). Once a poet recognizes defeat, he or she simply concedes, and the aitys comes to an end (Zharmukhamedoly 2001). However, in this contemporary venue there were two factors that made such an outcome impossible. First, the aitys was following a particular performance format: several pairs of poets would perform for a short amount of time, rather than two performing for several hours. Each pair was limited to twenty or thirty minutes, and thus no aitys reached any sort of traditional conclusion. Second, the entire aitys each week was televised on the country's main national channel, with its own set schedule and timing of commercial breaks. Thus, the televised format precluded the traditional resolution between poets.

Organizers were always struggling to come up with an alternative way to effectively judge performances, because the situation demanded not only one winner but several runners-up. Places (first, second, third, etc.) were required because different sponsors could award special prizes to various winners in this way. At the end of each show, sponsors could come to the stage and personally hand their chosen poet a special gift (ranging from flowers to cars to television sets) and say a few words of their own. Thus, the quality of each aitys had to be judged comparatively and relatively, and it was important in this context that winners of aitys be, if not fairly, then at least "correctly" chosen, as organizers had a variety of demands to satisfy. Typically, performances were judged by a panel of culturally and politically prestigious individuals who made up a local jury.

The jury represents an opportunity for organizers to recognize and reward select members of the community and for those community members to judge which version of culture is somehow "best." In the context of aitys, "best" by jury standards could mean many things: how well a poet dressed and presented himself or herself, whether or not the poet addressed a previously chosen theme, whether or not the poet was funny or responded well to his or her opponent, and whether or not the poet voiced some ideas and opinions with which the jury concurred. Juries were made up of individuals upon whose support the aitys organizers relied to keep the cycle of performances going—respected elder poets and writers, the editor of the literary newspaper covering all these events, local politicians, and sponsors. For most cultural organizers, juries are not only part of the

FIGURE 3.1. Spectators in an aitys auditorium.

proper protocol of performance spaces but also preferable in a practical sense to the perceived pandemonium and bias of audience voting (for example, one series of performances televised live in Almaty in 2004 allowed audiences to send in votes by cell phone, but this method was short-lived, as wealthier fans simply corrupted the system and started purchasing large blocs of votes from the cell-phone company). While juries may also be biased, they are at least physically present during performances, experiencing the atmosphere and the palpable energy of the auditorium as a dynamic space. While juries and cultural organizers are deeply caught up in complex relations of sponsorship and patronage, there is also a more direct call-and-response relationship in the theater between poets and their audiences, who come to see Kazakh language and culture lauded on a national stage.

The greatest poets are known for their own style, for their beautiful and wise words. In their confident self-presentation, they enact an idealized form of Kazakh culture, in which Kazakh language and traditions are overtly celebrated. Poets consider themselves to be speaking as and for *all* Kazakh people, past and present. Speaking as and for regional neighbors, kin, ancestors, and audiences, poets claim to voice "the truth of the Kazakh people." Aitys poets not only present a positive and inclusive model of cultural belonging but are also able to use that model as a position of historical legitimacy from which they can then evaluate the problems and issues of the day. Often over recent decades, performative and dialogic frames of kinship and ancestry have formed the basis for more direct forms of sociopolitical critique.

Talking to me about the social purpose of aitys, poets and their cultural sponsors usually invoked a mythic history, wherein the great khans of the Kazakh past had poets who would ride around the lands of the khanate, entertaining the people and gathering news of their current condition and concerns. After a period of time, the poet would return to the court of the khan to present all of the information he had gathered. Not all of the news was good; sometimes the poets would tell of problems, dissatisfaction, or criticism from the people. But this was the duty of the poet, called by God and the ancestors to represent his people with his *dombyra* and song; if the khan was angered or called accountable, the poet was not to blame, as his poetry was simply the word and music of the khan's own people, whom the khan had a responsibility to govern well. One contemporary aitys poet joked that "today we do not have a khan but an ostensibly democratically elected president!" Nonetheless, poets today see their duty or mission in the same mythic or historical terms: to report the condition, or "truth," of Kazakh people to their leaders.

Part of the purpose of this oral tradition, then, is to make leaders accountable to those they govern. Poets are intermediaries in a complicated dialogue not only between ancestors and the living, but also with a third category: contemporary leaders. Aitys poets often glorify the Kazakh leaders and warriors of the past, criticizing current leaders for their failure to live up to the example of their predecessors. Aitys poetry is efficacious as a political voice on a national stage because it invokes a shared past and present and because the tradition taken as a whole over time represents a timeless and extensive "Kazakh people," all of whom have a vested interest in sovereignty and good governance. The legitimacy or authority of this voice comes from that people, but ultimately poets must literally give voice to shared sentiments. In that regard, poets should also be known individually, for their ability to craft noteworthy and memorable language.

FROM WORDS TO VOICE

The public performance tradition of aitys is always invoked on national holidays and celebrations. However, the complexities and realities of a bilingual country are glossed over in presentations of Kazakh poetry, song, and other cultural forms of music and dance that together constitute an ethnic pageantry harkening back to the days of Soviet internationalist performance (see L. Adams 2004; Hirsch 2005; Rouland 2005). In this staged cultural world, Kazakh nationalism is presented as traditional—not in the sense of "backwardness" (as compared to Russian nationalism) but rather as occupying a space of exceptionalism and richness with a deep connection to cultural history. Aitys poets, particularly those in the president's new capital city of Astana, are sometimes criticized as representing "patriotism for hire." But in my years of living and working with poets and students in many different regions of Kazakhstan, I came to understand that, for many, Kazakh nationalism does not imply blind loyalty to government but instead includes the responsibility to advocate for ethnic Kazakhs in general, even if it means criticizing particular trends or leadership. This obligation to "stand up" for the people is one stemming from the mythic history of the tradition; the ideology of Kazakh language and culture structuring the aitys community is one that suggests "tradition" is also powerful.

As younger students move through mentorship relationships, initial performances, engagements with sponsors, and so forth, they are being schooled in becoming Kazakh in a pointed way. In order to attain legitimacy as the voice of the people, as well as to attain recognition as individual poets, students of aitys develop a style, the elements of which are symbolic of an inclusive Kazakhness: costume and decoration, gender and kin roles, and dombyra, the wooden two-stringed instrument.[8] Even the personality characteristics displayed by individual poets are deeply cultural; in aitys, any performance stems from the adoption of a kinship role, so personal styles (e.g., being funny or serious, brazen or coy, tending toward politics or not) are written over appropriate familial contexts. Thus, cultural ideals are enacted—spoiled younger boys, cunningly funny women, and venerable elders. When performances are taken together over time, it is clear that aitys is representative of some varying but idealized Kazakh relationships. It is interesting that what all these poets and personae ultimately are supposed to share is a deep knowledge of language and history, such that part of the legitimacy of poets and their performances comes from some aspect of an imagined ancestral community. The aitys tradition represents a form of cultural and linguistic knowledge, the long-followed practice of learning among generations of teachers and students that continues actively today, and it is considered by many to embody the performative ideal of Kazakh ethnic nationalism.

As a national tradition, aitys is staged in a way that is as Kazakh as possible: poets' modern versions of "traditional" Kazakh costumes, Kazakh stage ornamentation, symbols such as yurts, *shangyrakhs*, and pictures of ancestors.[9] Before an audience, two poets are seated on stage with their dombyra. They will play as they sing, ideally improvising in extended turns, seeking to outwit their opponent in some way, with greater cultural knowledge, humor, or offense. To "win" an aitys is to leave one's opponent without a way to respond, without words. Poets themselves draw a distinction between their words or phrases (*suzder*) and the concept of having a voice (*un*). From an analytic perspective, the relationship between an *akhyn* and his or her suzder correlates to that between an utterance and the person who "animates" or actively produces that utterance (Goffman 1981, 144). Poets want their words to be beautiful and powerful not just so that they themselves (or rather, their poetic personae) become famous but so that the words are memorable, iterable. Words that are remembered will be repeated in contexts ranging far beyond that of the immediate performance and will have an impact within a broader social world. Poets can create suzder that will be part of the un, the voice, of the aitys tradition.

There is no question for poets that their words are dialogic, that in the course

ANCESTRY IN *AITYS* POETRY

FIGURE 3.2. Poets Ait Akyn and Karima onstage during a performance.

of performance they are not single "authors" (where author is defined as "someone who has selected the sentiments that are being expressed and the words in which they are encoded" [Goffman 1981, 144]). At a basic level, aitys literally means "shared talk," and all poets know that the success of any given performance depends on their dialogue with an opponent. All poets have at least one mentor, as well as a group of peers with whom they perform and practice regularly. If they are old enough, they also have students. This group necessarily contributes over time to the quality of poets' words and phrasing, and if possible, they are usually present when the poet performs.[10] Further, as the poets explain above, the audience plays a major role in the success or failure of performance—the audible level of vocal enthusiasm and clapping (or lack thereof) encourages (or discourages) them.

At any one competition, several pairs of poets compete, each establishing anew relationships with their audience that may or may not be successful. And within the context of any one competition, there are also other types of "words" spoken regularly: a head cultural organizer sits on the stage with the poets and functions as an emcee, inviting the poets to perform and often commenting on the performance. After the poets have all sung, they are judged by the jury sitting within the audience; a representative of the jury often stands to explain who has won the competition and to offer the reasoning behind that decision. At the end of each competition, the poets all reassemble on the stage and prizes are handed out to the top performers. Prizes are given by particular sponsors, who often pause to give a small speech about local politics and cultural affairs to the audience. Poetic personae, audiences, cultural organizers, juries, mentors and students, and sponsors are all participants in the dialogic framework of performance and have various roles within that frame: some are designated to speak and/or hear, and they are thus responsible for the creation of what is said in performance.

There is another level at which aitys is dialogic: to fulfill a basic tenet of performance, poets must inhabit multiple social relationships: territorial, familial, historical. Poets always speak as and for a region; they are known and called by their first names and their region of origin. In order to aitysu, to speak with or against an opponent, poets must verbally establish a fictive kinship relationship. Poets also are always speaking as members of a particular maximal lineage group (Kaz: *ru*).[11] These groups are also loosely defined by territory. Another type of ancestry that poets claim is a connection with the famous *akhyndar* (poets) or *batyrlar* (warriors) who also come from their region. This process of progressively inclusive naming and claiming forms a "people," voiced by poets, who then have the legitimate authority to confront contemporary Kazakh leaders. In performances, in the dialogic frames of family and genealogy, poets wonder what Kazakh ancestors would think about the lives and trials of their descendants.

KAZAKHS AND THEIR ENEMIES

The first extended example I present here comes from a performance in 2004 of the poets Kenzhebai and Amanzhol in commemoration of eighteenth-century Kazakh hero warrior Raiymbek Batyr. Raiymbek is one of the many historical figures made well known in a wave of postindependence ethnic nationalism.[12] Figures like Raiymbek reinhabited the social geography of towns and cities across the country in the post-Soviet period, replacing the figures of the socialist, communist past: in street names, monuments, statues, and in days of commemoration in which aitys is almost certain to be a part. There is of course a particular reason and complicated ideological historical trajectory for the inclusion of various personages. Poets, *batyrs*, famous leaders, and judges—each contributed something to the creation of what is now understood (and deeply felt) as a distinctly Kazakh national identity.

These figures, and their symbolic histories, are part of the fabric of a new national life in Kazakhstan. In the city of Almaty, a boulevard was renamed in honor of the famed batyr, and a popular shrine was built in commemoration. There is now a Raiymbek Batyr stop on the new Almaty metro line. The first aitys I analyze here was part of a celebration on the 150th anniversary of his birth. The character and format of these anniversary celebrations come directly from the Soviet period, but they now include newer historical figures such as the president of the country and even the new capital city Astana, which also celebrates anniversaries of its founding. Figures like Raiymbek become blended in both the social geography and in the calendric cycle of the new Kazakh nation. But of course while many Kazakhstanis would be quite familiar with the name of the batyr, knowing the actual history of the figure and the subtle shades of inference it brings to a national history is not as common. That is one reason why aitys is a part of national anniversary and holiday celebrations. Because poets are educated in Kazakh history and literature, part of their social task in poetry is to share that knowledge (as well as to discuss current social and political events and/or joke with their opponent). Listening to an aitys competition about Raiymbek is potentially a chance to learn about the man's contribution within the frame of ethnic nationalism: why, exactly, is he considered an exemplary *Kazakh*?

What is most significant about Raiymbek in the context of Kazakh national history is that he was the military leader commonly remembered for his fight against the Kalmyks. From the mid-seventeenth century, invading Kalmyks contributed to a long period of war and disorder along the southern frontier of the Russian Empire, where Moscow negotiated contracts with regional khans and where Kazakhs were already fighting Oirats to the east. After a century of conflict, despite self-interested Russian attempts to negotiate with both groups, an invading Oirat army forced Kazakhs "to flee west across the Syr Darya river" in a panic (Khodorkovsky 2002, 150). Many died or lost their herds; this event is a tragic one in national memory. From the seventeenth to the eighteenth centuries, Kazakhs and Kalmyks engaged in a long series of raids, threats, temporary treaties, and continued hostilities. In contemporary nationalist discourse, this period is one of both pride, in Kazakh triumphs over invading Kalmyks, but also grief, at the loss to the Oirats. These histories have become conflated in popular imagination, with the result that the term "Kalmyk" (Kaz: Kalmak) has come to be a central signifier for "Kazakh enemies."

At the anniversary aitys for the warrior Raiymbek, Amanzhol opened the competition by welcoming the audience and his opponent. In response, Kenzhebai moves into a historical narrative mode quite common for aitys singers: he talks about the person of honor on that day, his qualities of character, and his role in the defeat of "Kazakh enemies," identifying him directly as a general Kazakh ancestor:

Көрсеткен қиналғанда көсем қайрат,	A leader shows courage when in trouble,
Жақсы ақын жауын тастар жіпсіз байлап.	A good poet finishes his opponent by tying him without a rope.
Қалмақ десе, басына қаны жауып,	If you say "Kalmak," with blood boiling in his head,
Райымбек атам өтті қылышын қайрап.	My brave grandfather Raiymbek passed, sharpening his sword.
Ой, аруақты аталардың арқасында,	Oi, thanks to the spirits of the ancestors,
Жатырмыз өмір сүріп, гүл-гүл жайнап.	We continue to survive and be happy.

Қазақтың сұрағанын беріп тұрған,	You have given what Kazakhs asked you for,
Арқадағы ақын едің толып тұрған.	You are a well-known poet from Sary Arka.
Әулие баба киеңнен айналайын.	I am grateful to the holy ancestor,
Арқа Сырды Жетісуда жолықтырған.	Who brought Sary Arka and Syrdarya together at Zhetisu.[13]
Болмасын қалмақ қазақ белдескенде!	There will be no Kalmak in a Kazakh fight!
Жаны барды жау дегенде сенбес пенде.	Don't believe that a soulless person is an enemy.
Аманжол, дүркіретіп айтысайық,	Amanzhol, let us have aitys loudly,
Жайлауда ойнап күліп ел көшкенде.	As the people play happily on the pasture.
Кайраттай Райымбек болса ортада-ай,	If energetic Raiymbek were here in our midst,
Ойпырмай, ойындағын арттырар ма едік?	Could we manage to know what he thought?
Қазақта небір батыр, шешен өткен,	Among Kazakhs there were many batyrs and orators;
Бірлік жоқ елден жауға есек еткен	The country with no unity is a donkey to the enemy.
Қарыс жерге қан төккен қас батырлар	True warriors shed blood across the land,
Ерін жастық, тоқымые төсек еткен.	Who made a saddle a pillow, a sweat-flap a bed.
Сырдан келіп Сартай батыр бың-баламен,	The batyr Sartai came from Syr with a thousand men,
Райымбектің сарбазын еселеткен.	[he] increased Raiymbek's troops by many times
Қазақтың бар батырын бас қосып еді,	If you want to know why Kalmaks were defeated,
Жеңілді десең қалмақ не себептен.	[It is because] he united all Kazakh batyrs.[14]
Дулаттағы Сәмен батыр орны бөлек,	The role of Samen [from the lineage of] Dulat is [also] special,
Райымбекті кім еді, десең еріткен.	He led those who asked about Raiymbek.
Біріккеді бөрі алмас деген сөзді,	There is a saying, "A wolf doesn't attack those who are united,"
Дәлелдеп, өтті батыр кешегі өткен.	Proving, that he was a brave hero of yesterday's past.

From the perspective of the new national history, Raiymbek distinguished himself as a true *Kazakh* batyr. A Kazakh batyr has certain characteristics: being a strong and capable leader, fighting for unity and freedom, having a vision about who and how his "people" (Kaz: *yel*) should be and which other groups threaten their freedom and therefore constitute enemies. A true batyr, of course, should be able to defeat his enemies. In this extended excerpt, the theme of unification is central to explaining why certain warriors prevail; united lineages and troops fighting together cannot be defeated by their enemies. Kenzhebai has already rhetorically "united" with his opponent Amanzhol, as they are from different regions critical in Kazakhs' history of fighting to control land, particularly around the Syr Darya river basin (Zhetisu).

There are two reasons why the general figure of the Kazakh batyr stands at the center of the national historical imagination. Batyrs who worked to unite the Kazakh tribes and who fought on behalf of a specifically Kazakh people against its enemies are therefore the heroes of that Kazakh history they worked to create and preserve. They represent all of the nation's historical lineages because the social histories of, for example, the members of tribes who were united or the soldiers who died fighting are conflated into the life history of one central hero. Talking about a batyr is also metaphorically or rhetorically a way of talking about the Kazakh people. If this hero is responsible for creating and protecting a Kazakh population in the world, then of course all living Kazakhs today owe him an ontological debt: they are all here because he fought. In this performance, Kenzhebai comments that listening to the history of these heroes is probably necessary in the contemporary world, where people are beginning to forget:

Бүгінгі қазаққа да керек шығар	It's probably necessary for today's Kazakh—
Батырдың, тарихын бастап кеттің.	You've begun to move away from the history of the batyr.
Қазаққа бұрын жауды жақтырар ма еді?	Did the Kazakhs approve of the enemy in the past?
Жау десе, шығатын жол таптырар ма еді?	If you said "enemy," would they let him escape?

Kenzhebai presents the perspective of Kazakh generations past: how would they respond to the life trajectory of Kazakhs today, to the loss of the path they set forth for their descendants? He states indirectly that in contrast to the past, when Kazakhs always confronted their enemies, something different is happening. Who are the contemporary "enemies" (literal and metaphorical) of living Kazakhs, and why are they not being confronted? Kenzhebai himself offers no direct answer for these questions, instead suggesting that Kazakhs are not as united as they should be, not as aware of what truly threatens them, not able to live by the example of their brave warrior ancestor(s). In a nationalist context, one could speculate that the issue here is some kind of Kazakh sovereignty, or self-rule, rather than the reality of continued Russian hegemony in the political and territorial leadership of Kazakhstan. Kenzhebai's purpose here is pedagogical: to set up Raiymbek as an exemplary hero in order to make Kazakhs today question their own potential. He wishes to criticize, but also to inspire. Therefore, in the last lines of his song, Kenzhebai turns the thematic focus from a shameful scenario in which the living have abandoned their ancestors, to a reverent one, in which ancestors are addressed with the formal "you" (Kaz: *siz*), praised, and promised that the generations to come will recognize their protection:

Әруағың, сан ғасырлар қорғайды әлі,	Your ancestor-spirit will protect [you] for centuries' time,

Ұрпағың сіздерге алғыс жолдайды әлі.   Your descendants will convey their gratefulness to you.

In this affirmation, praise, and thanks, Kenzhebai is drawing a genealogical link between Raiymbek Batyr and contemporary aitys audience(s), as Raiymbek's generalized "descendants." Speculating about what the batyr would have wanted or would have done in the present sets Raiymbek up as an idealized hero. This move also blurs eras of history, in which centuries past are set up as a practical guidepost for the present. As Nathan Light (2011) argues, such "mythic and genealogical bricolage" is a postindependence strategy common to all CIS states, one that is effective because these are "idealized narratives that explain in the most linear terms possible how the concrete present emerged from a more abstract past: they are parsimonious and comprehensive. Narrators of dynastic genealogies merge cosmological origins with descent through recognized historical figures and connect to the experiential knowledge of their audiences. They explain present social organization in terms of past kinship, politics, and cultural origins" (41). I would suggest that such rhetorical moves in aitys poetry, seen onstage at national anniversaries and celebrations, serve to amplify the mythologizing of Kazakh cultural history by the current nation-state.

What aitys contributes to a new national history, I would also argue, is not just a matter of form, but of content—the inclusion of social and political jokes, commentary, and criticism. Poets do not necessarily provide new historical or cultural content, in the sense that the topics and personages they are likely to mention are already well cataloged in Kazakhstan's national branding. However, by affirming and performing kinship and ancestry as frames for their dialogue, poets can exploit the trope of genealogy to create a discursive space maximally inclusive of "all Kazakh people." This is a position of cultural and historical authority, a "voice" with which aitys poets can help to create the new (and potentially subversive) "words" of Kazakh history.

KINSHIP AND CRITICISM

The second aitys competition I analyze here at length was between two fiery young poets, Orazaly and Renat, and took place as a part of the same series of weekly aitys competitions in the city of Almaty, staged at the Republican Theater. I was often part of the aitys audiences there, together with Kazakh research assistants, colleagues, and friends; as mentioned above, the competitions were also being broadcast live on the national television station Habar. The performances took place in the spring; parliamentary elections were to be held in the fall. The format of performances was zhek pe zhek (one on one), so as to highlight and encourage political commentary from poets. The chief organizer for the series was the poet and public figure Zhursin Yerman, and primary sponsors included a prominent business leader and a parliamentary candidate, both from the then-presidential party Otan (Patriotic fatherland).[15] Several of the performances in the cycle were quite critical of political leaders at the local, regional, and national levels, and the president himself was implicated on several occasions.

The series in 2004 represented an interesting moment in the recent history of the aitys tradition in that it fundamentally foregrounded the performance space as a field of possibility; for a time, poets could get away with social and political commentary that would normally be excluded in a climate of tight media censorship. (Indeed, as the parliamentary elections drew closer in the fall, aitys performances were closed altogether for a period of time, though a parliamentary candidate from Otan was one of its primary sponsors.) The aitys excerpts I present here come from a more permissive political climate that has since been foreclosed; however, what I highlight here are the ways in which poets exploit frames of friendship, regional origin, marriage, and ancestry, in order to facilitate social and political criticism. In fact, those frames serve to create a ground or field of interpretation—a way of understanding comments about current events.

The first poet to speak in this aitys was Orazaly Akhyn, who had a standard opening line: "Assalamalaikum, alty alashtyng!" In saying this, he names his contemporary audience the *alty alash,* an ancient alliance of Turkic peoples. The word *alash* itself is extremely meaningful and multivalent, a general referent for "independent Kazakh people." It also calls to mind for many nationalists the Alash political party and Alash-Orda government of the early Soviet period (1917–21), which stood for Kazakh autonomy from Russian rule. Thus, having named and claimed his audience as unified and independent Kazakhs, Orazaly begins immediately speaking from within a political frame about current events. However, this is also an excellent example of how the positionality of family and kinship relations can be used as a performative framework to "joke about" and/or criticize current sociopolitical conditions in the country:

Құтты болсын, Ринат, жуырдағы.	Congratulations, Renat—recently
Өзбекстанға күйеу болап деп келіпсің,	You went to Uzbekistan to become a husband,
Арзанға түседі деп шығындары.	You thought [wedding costs] would be cheaper.
Олар саған қалайша қыз беріп жүр,	How could they give you the bride,
Кимаушы еді, Құдайдың, сыйындағы.	They wouldn't sacrifice a gift from God.
Өңтүстікті науқанда судан қысып,	They limited our water supply in the south [when it's needed to sow crops],
Өтелмеуші еді халықтың, шығындары.	People couldn't recover their costs.
Жақсы болды сені енді жібереміз,	Good, we'll send you then,
Мақта жақсы шығады биылдары!	The cotton grows well this year!

Poets are typically responsible for defending their own region from any kind of criticism; the poet Renat is from northern Semei, while Orazaly is from southeastern Almaty. What Orazaly describes here is specific to a different region, southern Shimkent. However, because southern Shimkent is near the border with Uzbekistan, Renat's new Uzbek in-laws are enough reason to bring up the politics of the region. The issue Orazaly references here is the ongoing tension regarding water resources in the region, particularly waters being diverted from the river Syr Darya to Uzbekistan to irrigate crops (such as cotton), while Kazakh farmers are left without. A Kazakh audience in another region of the country might not know exactly what the regional water politics of the south are (to some audiences this might be new information), but they do have enough knowledge of the general political climate between the two countries to be sympathetic to Orazaly's critical joke. Kazakhstani-Uzbekistani political relations had long been tense at this time, with fights about dominance in Central Asia and frequent border closings and other restrictions.

The aitys competition from which this joke was excerpted took place in 2004, but the topic of water in particular has been resurgent in recent years and was highly relevant in 2012, when Uzbekistan and Kazakhstan signed joint usage agreements and considered a cross-regional water usage agreement with Kyrgyzstan and Tajikistan as well.[16] An audience member from western Kazakhstan would no doubt also be reminded of the tragic history of the Aral Sea, the fourth largest inland sea (half in Kazakhstan, half in Uzbekistan), which was mismanaged, overused, and nearly completely drained for crop irrigation through the late Soviet period. Today, there are many Kazakh and Uzbek families and kin groups split across the border, and political problems at the national level translate into the reality that these borderland populations (as well as labor migrants) lose practical mobility and economic opportunities.

Because the format of the aitys competition is a verbal duel, one classic strategy is to insult, criticize, or make fun of your opponent. Orazaly is able to use this strategy to project the strained geopolitics between Kazakhstan and Uzbekistan onto the marriage of the Kazakhstani Renat and his Uzbekistani wife.[17] In the context of a joking friendship, this is a creative and witty move. Because the wedding of two young people is bringing two families and kin groups into newly established but very important relationships of social and economic obligation, most Kazakhs (as well as other Central Asians with similar kinship practices) will recognize that Orazaly is using those practices as an analogy for social and economic relations between two countries. The frame of one man giving his newly married younger friend a hard time, joking about his new wife, reflects common experiences and relationships in the real world outside the aitys theater, and it is therefore funny and completely relatable for most audiences. It is a socially comfortable frame of interaction in which Orazaly can push the boundaries even further, critiquing the country's politics:

Қазақ қызын Өзбекстаннан алып келсең,	If you bring a girl from Uzbekistan,
Қосағыңмен қоса ағар, гүлдегейсің.	May you live a hundred years with your wife!
Оралманды оралға оралтып ап,	Having "returned" Kazakhs,

Үйсіз-күйсіз қаңғыртып жүрмегейсің.	You shouldn't leave them without homes or family.
Сөйлейін сөз кезегі маған келді,	The turn to speak has come to me,
Дәл бүгін жақсы басқан қадам болды.	Exactly today it was a good starting point.
Елбасы жолдауында қадап айтты,	The president explained this clearly in his address—
Тұрғын үйдің бағасы барар жерді.	He outlined the price of housing.
Енді соған құлақ асып ары қарай,	Now they pay attention,
Компаниялар арзан үй салар ма енді?	Will companies build affordable housing?
Басшылар жүр пұл санап, Арзан үйді кім салмақ?	The bosses [only] count money, who will sell these cheap houses?
Қарапайым халыққа,	For ordinary people,
Қайдан келсін мұнша бақ?	Where will such happiness come from?
Салынған мен ол үйлер,	Having built those houses,
Министрмен, әкімдер,	ministers, mayors,
Танысөтамырын тұмшалап,	having enveloped friends and acquaintances,
Соларға бырін жұмсамақ.	Will use up all the resources for them.
Қара халыққа тимейді,	Poor people won't get
Үй түрлі жіп те бір сабақ.	So much as a rope or a thread.
Аспаннан киіз жаусада,	Even if felt was falling from the sky,
Сорлыққа тимес ұлтарақ.	A poor person wouldn't even get an insole.[18]

Here Orazaly again presents the fact that Renat has recently returned with his bride from Uzbekistan, using it as an entrée to talk more generally about someone belonging to a certain social category in post-Soviet Kazakhstan: that of the *oralman*, a Kazakh returnee, a person who comes "home" from another country. The government program that invites people with Kazakh ancestry to move to Kazakhstan from wherever they are living projects the sovereignty of the Kazakhstani state backward through the Soviet and pre-Soviet period, simplifying the complicated multinational histories of Kazakhs in Inner Asia. In 1991 the Kazakhstani government began a large-scale program to repatriate its "diaspora" from Mongolia, China, and other countries, promising Kazakhs new citizenship, housing, and a head start toward a new life. Over the years, however, there were many problems with the program for the thousands of people who returned. While some families did receive the land and housing promised, there were many who did not and had to find housing or build their own dwellings from what resources they could. The oralman in reality has been a controversial figure over the last two decades.[19] Kazakhs in Almaty at the time of my research in 2004 were divided. Some felt strongly sympathetic toward their Kazakh "relatives," while others felt that the returnees had become a burden on society (see Kuscu 2008).

Orazaly deftly links the problem of oralman housing to another current housing controversy: the perception of widespread corruption and protectionism in the world of construction and contract builders. Orazaly notes that the president has promised these *oralmandar* (Kaz pl.) housing but that even if the homes were built, local contractors would make sure they ended up in the hands of their own friends and family. Of course this is a multilayered and complicated topic, and Orazaly is touching many bases in just a few lines. Poets are sometimes criticized by audiences (or potential audiences) for being too superficial in their social commentary. But I would note that, in constantly bringing up current topics of controversy in the social and political life of the day, poets are keeping issues on the radar and are unwilling to let them be covered over. Poets have the interesting quality of being champions of the Kazakh people (and even nationalists), but in their willingness to criticize they are also shouldering a certain social responsibility in their patriotism: there are few willing to routinely call attention to the problems and dynamics of real life, let alone to call on leaders to be accountable.

Most poets believe that responsibility in governance and social welfare is paramount, and they are encouraging their audiences to share the same opinion (and perhaps also to consider or advocate for these ideals in their own lives). They do so by crafting lyrics that exemplify their own persona and talent and that are thus beautiful, original, and provocative—each poet becomes known for his or her style. At the time of my research, audiences responded affirmatively to poets known for the political commentary (both serious and humorous) in their personal delivery, as well as their cultural and historical knowledge. But poets also speak from within a traditional poetic framework, which provides a strong basis of support from which to criticize contemporary figures and issues. Any one point of criticism is nested within the many performances and relationships of the aitys tradition as a whole. Taken together, all of these people and places have merged to become both a cultural and political "voice" in the post-Soviet period (Dubuisson 2009). That voice speaks from within the space of a shared cultural history, and thus claiming knowledge and ancestry becomes a critical means of demonstrating the power of this oral tradition.

For example, after Orazaly's speech(es), his opponent Renat provides critical commentary on current events in Orazaly's home city of Almaty. He uses the strategy of combining ancestral claims and social commentary, explicitly and directly linking them. Specifically, he talks about one of the city's largest universities, Kazakh National University, which was founded in 1934 in the Kazakh SSR and which was named for Al-Farabi (Abu Nasr Mohammed Farabi), a ninth-century philosopher. Al-Farabi is a fundamental historical figure in Central Asia. He is known as the scholar who brought the tradition of ancient Greek philosophy to the region, and his heritage has been claimed in many different ways in the region. Al-Farabi is firmly in the center of the canon of historical figures claimed to have generated a Kazakh nation; while historical material on the early life of the philosopher is scant and contested, it is important to note that the territory of Kazakhstan is likely the place of his birth.[20]

In his aitys to Orazaly, Renat is able to exploit Al-Farabi's fame and the general respect and pride Al-Farabi commands as a Kazakh ancestor, and by doing so he is able to launch a more subtle critique about nuanced political aspects of the university:

Алматы сенің мекенің,	Almaty is your place of residence,
Тарихы терең бас қалам.	A foremost city with a deep history.
Әл Фараби бабамның	My grandfather Al-Farabi's
Ордасы болды баспанаң.	Center is your dwelling place.
Ғасырдан ғасыр өткенде,	From century to century in the past,
Тасқа айналған, қас бабам.	My true ancestor turned to stone.
Ей, ұрпағыңды кеше гөр,	Oh, forgive your descendants,
Ескерткісіңді бұл күні	who this day have broken
Үшке бөліп тастаған.	Your monument into three parts.
Бұл әңгімені бастасам,	If I begin from this topic,
Тереңіне Ораз бойлай ма?	Will Oraz follow to its depth?
70 жасқа толғанда,	At the age of seventy,
Қарт КазГУ шаңырағы,	old Kaz-GU's shangyrakh,
Өкпесіз тойын тойлай ма?	Can we celebrate your *toi* without insult?
Әл Фараби бабамның	My grandfather Al-Farabi's
Ескерткішін жаңғыртып,	monument will be restored,
Қайтадан енді қоймай ма?	Won't they erect it then?
Баба мүсіні құласа	If the statue of the grandfather falls,
Сүйекке таңба болмай ма?	Won't the whole family/lineage be disgraced?
Жоқ әлде Сіздің басшылар,	Your leaders are not among the people—
Жаздың қамын асықпай,	[They're] thinking leisurely of summer's problems,
Күз келгенде ойлай ма?	Will it be like that when winter has come?

A large statue of Al-Farabi stands prominently on the campus of Kazakh National University, one of the preeminent schools of the Kazakh SSR. It is still one of the largest and most active campuses in the city. Thousands of students, teachers, and administrators have passed through the halls and rooms of the university over the years, and together they form the school's "family" (a term of figurative kinship). This family's "home" is the school, a metaphor invoked here by the term *shangyrakh*, the wooden structural element of a traditional yurt and sacred symbol for many Inner Asian cultures (it is, for example, on the national flag of Kyrgyzstan). As this university is named for Al-Farabi, these people are thus all his "descendants." In this context, criticism of current school administrators for failing to take care of the statue was actually a criticism of those school officials for failing to adequately prepare for that year's anniversary celebration of Al-Farabi. Further, every large celebration is an opportunity to publicly perform one's social position and connections; the implication of Renat's comments here is that the event may have encountered (or created) grudges among the organizers. It is a chance to shame those leaders for not respecting their own history and not living up to the respect so many have for their institution.²¹ Renat wonders in his last lines if the school administration has already neglected its fundamental duties and if it will continue on in this way.

GRIEF AND THE PAST, PRESENT, AND FUTURE

Orazaly takes Renat's criticism not as a personal attack but rather as an invitation to talk about the topic of history itself. The approach he takes is one of warning. As discussed previously in the example of Raiymbek Batyr, it is quite common in aitys for poets to name famous figures in Kazakh history and to celebrate their legacy as an example of how things should be in the present. This approach pertains to classical poets or batyrs and particularly to great leaders of the past such as the figure of the khan. One of the most well known examples in contemporary Kazakh national myth-making is that of Ablai Khan, the eighteenth-century khan of the Kazakh Orta Zhuz (Middle Horde) who refused to submit to Dzungar rule and who united the three *zhuzes* in a sovereign khannate for the epic fight.²² The specter of disunity among Kazakhs today is often described by aitys poets as a threat of tribalism.²³ The fear is that the three hordes will break apart again and thus abandon the project of a unified Kazakhstan to the more petty political interests among kin or relatives. Ablai, by contrast, was a great khan precisely because of his ability to keep people together, the implication being that today's leaders do not share this quality.

While mythologizing a great Kazakh past is certainly a common rhetorical strategy in aitys poetry, in the performance I analyze here, Orazaly takes the opposite approach—that of grief and warning about the past, rather than a celebration of it. He reminds his audience that Kazakh history was not actually a happy one and that the people have been through many difficult events, including the major disgrace of being defeated by Dzungar forces and evicted from their land in large numbers after the initial invasions. Orazaly also recalls the cultural and ideological domination of Soviet rule:

Тарихта тар жол, тайғақ жол кешіп ек.	We have passed a narrow, slippery road in history.
Елім айлап еңіреп, ата-жұрттан,	Singing sad songs for our country, from our fatherland
Адасып айдалаға ел ктіп еді.	We have strayed toward an uninhabited place, the people have left.
Ақтабан, алқа көл боп, бір кездері,	*Akhtaban, alkha køl*—many all at once,
Қайың сауып, қасырет шер кешіп ек.	[Which created] deep grief and sadness.
Дін мен діл тілімізден айырылды,	We lost our religion and language,
70 жыл Ресейдің пендесі боп.	Captured by seventy years of Russian rule.

In this verse Orazaly presents the major components of a general historical sense of grief and loss, the times when Kazakhs were taken over by others—the devastation Kazakhs suffered in losing to Dzungars in the seventeenth and eighteenth centuries (referred to colloquially in Kazakh as *akhtaban shubyryndy*) and the more recent domination by Russia. He makes a play on the word "alcohol" (in Kazakh the word *køl* means lake) and in this way paints a picture of Kazakhs losing themselves, their path, their identity. The way to overcome this grief is to reclaim sovereignty; in the present day this logic merges with ethnic nationalism. Renat responds by saying that he will follow this "new song" (topic) of Orazaly's and quickly follows him on this rhetorical trajectory by talking about the present and reiterating themes of today's sorrows, such as corruption, this time at the government level. He characterizes the national government as consisting of liars or manipulators in a series of sharp metaphors:

Егеменді ел болдық десек дағы,	Although they said the country was independent,
Зањлдандық кәріс, қытай, орыстарға.	We work for Koreans, Chinese, Russians.
Укімет ел қорғаны десек дағы,	They say government protects people,
Елге есеп беріп жатқан арыс бар ма?	But is there someone accountable to the people?
Тонап-тонап жеген соң тайып тұрар,	After having stolen and eaten they slipped away,
Тығылған шурегейдей қамыстарға.	Hiding like a duck in the rushes.
2030 деген ертегі айтып,	They've told the 2030 fairytale,
Ұстанып-ап бейкүнә барысты алға.	Supported by the innocent snow leopard in front.
Мұншама ұсақтасын деп тілеппе еді,	Did they wish for their descendants to be petty,
Бабамыз ұрпақ үшін алысқанда?	When our ancestors fought for the next generation?
Неге біз үндемейміз осы күні,	Why are we keeping silent now,
Ағайын осы бізде намыс бар ма?	Brothers, do we have honor at all?
Мұңсыз мүзгі берсек, мысық ұқсап,	If we continue to sleep like a cat,
Ші бөріге де таланар арыстанда.	Even a lion will be beaten by the wolf.
Жаңа үкімет келгелі,	Since the new government came,
Жағдай кетті күрт төмен.	Our material status worsened.
Депутаттар жүр баяғы,	There are still deputies around,
Ақылдаспайтын жұртпенен.	Who don't consult with the public.
Премьер деген көкеме,	To my godfather the prime minister—
Ойыншық болды жұрт деген.	People were game-pieces [for him].
Бірақ олда қуыршақ,	But he's also a puppet,
Басқарылатын пультпенен.	Controlled by the remote [control device].

In these excerpts, Renat explicitly implicates the national government (ostensibly the parliament and ministers) for their failure to create equality and social growth in the new period of Kazakh independence. He also suggests that government personnel are thieves or cowards who steal while hiding behind the allure of the beautiful snow leopard—an animal that, alongside the eagle, has become an icon of the new nation. A snow leopard was one of the figures uncovered in Kazakhstan's famous "tomb of the golden warrior," a fourth- or fifth-century Scythian burial site that the Kazakhstani government has explicitly adopted as a piece of Kazakh history.[24] Perhaps ironically (given Renat's accusation about stealing), until 2007 the snow leopard was featured in the design of the country's official currency, on the 10,000 tenge note. Renat also mentions the year 2030, a reference to the government's strategy for development, adopted in 1997. In the tradition of Soviet labor plans, the strategy outlines goals for security, economic growth, health care, infrastructure, and energy.[25] While social welfare was not a major element of the plan and the distribution of wealth and shrinking of the gap between rich and poor constituted subpoints of the plan, Renat simply refers to the whole thing as a "fairy tale" that cannot be realized.

Renat also gives a short but sharp critical commentary on the prime minister. The office of prime minister in post-Soviet Kazakhstani politics is one that rotates regularly, as it does for other regional officials, ministers, and appointees, according to the president's pleasure. In the year immediately prior to this aitys, there was a changeover of power, from Imangali Tasmagambetov to Daniel Akhmetov. These two were both controversial figures, and they had both shifted positions in the power structure several times in the previous years. Renat was reminding audiences that while these leaders can be criticized for their failure to take care of the people, ultimately they too are pawns in a greater game. This comment is an indirect criticism of the president himself and thus potentially inflammatory.

COLLUSION IN DIALOGUE

Renat was saying incendiary things, which were barely (if at all) within the limits imposed by the state censors controlling media and voices of dissent. While many people may share his opinion, it is extremely uncommon in Kazakhstan to utter such accusations aloud and in public. What's more, this performance was being recorded and televised live on the state television channel, thanks to the sponsorship and support of the national network of cultural organizers and sponsors, including representatives from the president's own political party. Renat's words were also written down by archivists from the Kazakh writers' union (the text printed here comes from them). Thus, Renat's performance within the context of the "voice" of the aitys tradition and its dissemination were not fleeting or ephemeral. Rather, they "stuck" in different ways, both in the recording and in the memory of other poets and audiences. Indeed, at the time of my research Renat was very much known as a hot-headed young Kazakh nationalist (see Dubuisson 2010), and he fed off the enthusiasm of vocally supportive live audiences. But adopting this kind of character or persona is risky in that, while he certainly created *memorable* words, as an individual he pushed the bounds of what was typically acceptable or normal, even for a political aitys. As a strategy in the verbal duel,

Orazaly could potentially condemn Renat or make fun of him for his wildness. Thus, it is significant that Orazaly instead praises him:

Айналайын Ринат,	My dear Renat,
Қазақ деген халықтағы,	It is said that a Kazakh is also the people,
Бейбітшіліктің сімболы.	A symbol of peace.
Бір Аллах берген бойыма,	To my God-given height,
Арқасында өнердің.	Your art is at your back [protects you].
Жырын жырлап халықымның,	My people's epic tale has been sung,
Алғысына бөлендім.	I share [their] gratefulness.

Orazaly says that "his people's epic tale [*zhyr*]" has been sung by Renat, that "his people" agree with what the poet had to say; Renat has been successful in giving voice to the Kazakh people, and he stands for them. Orazaly directly aligns himself as a supporter and notes that aitys is a protective framework for Renat. In his closing lines, Renat then responds to this affirmation by explicitly reiterating the link between independence, good governance, and ancestry:

Еркіндігімді қол жайып,	Pray for liberty,
Ешкімнен енді сұрат па?	Is there a demand from no one then?
Егемендігім ел күткен,	Sovereignty, my people waited for you,
Еліме мәңгі тұрақта.	Please settle in my country for eternity.
Жеріңе ие бол дегендей,	As goodness comes to your land,
Бабалар дауысы күнбе-күн	Ancestors' voices every day
Естіледі құлаққа.	Reached the ear [were heard].

When one poet acknowledges and accepts what his or her opponent has given as a topic or relationship, the two move forward (whether overtly agreeing or fighting), and they do so before the audience(s) they have named and claimed as shared ancestors. The poets' words, then, become part of the voice of some historically legitimate groups of "descendants," who are unified by a desire to be part of an independent Kazakhstan. The critical turn made so often in aitys poetry is that independence becomes a metaphor for good governance: it is not enough to be free, but leaders should also show social responsibility to those they purport to govern. This demand, made by poets in performance, is done from within the culturally and historically legitimate space of ancestry. Indeed, this is what Renat accomplishes in his closing lines, proudly proclaiming, "Kazakhtyng ulymyn!" (I am a Kazakh son!).

FOUR

DIALOGIC AUTHORITY

> May there be respect from the people,
> May our road be the right one.
>
> —Karima Akhyn

SPONSORSHIP IN THE *AITYS* TRADITION

The word *aitys* comes from the Kazakh verb *aitysu* (to talk to each other). This form of poetry itself is a back-and-forth composition—a dialogue—and the relationship between poets and their sponsors, who are typically national- and regional-level politicians, is also a two-way street. In the case of aitys (as well as many other philanthropic and cultural projects in the region), cultural sponsors from the ranks of the country's political and economic elite have stepped forward with practical, monetary support for the performance tradition. That form of cultural patronage is quite common both historically and currently (Levin 1996; Prior 2000). It is a component of "patronage politics" (McGlinchey 2008, 2009), a way in which individuals can establish and reaffirm their position by being visible in the culturally legitimated places occupied by the powerful.[1] Cultural patronage is also a mechanism by which individuals located outside the networks of wealth and privilege operating at the top tiers of the economy (centralized under autocratic rule) can substantiate and build up positions within kinship networks, communities, regions, and political parties.

The aitys tradition embodies an idealized, khanlike form of Inner Asian leadership, wherein a strong ruler makes himself available and accountable to the people he governs. The arguments and examples presented in this chapter exemplify the paternalistic nature of state authority (see Liu 2005, 2012), which characterizes Inner Asia more broadly and which is rightly understood as a legitimate alternative (or challenge) to democratic reform in the region. This alternate form of authority at the local level is also described by Judith Beyer (2014) in her ethnography of *aksakal* (venerated elder) leadership: authority is not given but earned and enacted in relationships over time. Personal relationships and networks form local political microcosms, which provide a local legitimacy even to external state politics, as in the case of elections (Ismailbekova 2014b); these networks arise within and across regional and state governments and are an addition or alternative to state party power.

A paternalistic form of authority is operative in the sphere of aitys poetry in the performative relation of poets to contemporary leaders, as well as in the activity of the tradition's wealthy sponsors. I describe these as a dialogic form of leadership: performance and sponsorship presume an ongoing conversation between poets and leaders, one to which both sides are accountable. Dialogism entails co-performance (Madison 2012). Here I describe the concept of poets' voices being particularly valuable in the context of censorship under a repressive regime, one in which other voices of criticism or dissent are actively silenced.[2] I explain how members of the economic and political elite, even from the innermost circles of power, can effectively collude with poets in their criticism of government: poets draw upon sponsors' economic and political capital in order to stage their performances, while sponsors draw from poets' cultural and historical legitimacy in front of the people they both serve.[3] While sponsorship contexts vary, I argue that aitys is most successful in maintaining a cultural and critical voice when sponsors collaborate with poets: together they can demand accountability from government leaders and can enact a "life-changing dialogue" (Attinasi and Friedrich 1995).

The largest threat to this dialogic form of leadership and critique offered by aitys poets and sponsors stems from the fact that money is involved: poets might "sell out," and their voice would be nothing more than an outlet for sponsors' interests. The process of sponsorship is itself an exercise in the simultaneous accumulation and expenditure of social capital. The more wealthy and popular the sponsor, the more successful and consequential the sponsorship projects can become. However, because there is often a wide gap in wealth between typical sponsors and their poet counterparts, there is always the risk that sponsors will not support poets' *own* words or voice but rather will tell them what to say and pay them to say it. In the figure of the sponsor lies the threat that what should be a complex and intangible relationship will be reduced to a moment of capitalist exchange: buying the "commodity" of aitys for money.

FOLKLORE, SHOW BUSİNESS, AND THE THREAT OF SALE

Aitys is recognizable as a cultural form in part due to the work of ethnographers and folklorists at the Academy of Literature and Arts, a primary site of cultural description and production in the Soviet period and today.[4] The characterization of aitys as a (prolific) *genre of Kazakh oral literature* or *folklore* is formulaic in academic articles and dissertations produced by those associated with the academy. In the Soviet formulation, folklore is something that national (ethnic) cultures had; various forms of poetry and music became identifiably "Kazakh," as opposed to being characteristic of any other (similar) cultural groups; that is, these forms can be bound to a particular group of people ranging over a particular territory. In the encyclopedia articles compiled by the Academy of Sciences and by local universities, this characterization becomes definition: "folklore" becomes fact.[5] Spanning several decades, these articles vary only slightly in their content; all describe aitys as an art (*uner*) and identify it as a Kazakh custom or tradition (*dastu*). All present examples of and quote extensively from very well-known aitys from the past, texts of which are to be found in the archives. The names of poets who performed are listed, but descriptions are largely devoid of details about their performance context, particularly information about what audience(s) might have been present. Also well known in the academy are the folklorists who documented various cultural traditions. In the case of aitys, that role is occupied firmly by Mukhtar Auezov, famous for his work documenting Kazakh folklore and now also recognized as a kind of national hero (see Auezov [1959] 1964, 1997).[6]

Within each republic, the Soviet Union established a hierarchy of cultural organizations; there is not only a republican-level ministry of cultural affairs but also to this day a very active network of regional offices of cultural affairs.[7] These offices function as local foci for artistic communities and networks; they serve as places where musicians, poets, and their students come together to collaborate and to perform. While in the Soviet period cultural production fell more into the domain of the academy, today the national network described in the previous chapter has taken up the mantle of that historical legacy, and regional cultural affairs offices typically play a mediating role among publics, poets, organizers, and sponsors.

This widespread network of "culture producers" (see L. Adams 2010) continue to work together to perpetuate aitys as the genre of Kazakh folklore, as "authentic culture." Within that genre, poets become canonical representatives not just of a tradition of verbal art but of Kazakh culture more broadly. This is a process of intentional retraditionalization, the endowing of "tradition" being considered not as an inherent quality but rather "as a symbolic construction by which people in the present establish connections with a meaningful past and endow particular cultural forms with value and authority" (Bauman 1992, 128). A mantle of authenticity ultimately serves to protect poets when they criticize the government: they are safe occupants of the innocuous space provided by folklore. However, while there is much overlap in their object or intentions, these fields of cultural production are not entirely unified or without disagreement.

Researchers at the Academy of Literature and Arts do not tend to include contemporary aitys poets in their canon, and the contemporary performance network is rarely mentioned in scholarly works there, if at all. Indeed, the academy maintained a somewhat distant relationship with the national circuit of performing poets. Theirs is a position widely shared among the cultural intelligentsia and perhaps best summarized by the ethnographer Gulnar Kendirbaeva (1994, 100), who distinguishes "scientific folklorism, i.e., authentic folklore that is consciously studied, reproduced, and popularized by specialists and amateurs to preserve and better understand it" from both "ideological folklorism" (driven by state policy) and "pop music" or "professional art." Scientific folklorism is the work done by urban intellectuals, like those at the academy. Kundirbaeva claims that the tradition of aitys suffered in the hands of both ideological and "pop" folklorists. In the Soviet period, aitys, like other popular forms of poetry and music in Central Asia, was co-opted by the state as a political and economic set-piece: "this ideological aspect ultimately led to the genre's deterioration and loss of uniqueness" (99). Similarly, in the contemporary performance context, on stage and television, Kundirbaeva argues that "the very soul of the *aitys*—its sparkling, instantaneous, and situation improvisation [*suryp-salma*]—is lost." She feels that in today's aitys, topics such as "production, patriotism, and (especially) everyday life [have] watered down the aesthetic content of the *aitys*" (106).[8]

Some of Kundirbaeva's colleagues at the Academy of Literature and Arts shared similar sentiments. The director overseeing the aitys archive, upon learning that contemporary aitys was the focus of my research, dismissed me out of hand: "That is not a project." The vice-rector of the academy at the time was not dismissive but rather a combination of bemused and bitter. He and some of his colleagues had not been invited to the recent performances in Almaty (where the academy is housed just blocks away from the national theater), and he felt slighted. He also felt that the tradition today did not represent "real" aitys but was rather a type of show business propped up simply for the purpose of making money. The poets were either selling out or being taken advantage of.[9] Ideally, he believed, beyond flashy prizes and cash ceremonially awarded to winning poets, money should remain but a side aspect of the mutual relationship between performers and their sponsors: while cash or goods are always involved, what is actually exchanged is a mutual form of legitimacy—not currency.[10]

The offices of cultural affairs work on an annual budget approved by the regional government, with monies channeled from the state level. Generally, there are enough funds to host one or two aitys competitions per year, as part of broader holiday celebrations such as the Kazakh New Year or in recognition of the anniversary of a famous cultural figure from the region. The head of one regional office with whom I worked in 2005 and 2006 complained that local employees do all the work to prepare for aitys (renting the theater, staging, recruiting poets and arranging their accommodation, advertising the event), but national (republican level) organizers and sponsors come in at the last minute to rig a jury, arrange flashy and expensive prizes, and take all the credit. Other local organizers with whom I worked in different regions of the country agreed about the uneven distribution of work and credit but recognized that their association with the national network was ultimately beneficial. Not only did its presence increase local audience enthusiasm and attendance, but cultural organizers could use their association with it as a way to promote their region's talent across the country: local cultural affairs offices ultimately want their region's poets to ascend to the national network.

The final and obvious category of persons deeply implicated in the cultural production of aitys are poets themselves. Many poets working regularly at the national level have a very complicated relationship with their elite organizers, upon whom they are largely dependent for the opportunity to perform and, therefore, for any individual success they may enjoy. But the environment of the national circuit is incredibly demanding, in both pragmatic and emotional terms. First, though the circuit does have the negative reputation of being "show business," poets themselves, despite flashy prizes like cars and bundles of cash, are actually not wealthy. Whether men or women, poets tend to be the sole wage-earners for their families, both immediate and often extended. Most have another job as a teacher or journalist in their region. Between performance and other work, their schedules are demanding. Because they are famous public figures, their presence is also requested at myriad social events, often on very short notice. Poets are themselves also a product of cultural production, and they are somewhat misunderstood as a group by the wider public. Each member of this community has to live with a struggle over the figure of "who" they are and what their significance is: as a poet of the people? or as a family member with very real day-to-day concerns? They have to constantly juggle a popular perception that they are "wealthy stars" with a much busier and more modest reality.

Poets wrestle to find some degree of autonomy within the national performance network. During my first year of research, three poets tried to do this in different ways. Two poets attempted to set up an external sponsorship relationship through the ministry of culture, a line of support that would be separate from the elite group in Astana. They were ultimately unsuccessful, and the effort was quickly swept under a figurative rug. Another poet, one who had been successful in finding private sponsors, attempted to move into local politics. She was envied and gossiped about within the ranks of poets themselves, most of whom do not have the luxury of private sponsorship and who resented her success. A third poet left the national circuit altogether and made poetic and musical recordings on his own and in conjunction with the Academy of Sciences.

At this point in the contemporary Kazakhstani tradition, which over recent decades has become a televised and published national performance network, the question is one of cost. Theaters must be rented, costumes and instruments provided, and cross-country travel and accommodation taken care of, not to mention the necessity of substantial prizes for competition winners. Poets themselves, who generally eschew the accumulation of wealth as antithetic to their social and artistic ideals, are not in a position to pay for any of this. Nor are the majority of their audience, who tend to be middle- to low-income families. Today the aitys

FIGURE 4.1. Poets rehearse for an upcoming competition.

tradition, with its cycles of learning and mentorship and the performance frameworks it can create, is part of a broader political economy.[11] The final category of relationship that poets must cultivate, along with their mentors and/or through the offices of cultural affairs, is with sponsors. By the time most poets are successful enough to make it to the national circuit, they have almost always established a relationship with one or more local or regional sponsors—local politicians, rectors of universities, or prominent businessmen. These relationships are, by and large, some form of the patron-poet ideal discussed here.

On the national level, however, sponsorship becomes far more elite, and the relationship between poet and patron becomes more distant. Whereas in regional sponsorship relationships, poets and patrons tend to meet frequently and socialize within the same cultural circles, on the national level the two figures may live in different regions and may rarely (or never) actually meet. The national circuit thus introduces a threatening dynamic: unfettered by mutual acquaintances and a personal accountability, the influence of elite organizer-sponsors will predominate. Sponsors' interests might overshadow a poet's relationship with his or her audience, as well as with some imagined "Kazakh people." This dynamic could ultimately undermine a poet's relationship to his or her own words, as well as to the voice of the oral tradition as a whole. If aitys is commodified, it is ultimately the people who are left without a voice.

The fear or threat of sale has, indeed, become part of the discourse among aitys poets, both in private conversation and in performances. Here I argue that the real value of aitys, in the eyes of its supporters, is the voice of the oral tradition as a whole, which embodies a positively valued Kazakh cultural identity as well as sociopolitical criticism. Aitys represents a positive medium of belonging as well as a pragmatic means of participation in a climate of repression, censorship, and political violence. Even the threat of the potential "sale" of this poetic tradition metaphorically represents the removal of an alternate form of dialogic leadership.

A SOCIAL AND POLITICAL VOICE

"Voicelessness" (*unsizlyk*) is one of the harshest criticisms poets hurl at politicians, particularly seated senate members. What they mean is the practical inability to effect change—impotence. The insult is loaded because poets throw it from the relatively powerful position of inhabiting "the voice of the people," weighted with the authority of the ancestors, such as the poets of old, khans, and warriors, as well as the various figures assembled at performances. To call leaders "voiceless" is to call them powerless—individuals who cannot effect any real change. It is a move that radically inverts the actual structure of power in Kazakhstan: poets are speaking as and/or on behalf of those who are more literally "voiceless" or powerless and condemning leaders who wield wealth and authority on a day-to-day basis. In the light of a broader political context of media restrictions, though, there is another meaning to "voiceless"—a more literal form of political silencing.

Few people or groups in Kazakhstan today are in a position to publicly criticize the seated government (let alone the president), and those who do are usually silenced. At the time of my research, there was an ongoing series of arrests and jailings of opposition politicians and journalists. Two former members of the president's administration shifted to opposition politics during my time in the field and were dead by the time I left.[12] One of these was Altynbek Sarsenbayev, who at the time I arrived in the field was serving as minister of communication in the government and making broad strokes toward breaking up the government monopoly and censorship of the media. Indeed, when I met him the first time, it was at the taping of a debate on freedom of the press, to be aired on national television. But his reform policies did not make much headway, and in 2005 he left the administration in frustration to become cochair of the country's largest opposition party, Naghyz Ak Zhol (True White Way).

In the presidential election that year, Naghyz Ak Zhol put up a viable candidate who actually won the vote in Almaty. Less than a year later, in February 2006, Altynbek Sarsenbayev was found murdered in the mountains outside the city, along with his driver and bodyguard. All three men were found with their arms tied behind their backs and shot in the back of the head. The FBI in the United States was in the midst of organizing and sending an investigation team when their Kazakhstani counterparts suddenly "found" the killers: five men in the ranks of their own secret service. These men had all allegedly been paid thousands of dollars to take part in the assassination. The party who had hired them was never clearly identified, and these murders set off a harsh and ongoing volley of accusations among the highest levels of government, including President Nazarbayev's daughter, son-in-law, and nephew.[13] These accusations became part of an ongoing jockeying for power in anticipation of the 2012 presidential elections, which led to some speculation that President Nazarbayev might be replaced.[14]

A few months later, in the early summer, Naghyz Ak Zhol organized a large protest rally in Almaty. Some fifteen hundred persons assembled in front of the Academy of Literature and Arts, in the center of the city, to mourn his death and to demand accountability on the part of the president's administration. Midway through the protest, crews began to set up large speakers on one side of the crowd, claiming that there was to be some kind of public event there that day. The speakers began to blare pop music, which drowned out the opposition speakers and destroyed the call to silence in honor of the dead. As the rally finally began to disperse, the speakers were taken down, but the event of which they were supposed to be a part had never happened. A friend who attended the rally was disgusted, because just like the murder of Sarsenbayev himself, this scuttling of the event was very transparently an act of government, and it was insulting in its simplicity.

Sarsenbayev and the media reforms and opposition politics he represented were actively silenced in this example—ultimately washed up in the complicated antagonisms between dominant members of the elite. Poets are not in such a conspicuous position as he was, nor are they demanding the degree of change that Sarsenbayev was. Poets are not seeking democratic revolution but simply accountability and attention from government. Their position is nicely summed up in the phrase of Koishyghary, a well-respected historian I interviewed at the Eurasian University of Astana: "politics are not forever, but the people's interests are."[15] It is far easier to silence a dissenting politician than a dissenting citizenry.

Returning to poets' claim "to voice the truth of the people," I turn to the things that that collective voice is seen to accomplish: cultural unity and sociopolitical critique. What is enabled by this voice is ultimately a demand by the people for answerability on the part of government leaders. It is a way to participate, however minimally, on a national political stage.[16] Given the centralized and autocratic nature of power and the strong censorship of dissent in Kazakhstan, the majority of Kazakhstanis (of any ethnicity) disenfranchised from the elite networks of government and business do not have much opportunity to have a voice, in the sense of having a say, in the forces that exercise control over their lives and well-being. Aitys poets must turn the tables and voice that same "ordinary people" in performance in order to have the strongest position from which to launch criticism: the position of a citizenry embodying an idealized (and inclusive) Kazakh cultural identity and historical legitimacy. So long as the conditions of performance are maintained in a practical sense, so too will poets have the literal platform from which to accomplish those cultural and political ends: their doing so depends directly on external sponsorship. While less obvious and immediate than the murder of an opposition leader, the compromising of aitys competitions (by sponsors' interests) can also be seen as a complicated silencing.

As described above, sponsors are typically in a position to advance their political careers and thus patronize aitys (and other social projects) in order to garner cultural legitimacy in the eyes of their constituency. The relationship between poets and patrons is ideally one of mutual legitimation: both sides need the other to achieve their public persona and the political voice it affords.[17] This vision of the relationship among people, poet, and patron (or politician) stems from a mythic history of the aitys tradition in which poets were tasked with mediating relationships among wealthy patrons, like the khans of Central Asia's great khanates, through the centuries. This is a critical point, because it is precisely this type of mutually informed and dependent leadership that is modeled by contemporary poet-patron relations and that poets further advocate as a model of leadership for the contemporary government of the Kazakhstani nation-state.

KHANDAI

Poets' demands for accountability are, in the performance framework, couched within the figurative frame of poets speaking as and for "the people" to their khan. Aitys poets romanticize the era of the khanates as a time when a strong and powerful leader listened to and was responsible toward the populace under his stewardship. When successful sponsors are named or involved in poets' performances, the implicit message is that these men are, or have the potential to be, *khandai*, or khanlike. As I noted in the introduction, such leadership can and should be seen as characteristic of the region. Attention to paternalism at multiple levels reveals that the country and its regions do not function under a completely totalitarian regime. Rather, politics is a space where many forms of social authority (and attendant spheres of social relationships) jockey for recognition (see Jones Luong 2004; Liu 2005; Beyer 2010; Gullette 2010).

Persons were considered to have "sponsored" aitys if they provided material support for any of the following: theater rental, travel, costumes and instruments, accommodation, or awards and gifts for poets. There were two primary sponsors through the spring cycle, and many minor sponsors who came and went. Because aitys was held in the city's largest theater, because it was televised live on one of only three channels to reach all of the country's television sets, and because aitys is considered to be "authentic Kazakh culture," sponsors benefited greatly from associating their names and agendas with the competitions.

One of the tradition's foremost sponsors during the years of my fieldwork (2003–6) is typical of such a model of success. Having headed the presidential party Otan for three years and leading one of the country's powerful holding companies (based in Almaty), Amangeldi Yermegeayev (hereafter, A.Y.) himself echoes the mythical khanate framework of aitys performances and his own role therein. He praises poets for their wisdom, their meaningful words, their "open eyes," and their refusal to back down in the face of power. Congratulating poets for their "sharp" criticism of contemporary government, including his own party, A.Y. quotes a proverb: whips break the skin, but words break bones. In an extended interview given to explain his point of view, A.Y. shifted to a generalized historical frame of reference: "Before, the most important khan was Abylai Khan. And in front of him was [the epic poet] Bukhar Zhyrau, who could tell him what even his highest commanders and advisors could never say straightforwardly. Sometimes the words [that Bukhar used] were unflattering, even hurtful. But [these words] were what the people were saying, so Abylai Khan had to accept them."[18]

Abylai Khan is the eighteenth-century khan responsible (and famous today) for the unification of the three Kazakh *zhuz* (the Kishi, Orta, and Ulken hordes) on the territory of Kazakhstan (see Soucek 2000; Grousset 1970). The mythology of Abylai Khan and Bukhar Zhyrau, the epic poet who supposedly worked by his side to tell the khan about his people, is well known in aitys circles. Indeed, poets often compared themselves to Bukhar Zhyrau when explaining to me how they saw their role with regard to society and power. Here their sponsor A.Y. is also likening himself to one of the khan's inner circle members—a position at once privileged and restricted. While A.Y. is powerful, he also cannot tell his "boss," Kazakhstan president Nursultan Nazarbayev, directly if he disagrees with him. By telling his experience metaphorically through that of Bukhar Zhyrau, A.Y. tries to blur what is a real distinction between *any* patron-client and *this* particular politician-poet relationship, making it into a mythic history with no distinction. He further locates this dynamic in culture, writ large: "Kazakhs never say anything straight out. They start to speak and turn things around [such that] if you listen to the middle of what's said, you wouldn't understand." So too in aitys, he explains, do poets create "a chain of words and thoughts from the beginning," comprehensible only in its entirety.[19]

A.Y. at that time dissented from his boss in one fundamental way: he was a Kazakh nationalist. This meant that he thought Kazakh language and culture should be a priority in this still-developing state. His (Herderian) point of view was quite clear: "The spine of the nation is language. Language, culture, traditions—these are the center of the nation, not eye color, not territory. A Kazakh might live anywhere—even religion doesn't change it . . . [but] if you lose language, you lose everything. For us Kazakhstanis, if we lose our language then we lose our people's government [*yel*]."[20] At that point in the country's post-Soviet history, however, despite President Nazarbayev's initial nationalist platform in the immediate postindependence period, by the mid-2000s he had increasingly begun to support an internationalist vision of the country, which, by virtue of its wealth of natural resources, could act as a power among such players as Russia, China, Europe, and the United States. In a forward-looking and economically based model of state power, rather than wasting financial or human resources on traditional or "backward" linguistic or cultural forms like Kazakh, internationalist leaders advocated knowledge of the Russian, English, Turkish, or Chinese language as a better indicator of outward-oriented or global practical progress.[21] Ethnic nationalist politicians like A.Y. found a relatively easy connection with the tradition of aitys, as it is inherently a celebration of Kazakh language and culture.

The view of Kazakh language in nationalist spaces—as positive and valued—is constructed specifically against continued Russo-hegemony in the post-Soviet period, whereby Russian stands as the language of progress and future, while Kazakh is characterized as backward or increasingly unnecessary. These attitudes are a continuation of Soviet-era social-evolutionism, which dictated an understanding of Kazakh folk "lore" against Russian civilized "literature" (Hirsch 2005) and which also informed ideologies of Kazakh language as being local in comparison to the internationalism of the lingua franca, Russian. Today there is still a very real divergence in attitudes toward Kazakh versus Russian and the cultural and historical trajectories each language is seen to represent. Kazakh language is tied deeply to family and to rural spaces, especially in the southern and western regions. Russian is more predominant in the north and in urban spaces, and it is of course still a political and economic link to the entire former Soviet Union. These questions become more complicated in the tides of ethnic nationalism; while Kazakh language and culture are now a required part of the educational curriculum at many schools and universities, it is still the case that such programs and materials are not equally funded across the country. Nationalist leaders not only want to celebrate Kazakh language and culture; they also want more concrete leadership and reform for education and employment opportunities (Fierman 2006). This is an uphill battle, given the continued political and economic dominance of the Russian language in the region.

Because language serves as a metaphor in state-level politics for differences between Kazakh nationalists and internationalists, aitys poets performing in Kazakhstan (as featured in the previous chapter) are also able to use language as a metaphorical bridge for talking about the concerns of some broad category of "Kazakhs." But that license also comes "from below," from the ways that poets themselves have been indoctrinated and socialized into aitys poetry and into performance. Poets come to be poets through a series of training and mentorship relationships, which are underwritten by particular conceptions of and attitudes toward Kazakh language itself. In their language ideology, those within the world of aitys conceive of Kazakh poetry as traditional, of the ancestors, as unique, and difficult to learn.[22] That ideology of Kazakh language (and culture) structures and safeguards the ways in which young artists come to be socially legitimated as culture bearers. This legitimation is twofold: poets should not only have a unique style and mastery of their own words in performance, but they should, after a time, move into a position in which they can represent their regions and eventually lay claim to the "voice of the people." In aitys performances, speaking the Kazakh language becomes a broader metaphor for representing the concerns of the Kazakh people.

During the years 2004 and 2005, parliamentary and presidential election years, respectively, when the president's political party Otan was advertising itself countrywide, A.Y.'s affiliation with the poetic tradition was widely publicized. While sponsorship monies came directly from his own pocket, at performances large Otan banners hung prominently around the theater, such that the actual sponsor was ultimately overshadowed. Aitys performances at that time were well attended in the major city of Almaty, where a series of scheduled performances ran for nearly six months in 2004. However, they were also televised on the country's national television station Khabar (News), a major arm of the media conglomerate controlled by the president's daughter, Dariga Nazarbayeva. When poets began to criticize leaders in those performances, even directly targeting the president, A.Y.'s prominent sponsorship and inclusion of Otan was contributing to a confusing context in which it was not easy to simply keep poets from singing (though it should be noted that performances were stopped entirely by the state government at the actual time of elections in the fall).

The example of A.Y. shows that while sponsors and poets have their own agendas and ambitions, in nationalist contexts they can collude to promote Kazakh language, culture, and history. Poets could describe poor national stewardship as characteristic of particular leaders' continued Russo-hegemonic worldviews, which they could contrast directly with the positive example of A.Y. In this formulation, although at some point money changes hands, the actual finances are somewhat beside the point. The more important products of this collusion are mutually legitimated cultural and political leaders—co-advocates of a specifically Kazakh polity-in-the-world.[23] It is precisely this form of leadership—at once attendant and dependent, taking the form of an ongoing dialogue, ambiguously public in its paternalism—that best exemplifies khanlike authority in Kazakhstan.

Many sponsors do not (or cannot) fit so nicely into this collaborative mold. One particular problem is that, as sponsors do tend to be members of the wealthy and powerful elite, they may assume their position of power a priori rather than as a product of an ongoing relationship with poets or other cultural figures. It is this misrecognition that makes the sponsorship relationship fail. Each failed sponsorship relationship, however, calls to mind a basic truism: the aitys tradition cannot continue or grow without practical support. Lack of understanding sponsors seems to signify a lack of powerful individuals who value poetry for its own sake. Bad sponsorship is characterized by an overly commercial quality; in the following extended example, it is possible to see how the "sale" of the tradition stands as a broad metaphor for the devaluation of Kazakh culture and people.

POETRY OR PIETY?

In 2006, Zhursin Yerman, head of the national aitys circuit, came forward with a new primary sponsor. It was to be Ak Orda (White Horde), a burgeoning pan-Islamic movement headed by the president's nephew, Kairat Satypaldy, an individual then clearly positioned within the country's top circles of power. When Yerman and Satypaldy met initially to discuss the financial backing of aitys, Satypaldy explained that he was opening offices of Ak Orda in every region of the country and that he needed help spreading the message of the movement. Aitys poets were to be enlisted in that project: in performance they were supposed to discuss and share the tenets of the movement, primarily *imanshylyk* (piety). Ak Orda would host a two-day aitys competition in every region over the course of the year, paying for theater rental and poets' travel and accommodations and providing cash and other large prizes.[24]

In the months prior to this aitys, leaders of Ak Orda had established a regional office and, in an initial meeting with local religious leaders, had firmly established their own presence and agenda regarding the upcoming aitys performance: poets who were to perform were clearly instructed to propagandize the goals, activities, and underlying principles of Ak Orda. The performances were judged by Ak Orda leaders and their friends in the community. Ak Orda had also done the great honor of sponsoring a hadj (pilgrimage to Mecca) for Yerman and six poets from around the country, as well as the elderly parents of Bakhytzhan Ospanov, head of Ak Orda's regional chapter in Shimkent. Ospanov referred to the task of his representation as *politika* (politics). The religious movement was quite transparently laying the groundwork to become a political party in the next few years, in order to prop up Satypaldy's possible ascension to the presidency after the end of Nazarbayev's last term. Thus, at the time, Ak Orda was actively pushing its philanthropy and piety message across the country, seeking to insinuate itself firmly in Kazakh life.

Ak Orda's focus on religion backfired in aitys performances in Shimkent, even though the southern region (particularly the city of Turkestan) is widely recognized to be a spiritual center for Kazakhs. The Ak Orda aitys events were, in the opinion of audience members I interviewed, very preachy and less funny or engaged with audiences than the form usually allowed. I attended two days of performances, ranging from three to six hours each, and sat next to a large elderly woman named Mira Apai, who kept me company and fed me candies. She and her husband had traveled three hours by bus to attend, having saved money from the sale of *kymyz* (fermented mare's milk) on the roadside in their village. At the end of it all, she seemed deflated. I asked her what she thought of the event. "I don't know," she said. "Of course it's nice to see our culture and our tradition, but these . . . all they did was sing about piety. It wasn't a real aitys."

It is important to note that while a majority of Kazakhs would identify as Muslim, that category is as much a cultural one as a religious designation. Kazakh Muslim identity, largely centered on family and the figurative "hearth" of the home, includes ancestor reverence, as well as a relationship with the natural world and its elements (as described at length in chapter two). This culture tends to be inclusive and flexible, rather than orthodox, and so preaching about "correct" Islamic morals and virtues rubbed many audience members the wrong way. Further, it was culturally inappropriate that poets, rather than mullahs or muftis, were taking on the role of religious advisors, especially in the performance genre of *zhek pe zhek* (one on one), which is designed to encourage social and political commentary as well as interpersonal rivalry.

Poets in the region were conflicted about the role of Ak Orda and the type of sponsorship it represented. One of the region's most successful and well-known poets, Karima, talked to me at length about the difficult situation in which contemporary poets find themselves. I asked her to compare what goes on today with the atmosphere when she first started, in the late 1980s. Answering me, she was clearly frustrated:

> In those times aityses weren't bad, they were good. Then in the best people's aitys performances there were poets like Aselhan and Taushen. They have their own beautiful words, which people still remember. They were stars of their time. In those times, what I really liked was that there wasn't any kind of bartering or unfairness—whoever had the fastest horse in the race won. But today [the prizes are] cars, they say that you can't stand your ground in the face of wealth, and so like that [poets are] not shy of their elders, they don't give you the road. As if winning that car was the meaning for them. As if it all ends in this life. They do everything for the car. And here's how they're forgetting about art, forgetting why they came. This isn't aitys but some kind of bargaining. In those times it wasn't like this. In those times prizes were like tea services, rugs. The most expensive prize was a TV. Now even students wouldn't take a TV. And then they gave us certificates. We're up to here in that kind of thing! Property has ruined aitys.[25]

The reason that the prize issue is such a sticking point for Karima and other poets is that prizes are provided by sponsors. But as was the case with the Ak Orda aitys I saw, sponsors and their important colleagues and friends are usually also the ones who sit on the juries that judge aitys competitions, so obviously those poets who best represent sponsors' goals will win sponsors' cars, money, and other prizes. Karima noted that sometimes a private sponsorship relationship develops, and it does happen that one sponsor can buy off an entire competition such that his or her poet will win. However, later in our conversation she gave a contradictory point of view, reflecting that, just because Ak Orda spent big money on prizes, even if all that money is called in from those higher up in the president's administration (Kaz: *Nazarbayevting khozghalysy*), perhaps it is not inherently bad. As long as the poets consider equally their financial situation and "moral jaw," Karima ultimately decided, she can support them.

"AITYS IS NOT FOR SALE"

Karima's frustration came out not just in her reflections on the situation but in her next aitys performance as well. It so happened that a little over a month after the performance sponsored by Ak Orda, the city government held a regularly scheduled aitys to celebrate the Kazakh New Year (Nauryz). That is, the aitys was funded by public (government) sponsorship, with the regional budget covering the bulk of the costs. The state ministry of culture typically allocates enough funds to sponsor one aitys in each of the country's regions per year. Zhursin Yerman and his elite cadre of sponsors did not participate in this aitys, which meant that the only extra prizes were small in nature and given to poets personally by local community leaders. In that second aitys, Karima met her friend and colleague Marzhan in performance.

Marzhan is a professor of Kazakh literature at the local university and sometimes lectures at the school. These two women are widely known and respected as pillars of the regional cultural community. They are also good friends. While Karima is sometimes more humorous or daring in her performances, Marzhan is quite serious. Her dignified persona (and deep voice) command attention from her audiences and students alike. She considers it her priority as a poet to support and promote respect for the Kazakh language and traditions such as piety and respect for elders.[26] Marzhan had recently returned from an Ak Orda–sponsored aitys in the far southwestern city of Aktau, Mangystau oblast' (region). While she certainly considers herself to be religious, Marzhan noted that she was not *hadjy* (someone who has made the pilgrimage to Mecca) like many of her opponents, and so she prepared for the aitys by reading and memorizing passages from the Koran.

However, she ultimately won the competition against the poet Nurlan, from Mangistau. As she described it, she bested her opponent by representing her own region in a political way that was more in keeping with the traditional politics of the zhek pe zhek format. Nurlan initiated the discursive shift in a classic aitys move, by finding something about Marzhan's region, Shimkent, to criticize (a fact that he had undoubtedly researched before the performance). He noted that a statue of Ahmet Baitursunov stands in the city of Shimkent. Baitursunov was an author and linguist who, due to his "Kazakh patriotism" in the Soviet period, is now lauded as a cultural hero. However, Nurlan said that Shimkent citizens have "cut off" the figure's legs for the scrap metal—an unexpected and critical comment that calls to mind certain stereotypes that Kazakhstanis elsewhere have about people in the southern city—poverty and banditry. The thought that people would be so desperate and/or so disrespectful as to sabotage the figure of a Kazakh hero is a real insult to Shimkent and to Marzhan, who is representing the city and the southern region in this aitys competition.

Marzhan would typically have two possible responses to this tactic: to show the untruth in Nurlan's claim or to criticize Mangistau in return. She did neither. Because the aitys was taking place in Mangistau, it was not necessarily in Marzhan's interest to directly criticize the region in front of that audience and jury. Further, she wanted to establish herself as far stronger than any "typical" opponent. So she answered Nurlan, the poet from western Kazakhstan, as herself—a poet from southern Shimkent and a Kazakh patriot:

Өсімнің, ешбір мінім болмаған соң,	As if [you] don't have any flaws,
Шімкентке сен айтып зорланасың.	you're compelled to speak to Shimkent
аулыңның еті жаман десе біреу,	Of course some say your *aul*'s meat is bad,
Қараптан қарап тогып қорланасың.	It's not for nothing you fill up this stand.
Біреулер Махамбеттің басын кескен,	Some people cut off Makhambet's head,
аяқ кессе сен неге таң қаласың?	if a leg is cut why would you be surprised?
өсіңе келер сөзді білмейсің деп,	If you don't know the word [coming to make you grow]
ертеңгі күні береді саған ел бағасын.	Tomorrow's day will give you the people's worth.

Marzhan calls to mind the story of Makhambet Utemisoly, a poet and leader of anticolonial uprisings in the early nineteenth century. Makhambet was born and raised on the territory of the Bukayev horde (now Ural and Orenburg districts, Russia) and attended *madrassa*. The leader overseeing the horde and the region at that time was Khan Zhangir, who was profiting under Russian (Cossack) control of the region; grazing lands had been very unequally distributed, and in addition to confiscating lands under dubious claims, leaders were collecting taxes from ordinary villagers. In 1936 the *batyr* Isatai Taimanov led an uprising of Kazakhs against Khan Zhangir; fighting alongside Isatai was Makhambet. The rebellion lasted several years but was ultimately defeated, beginning with the death of Isatai—he was killed fighting the combined forces of the khan and the Cossack regiments in a large battle at Tastube. Makhambet went into hiding but was eventually killed less than a decade later, in 1846, in the western region of Atyrau, apparently assassinated at the hands of his enemies.[27] As is often the case in aitys performances, by simply mentioning the name of Makhambet, Marzhan is invoking this entire history and nationalist moral narrative, which any true Kazakh patriot should know. Here she draws on her strengths as a teacher of Kazakh literature and flatters her western audience by indicating that she knows the history of their region.

Marzhan speaks a bit scornfully to Nurlan, reminding him that every place has its flaws and that if he can't speak well, the people will judge him. In a few short lines, she has turned his joking criticism on its head—if western Kazakhs have such a tragedy in their past as a Kazakh hero murdered by Russians (or

Russian sympathizers) and they can still feel like nationalists in the west, then what difference does it make that another hero's statue has been damaged a bit in the south? Kazakhs there can still be proud too! (It should be noted that in taking this ethnic nationalist direction in performance, both Nurlan and Marzhan evade a wide complexity of issues, such as ethnic diversity and forms of discrimination or exclusion in both regions.) As it turned out, the jury gave first place to Nurlan, but he decided to give that place along with its prize, one million tenge (roughly US$8,000), to Marzhan, as a way of recognizing her stronger performance.

Marzhan's return to Shimkent after her win coincided with my own arrival there to start working with Karima at the school where she taught. When I first interviewed Karima's mentor, the school director and poet Sabit Agha, in his office, Marzhan came to tell him about the aitys, the exchanges therein, and her winning words. Sabit nodded, smiling proudly as she talked, saying over and over, "*Molodets! Molodets!*"[28] Later that day, she came to Karima's crowded classroom, which had swollen from its normal size of ten or so to more than thirty students, to listen to the same speech Marzhan had delivered at the competition. Here again she repeated the phrases of her own winning aitys, as well as from other poets' performances past and present, to emphasize the importance of *akyly sozder* (wise words) in competition. Marzhan's win in Mangistau represented a huge victory for Shimkent, and the aitys community there was very proud.

When Marzhan faced Karima in a small regional competition a short time later, it was a local (non-national, non–Ak Orda) context, and it would have been very likely that Karima would use the public stage to congratulate her friend once again. However, while the New Year's aitys between Marzhan and Karima was largely cordial, in her last turn Karima warned her fellow poet Marzhan about the danger of "selling out." The competition was emceed by Sabit Agha, who knew both women very well. I would emphasize here that because these two are friends and collaborators, it is most likely that this performance was anticipated or at least clearly understood by both. Further, Karima here is rhetorically using the figure of Marzhan to stand in as a general referent for any poet who may start to sacrifice poetic virtue for monetary value (addressed further below). While winning poets almost always receive cash prizes, the problem was that Ak Orda's prize was far too large, giving Karima a metaphoric opportunity to comment on its inappropriateness and the general situation:

Саудалап біттік жерді де,	The riches of the land are appraised for sale,
Саудалап біттік төрді де	the riches of *tør* are appraised for sale.
Ақындықты енді саудалап,	So then poet-ness is being appraised—
Болып қалмайық сорға енді!	let's stop this grief!
өнердің жолы тар болмай,	The path of art will not be narrow,
Тонығымыз лайланбай.	our clarity will not be muddied.
Ақикат болсын айтыста,	Let there be truth, like authority

Таразға тең сағандай.	hidden in aitys.
әділеттен сыйды алғандай.	Let's be cursed further,
әділеттен сыйды алғандай.	confusion just takes away from fairness.
Арыныз таза боп қалсын,	Let honor keep clean,
бес күндік мына жалғандай.	this kind of unity, five times a day
Арзан сөзге бармайтын Маржан десе.	Let Marzhan not go to cheap words.
Маржансын,	You, Marzhan,
басқаны білмеймін,	I don't know another one;
Мен үшін бағасы биік жаңғарсын.	For me you are tall, awash in value.
арқасында айтыстың батыс	You went supported to the eastern and
Шығыс барған соң,	western ends of aitys.
Оңтүстікке де барғансың.	And to the south you also went.
Он сегіз жыл дегенде миллион да алғасын	You wished for eighteen years, you took a million.
Сол миллионың, енді сен тым болмаса,	But it is not to be entirely your million—
Жартысын.	you are only half.
Алуан бізге қамдарсын,	Different to us you are prepared,
Ырысты болсын сіңліңе.	May you be happy with your little sister.
Жұғысты болсын сіңлің	May you be close with your younger sister.
Ізгілік сенен жолға алсын	Take a sacred path, [where]
Еңбегінді бағалап.	Your work is worth something.
жолдасын деймін аңғарсын,	You are a friend, I say, a ravine—
Оңтүстік осындай.	Your south is like that.
Аққудай қос қыздай	girls like swans, like sown fields
Тәнті етіп ел жұртты	Satisfy the people's country.
Халықтың бүгін таң қалдыртсын	It is the people you are making blossom today.
Жылдызымыздың саулесі ол	The light of our stars,
Қыздарымызға жалғансын.	you join to our girls.
Халықтан болып қошемет,	May there be respect from the people,
Жолымыз біздің оң болсын.	May our road be the right one.[29]

Due partly to time constraints, Sabit Agha stopped their poetic duel at this point, so Marzhan was literally unable to answer Karima. Rather, in this case, Sabit himself had the last word, because as Karima finished singing, she was looking not at Marzhan or at the audience but directly at him. Sabit picked up the cue, and, after the audience had finished wildly applauding, he affirmed that Karima's words were right, that we should never bargain for our art. Their collusion trumped Marzhan, and in fact Karima did win.

Karima's aitys is multilayered. At broad strokes she is describing the meaning of what aitys does for the people. She uses several different terms to name the latter—*yel* (country), *zhort* (public), *halykh* (people and/or nationality), and *biz* (us). Karima names the elements of this world that belong in this nation: land, poetry, cleanliness, respect, fairness, honor, and unity. One of the elements with which Karima plays in her poem is the idea of *baghy* (value). In the first four lines of song, she uses the term to appraise: (1) the riches of the land, (2) *tør* (see below), and (3) poet-ness (*akhyndykh*). Karima articulates the concern that these standard bearers of cultural value are being transformed from unifying concepts to commodities. Karima and other aitys poets continually bemoan both the removal of resources and the absence of clear material benefits for their people.[30] Indeed, to take resources without caring for the land or its people is a base affront in a cultural mythology predicated on a nomadic, herding lifestyle, a ripping apart of traditional values and systems of sustenance and support.

Tør in particular expresses the indignity or inappropriateness of invasion, as it is also the spot within a Kazakh home of highest value, the spot farthest within, farthest from the door, and reserved for guests as a powerful sign of hospitality. Keeping guests away from the door demonstrates the host family's willingness to feed and shelter them, no matter what the duration of their stay. Land, poetry, *tør*—these are all aspects of a Kazakh world to which it should be impossible, by cultural and historical standards, to attach a price tag. Yet it is happening, and Karima worries on behalf of some general "we" whether poetry itself could be commodified and sold like other vital resources of the people.

Karima has even characterized Kazakh unity in spiritual terms: let us keep our honor clean, this kind of unity, five times a day. Here she refers to the practice of reading *namas*, Muslim prayers. She exhorts Marzhan to "take a sacred path [to where] your work is worth something," and here she means a place clearly of cultural, rather than strictly monetary, value. The metaphor of a pathway is a very common one in aitys: *ak zhol* (white way) means a path to religious clarity and goodness in a culturally Muslim context, but in Central Asia it also means, more colloquially, the virtuous path.[31] The metaphoric path could be characterized in many ways, but it has at its core themes of ancestry, respect, and obligation. That is, it is a path "we" take together. The fear expressed in Karima's aitys and the very real threat that exists in cycles of sponsorship and performance is that the tradition itself could become, literally and figuratively, a sell-out. I think that these comments reflected the climate of sponsorship under Ak Orda: financially rich, but (ironically, given its Islamic bent) spiritually poor for Kazakhs.

TURETAM

What counters the threat of selling out, then, is successful sponsorship by leaders at all levels of government (national, regional, municipal). In the aitys tradition as a whole, the forms of patronage described by poets in performance and embodied by politicians in real life are clearly tied to a quality of leadership. A "successful" patron is one who is accessible and accountable to the people. There are many ways to be khandai, the benevolent benefactor, as a cultural sponsor of aitys. It may mean being highly visible and involved, as in the case of the national sponsor

A.Y., mentioned earlier. Or, by sponsoring aitys, leaders may also make themselves present to their people in the conditions of performance, simply by making aitys possible and by emphasizing the relationship of poets and audiences (rather than having a personal emphasis or focus on their favored special interest groups). The final example I give here is of precisely that: a quiet patron behind the scenes.

In June 2006, I was fortunate to travel to western Kazakhstan for the last aitys of my field research. Together with regional cultural organizers from Kyzylorda, I went to a small town in the territory of Baikonur. Baikonur, the missile launch site for the former Soviet Union, is now Russian federal territory.[32] Our entire group therefore had to arrange visas and special permits to travel there. But Kazakhs call the area or town Turetam, which is also the name of the train station there, a stop on the Moscow-Tashkent line. *Ture* is a generic term for a person in the lineage of a khan—something akin to having royal ancestry. The president of Kazakhstan has suggested more than once that he, too, is *ture;* it is a way of pointedly staking and/or legitimating political authority that long predates Russian rule. *Tam* means home; in a metaphoric sense then, this aitys did not take place in Russia but in the home of the Kazakh khan.

Aitys was coming here for a simple, practical reason. A former employee of the regional cultural affairs office in the city of Kyzylorda had become head of the cultural administration for the Baikonur region, and she maintained close ties with her former office. She came to meet our group when we arrived, like so many arrivals in Kazakhstan, seemingly in the middle of nowhere on the steppe, after a five-hour bus ride. One of the first things she joked about was her workload: "Here we have to celebrate all the holidays—Russian holidays, Kazakh holidays, there's a holiday every time you turn around! But we have to fulfill them all equally." She came with the *akim* (mayor) of the town, who was single-handedly sponsoring this event as a part of his political self-legitimization—he had just become mayor the previous year. They came with a small caravan of black SUVs, into which we clambered for the short sojourn to the territorial border.

In the classic fashion of Kazakh hospitality, we had just dropped our bags in our hotel when we took off again to the home of a former *akhyn*, Turoly, who now works as a *tamada* (improvisational host of major events like weddings). He was to serve as emcee at the following night's aitys. Having also been there to greet us in the steppe, he now received us in his home, a modest three-room apartment in a local block. His wife, her sister, and three female neighbors were cooking dinner for us. After a generous multicourse meal and conversation, the poets regrouped in the living room with Turoly Akhyn. When I realized our company had become divided, I went to see what they were doing. I found the group of poets comfortably lounging together on *kurpe*s (floor pillows), watching videos of aitys performances from over the years. They were animated and happy, talking to each other about each competition, which poet had participated, and what they'd said. They repeated the words of their friends and laughed together at their jokes.

FIGURE 4.2. Nighttime aitys event held outdoors in Turetam.

Older poets explained to younger poets about their colleagues' performances and styles. In the life of these busy artists, who are constantly on the road working or teaching, it was a great chance to relax and share one another's company. When we finally left it was nearly midnight, and we rejoined the cultural organizers to finalize preparations for the following day.

The Turetam aitys was a bit unusual in that it was to be held outdoors in the central square, rather than in a theater. By early evening on the day of the performances, nearly eight hundred people had assembled; benches and chairs were found for community elders in the front rows nearest the stage, adults found standing room behind them, and children played around, in, and throughout the crowd. Typically, a smaller regional aitys competition lasts two or three hours, but this night's performances began at dusk and lasted through the night, and the crowd stayed for the entirety of the event. The performances remained relatively nonpolitical, focusing instead on poets' interpersonal relations and mastery of the Kazakh cultural canon. A few poets, including Marzhan, who had come from Shimkent, commented on our strange political geography only in a passing joke: it is fine for Kazakhs to read Pushkin, as long as Russians read Abai.[33] The evening outdoors felt very special, and it was a fantastic success for this small Kazakh community. The crowd cheered, laughed, and clapped all night.

When the aitys finally drew to a close in the wee hours of the morning, most of the group (poets and cultural organizers) headed back out for a *dastarhan* (table of hospitality) at a local restaurant. This tuckered ethnographer took a bus home with the town's vice-mayor, a small, ebullient woman in her mid-fifties. I asked her what she thought, remarking how amazed I was that everyone stayed so long, even though they had to stand outside. She laughed, "They're still enthusiastic! Tonight they forgot about eating dinner, forgot about washing the floor. It was remarkable! Something like this has not happened here before." She seemed to echo the poet Marzhan, who, when we arrived and saw the amassed crowd, said, "A free aitys is a huge gift for the people."

The man responsible for this "free gift," Turetam akim (mayor) Kenzhibek, remained behind the scenes the entire time. He was present at our dastarhans but didn't take a seat of honor. His sponsorship was mentioned in passing during the course of the night by the master of ceremonies, Turoly Akhyn, but no one made much of it. This was highly unusual, given how generous he had been (he had personally funded the entire event) and that he'd done so specifically in order to legitimate himself in front of the community. It was a risk for him, to host what could be perceived as a Kazakh nationalist event under the immediate gaze of Russia; that he had done so was much appreciated by his constituents. Some cultural organizers managing the event also speculated that because Kenzhibek Akim was ethnically half Tatar, he also had a personal investment in publicly enacting his Kazakhness.

Over the years I have met many regional leaders (who tend to be showy or even brusque or inaccessible in their power), but Kenzhibek was different. This may be in part because at the time he was a relatively new leader, one who did not feel as comfortable in a dominant role but instead needed to demonstrate cooperation and respect to other community elders and leaders. Whatever his reasons, his sponsorship of this aitys event was successful. Indeed, the mayor's generosity and apparent modesty allowed the primary focus of the event to be on the relationships between poets themselves and their audience, rather than on political pageantry.

KHANS AND POETS

The evening in Turetam was an opportunity for an enthusiastic audience to meet and greet beloved poets—children clamored for autographs, adults came to shake hands and to extend their congratulations. A great deal of attention was directed toward one poet in particular: Kenzhebai Akhyn. Having performed in the region for several decades, he was well known and respected. As an older poet, he serves as a mentor and leader in the aitys community and beyond because he is deeply committed to bringing a sense of Kazakh history and culture to the area. Kenzhebai himself also has personal sponsors, including his regional akim and others he does not personally know. The night of the Turetam aitys, a private individual gave him a special prize of 150,000 tenge (approx. US$1,200). A similar thing had previously happened after an aitys in Almaty in celebration of Raiymbek Batyr (described in chapter three), when an anonymous individual gave him a new car. Kenzhebai found out later that this person was actually someone very well known, a personal friend of the president.

Reflecting on that incident in a later conversation with me at his home, Kenzhebai explained the perceived relationship between his sponsor and the country's president like this: "My sponsor addresses [Kazakhstan's] president as '*sen, Nursultan*.'" In other words, the sponsor uses the informal "you," *sen* (as opposed to *syz*, the formal "you") and the president's first name, which implies both closeness and equal footing. When Kenzhebai told me this story, he quickly followed it with one about Bukhar Zhyrau.[34] "If anybody wanted to know what was going on in the region," Kenzhebai explained, "they knew they could ask Bukhar and he would tell the truth." Kenzhebai hopes that one day the president will call all the poets to him and say, "You can come to me and tell me the truth about all the regions."[35]

Kenzhebai here echoed the national sponsor Amangeldi Yermegeayev (A.Y., described above) in his invocation of mythic history and the figurative role of the poet in relation to his leader and his people. In his hometown in western Kazakhstan, Kenzhebai very much enacts this responsive and personal form of leadership: he is an active and well-loved community leader, every day in conversation with members of his village, in organizing events, and in encouraging relationships. On a more local and modest scale, Kenzhebai also defines the model of dialogic authority I describe here: it is a relationship not of dominance but of involvement and communication.

But when I returned to visit in the summer of 2011, Kenzhebai Akhyn was deflated. Confirming what other colleagues and informants in the aitys sphere had been telling me, he explained that for the previous two years aitys had been effectively "closed from the top." This does not mean any direct order or overt censorship of the tradition: performances still regularly occurred in the country, including in Kenzhebai's region of Kyzylorda. In fact, the offices of cultural affairs there celebrated the publication of a research volume on historical and contemporary aitys, an elaborate effort funded in large part by government monies. What had changed, gradually, was more subtle: it was the tone of performances and the increasing pressure against critical political content. That pressure may have come from the president, or from those who control his popular and cultural image, but it was diffused through many different lines of access—media, cultural organization, and financial support. A former research assistant of mine in Almaty wrote to tell me that performances had been closed after (and perhaps because) one poet had said, "Not the light of our fatherland, but the thief of our fatherland" (Kaz: *Nur Otan yemes, Ury Otana*) in reference to the president's political party, which was renamed Nur Otan in 2007.

In the case of aitys in Kazakhstan, limiting the practical conditions of performance hinders its content, hinders its dialogic potential. While not as overt or extreme as the murder of an opposition politician, this, too, is a form of silencing.

That the state government has acted to silence this oral tradition reflects the poetry's potency as a vehicle of expression and experience. In poets' claim "to voice the truth of the people," there are two aspects: cultural unity and sociopolitical critique. What is enabled by this voice is ultimately a demand by the people for accountability on the part of government leaders. Performances are addressed to state officials, who fail to listen and take care of the very people they purport to represent.

CRITICISM AS NATIONALISM

Sponsors' elite status and the status of aitys as authentic-but-innocuous Kazakh culture serve to protect the tradition when performances get political. But critically, it is also the very form of the poetry itself that serves to safeguard poets. Here I show that the pointed critique emerging over the course of these performances was successful because it took the form of a dialogue between Kazakh nationalists and Soviet Russia, their former colonizer; poets embedded in their performances some sharp criticism of Kazakhstan's current national government regarding the continued Russo-hegemony and corruption in a broader argument about cultural and political nationhood.

In the extended example I give here, the poets Aibek from Astana and Mels from Almaty in 2004 colluded to create in their performance particular frames that allowed criticism to emerge indirectly.[36] Aibek directly addressed the president in the form of a *dat*, a three-part advisory speech given to the khan that is a form of cultural permission to speak openly. He announced the shift to the dat frame in this way:

Үш ауыз ханға айтатын датымыз бар	Three of our dats are spoken to the khan
Аллаһның да ауызында заңыңның да	In the mouth of God and law
Үш ауыз дат айтуға хағымыз бар,	It is our God-given right to speak this dat,
Замандың зарлы өнін ханға айтуға,	to voice the suffering of our times to the khan;
Ақиқатын ашатын датымыз бар.	there is a truth opened by our strength.
Датымыз шекпеңдіге ұнамаса,	If our traditional dat is not liked,
Міне бас асыңыздар атыңыздар.	Here is a head: blame it, shoot it.[37]

In regard to Aibek's performance, another poet from Astana joked wryly that "today we do not have a khan, we have an ostensibly democratically elected president." But Aibek's dat stood unchallenged. (He did receive a threat from an anonymous caller the following week when he returned to Astana, but when I spoke to him at that time he was unfazed.) The three basic points of his dat, which I excerpt here, were that the president should: (1) support the language and the religion of Kazakhs, (2) stop selling land and resources to foreigners while Kazakhs themselves cannot afford to buy them, and (3) take care of people in rural villages (aul), who, lacking work and support, turn to addictive substances.[38]

Жастарымыз наркоман шұбырынды,[39]	Our youth's [disordered] drug movement,
Алқа көл солама бор, жын қиып жур.	Alcohol out in the open, a bad spirit is burning
Тас Қодайға табылған шоқындылар,	Christened and worshipping a stone god,
Исламның діңгегін сындырып жур.	Breaking the pillar of Islam.
Мұнай, темір пайдалы қазбалардың,	Oil and iron have been used up,
Қайда кетіп жатқанын кім біліп жур?	Where they've gone no one knows.
Zheri Жерімнің астын сатып үстін сатып,	They sell what is on the land, under the land,
Укімет жүрегімді құм қылыпр жур.	Government stops up my heart with sand.
Аты барда заты жоқ Казақ тілі,	Kazakh language has a name but doesn't exist,
Орыс тілдің қолына су қойып жур.	[they] pour water over the hands of Russian.

Of particular interest is the last line, "they pour water over the hands of Russian." (He is referring to the Russian language.) It is a custom that when guests arrive at the home of Kazakhs to eat, younger children in the family will pour water over the guests' hands into a basin so that they can wash up before everyone sits down to the meal. It is a literal cleaning but also a strong sign of hospitality. In addition to the direct criticism of language politics, as an oblique metaphor here Aibek is criticizing Kazakhstani leaders generally for being so generous and welcoming to Russia in political and economic affairs.

This dat came as a culmination of Aibek's fiery tirade about *lepirip* (pompous) rich officials, the bureaucrats who got their jobs through nepotism, who never consider the real, everyday problems of Kazakhs. In reference to state senators, he uses metaphors such as being made of stone, wearing concrete makeup, wearing a hole in their armchairs by prolonged sitting, and thinking only about their own stomachs. Aibek is likening them to an artificial edifice of power, calling them impassive and greedy. He also directly calls them false democrats and warns that following such leadership will lead to a country of *mankurttar*—those who have forgotten (or forsaken) their culture and history and therefore do not fight against unjust power. He contrasts such figures with "real heroes" (i.e., opposition leaders), who are suffering in prison.[40]

There are many aspects of the performance that lend it legitimacy and serve to safeguard Aibek's words, not least among them the ambiguity of voice in his presentation. When he began his dat, Aibek no longer used the first person singular, opting for more vague pronominal referents such as "we" and "you" (plural), as well as making statements about the world in the deceivingly simple frame of "it is so" (past perfect verb tense, *-yp zhur*). Further, Aibek spoke not as a citizen of a nation but as an akhyn to a "khan." He spoke as the student of the person who had taught him the dat form. He spoke in front of and ostensibly both to and for the people in the live audience. He spoke in a live televised format, which naturally includes everyone watching and which runs in real time, so it cannot be edited or changed. He spoke as a younger brother to his opponent Mels, which is significant because young boys in many Kazakh families are very spoiled by their relatives and allowed to get away with behavior that older siblings are not.

It is this last element that allows Mels to become involved. Mels's cooperation, however, is necessary to ensure the felicity of the speech event.[41] Here, though, cooperation takes the form of argument, a second frame different from that of the previous dat. Now Mels, in his next turn in the role of older brother (a tolerant, advising position), scolds Aibek for misusing his aitys performance, telling him that this is not an appropriate place for criticism. Aibek responds by criticizing his opponent's name (Mels is a Soviet-era acronym for Marx, Engels, Lenin, Stalin): "I name you Makhambet / Because I don't want to say your name." Like Marzhan in the previous example, Aibek is also referring here to the historical figure Makhambet Utemisoly. After Mels objects, Aibek explains himself:

Атыңыз оғаш екен Мелс деген	It seems your name Mels is strange,
Ұлтының ұғымымен келіспеген	Your ancestors didn't knowingly agree,
Атаңыздың еш қандай шатысы жоқ	your grandfather had no kind of connection,
Орыс, Еврей, Грузин, Неміспене	not with Russians, Jews, Georgians, or Germans.
Аз басында онанда алмайсың ба?	Why didn't you take [it] from a wise head,
Адайды есім қылым Берішпенен	why not from Adai or Berish?[42]
Төрт капердің бас арпын арқалатып	You carry four nonbelievers' heads—
Атыңды қойған екен теріс неден?	where did they steal that name from?
Оларың, Мелс аға Қазақпенен,	Not from Kazakhs, Mels's older brother.
Байкасақ ештеңе алып беріспеген.	Together, let us not concede!
Соңы екеуі Қазақты қойша қырыр	The last two killed Kazakhs like sheep
Бабалардың моласын терістеген.	and razed our ancestors' graves.

This aitys serves to invoke another conversation between historical figures, here between Kazakh ancestors and members of other nationalities, but it is specifically Soviet leaders who are the object of Aibek's criticism. In this rhetorical frame Mels, because he has not changed his name, ostensibly supports those leaders and their policies. Aibek thus positions his opponent Mels as a murderer, a clearly despised "other," and berates him. Aibek himself appears as a brave and loyal Kazakh, rallying against a cultural traitor. Mels quickly concedes:

Айбектер өлең айтса өнергенде	The songs of poets like Aibek grow tall,
Сөзіне қалың елді сендіргенде	in the words the richness of our country is affirmed.
Қайтайын атам қойған атымызды	You return the name that was taken from my father,
Айтыста талай мені жеңдіргенде	In this way I've been beaten many times in aitys.

This concession, coming at the end of two shifting cycles between the poets, is the way in which Mels moves from scolding Aibek for his dat to supporting it as a part of the stronger overall poetry in that particular pair's competition. Poets are able to use the frame of an argument between an ostensible "Soviet-supporter" and a "Kazakh nationalist" to criticize Kazakhstani leaders. Leaders' inattention to the basic needs of their constituencies is ultimately characterized as leaders' inability to shake off the shackles of Soviet rule and to lead the nation in a new direction.

Aibek was able to criticize the president (the figurative khan) and his government with the collaboration of his opponent. The competition in which he performed was paid for by Yermegeayev together with Nurtai Sabilianov, who was at the time an Otan Party candidate and later became a seated member of parliament. Like the sponsor A.Y., what Sabilianov also has in common with aitys poets and organizers is that he is a strong proponent of the Kazakh language; nationalism is part of his political platform, and he is unhappy with the continued predominance of the Russian language in Kazakhstan. However, given the current political climate, direct dissent from the president's agenda is impossible. In private conversations, both sponsors explained to me that they want to attach their own names as well as the president's political party Otan clearly to this "authentic culture," to this tradition whereby knowledge of Kazakh language is lauded.[43]

The inclusive and participatory politics that aitys embodies is very much part of the "value" of the tradition of which Karima and Marzhan and other poets speak; it is this value that is threatened by the sponsorship relationship. If sponsors' interests dominate, the precarious relationship of mutual legitimacy with poets is tipped out of balance the people are left without a voice. By contrast, a successful collaboration between poets and sponsors results in the enactment and emergence of a particular dialogic form of authority, one of mutual respect and legitimacy in which both parties are active and accountable to one another. When we consider that both sides, in their representative capacity, make claims to represent "the people," that dialogic relationship becomes political. In that sense, cultural patronage is a form of political activity and authority that is very common to Inner Asian communities more broadly. These are relationships in which governance is embodied and performed. Further, when poets and sponsors collude, the framework is created for them, together with the people, to speak to contemporary leaders of the nation-state and to demand of those leaders the same level of presence and accountability. The dialogic model I present here is at once a literal and a metaphoric performance of an idealized state: a possible present of participatory politics.

CONCLUSION

PARTICIPATORY POLITICS

A man must answer for his deeds.
The State should account for its actions.
This is called Justice.
The same ordinance was in place in [Chinggis Khan's] times as well.
And it must prevail today too.
Such an established good order is known as the worth and value of humankind.

—Mongolian president Tsakhiaghiin Elbegdorj

DIALOGUE AND ANCESTRAL CARE

One fundamental problem that many Central Asians experience is a distinct sense of distance from capital cities and centralized governments; in Kazakhstan the seated parliament has been enshrined in the new capital city of Astana, where the presidential power of Nursultan Nazarbayev has reached mythic proportions (Laszczkowski 2014).[1] As government ideologies, decrees, and plans form and shift in the capital, how are those changes received or experienced in other towns and villages, in the peculiarly large "margin" of Central Asian states? (see Das and Poole 2004).[2] In a more immediate or local sense, people are most likely to interact with bureaucratic offices or forms of law enforcement perceived as a hassle or even as corrupt. Because regional and city mayors (Kaz: *akim*) are rotated regularly by the president, they hold power, but their leadership is not fully rooted in local dynamics.

By contrast, forms of leadership with which people can more readily connect do exist, but they are less overtly visible in a regional environment dominated by spectacle states and the rhetoric of master narratives of, for example, a "failed liberal or democratic transition." Recent ethnographic attention has focused on local forms of authority, leadership, conflict resolution, and community building (Reeves, Rasanayagam, and Beyer 2014). In this volume, I call attention to forms of ancestral leadership and care that are immediate, co-present, even embodied in the wishes, dreams, and prayers shared by people both living and departed. The example set by the "ancestors" is that of blessing, upbringing, and moral education.

Brave *batyrs* fight to protect Kazakhs from their enemies. Leaders of the past watch over their *shangyrakh*s within the present. The ancestors bring to bear a lived model of community building. Their presence and guidance also bring comfort and care. The words of loved ones can be held, touched, taken in as a source of strength. The holiness of enshrined ancestors is transmutable through copresence, blessing, and prayer. Their miracle stories are a source of inspiration. Ancestors provide a model of instruction and support within, beyond, and sometimes as an alternative to the government of the nation-state.

Cultural orators such as *aitys* poets, for example, emphasize the greatness of warriors and leaders in the past in order to criticize seated government officials in the present. That rhetorical strategy serves to link populations and their leaders across generations through a genealogical imagination, a discursive environment in which ethnic sovereignty is natural and paramount. Within that space, aitys poets are in a position to describe and demand a "correct" form of leadership, one of unification, protection, and accountability. Further, if such strategies in oral tradition and public [political] performance are taken together with other "conversations with ancestors" in an emerging contemporary worldview, it becomes obvious that these different forms of dialoguing are an active means of sense-making in the present. Ancestors come forward in the here and now, to protect and comfort their descendants, as well as to help show the way forward for contemporary populations.

The invocation of ancestors in aitys poetry and performances overlaps heavily with an ethnic nationalist sponsorship context. However, it would be a mistake to reduce the role of ancestors in oral tradition to the nationalism of the state. It is more important to examine the words and intentions of ancestors in the broader contexts of other oral and musical traditions, such as epic poetry (*zhyr*) or song (*kyi*). In them we can see a broader historical conversation extending back centuries across the steppes of Inner Asia. We can also see the role of various forms of cultural leadership in that mythic history, centering not only upon sovereignty but also recognition of the population and good governance. Mythic history becomes a discursive ground against which to evaluate and criticize the politics of the present, in which the Kazakh people may not be valued or heard. It is also imperative to contextualize poetry further within oral expressive culture more generally, as well as to look at the wishes of ancestors in poetry against their position and blessings in pilgrimage and everyday life. My ethnographic argument is that precisely because ancestors are already present in so many contexts, always working to watch over and protect their descendants, or the "family" of all Kazakh people, it makes a great deal of sense to turn to them for guidance and for a positive model of social and political inclusion.

The levels of interaction I present here are meant to demonstrate different moments of dialogue with ancestors, understanding that "dialogue" itself has two blended forms of significance. First, those in dialogue are both speaking and listening. As I describe in this concluding chapter, dialogue implies mutual accountability for having (and maintaining) a conversation in a given moment, or over time. Further, that which is dialogic is also emergent—in a perpetual state of coming into being. Dialogism, the ways in which the multiple voices and experiences of many social figures over time come to bear on interactions in an unfolding future, can be part of a model of inclusive leadership. I would argue that dialogic models of ancestral care are ubiquitous throughout Inner Asia, bringing modern citizens into a lived relationship with ancestors and ancestral land. In a different—dialogic—landscape, individuals, families, and local communities can take charge of moral upbringing and care, with the help of elders and those who have come before.

In this view of a sacred geography, contemporary nationalizing states are but a part of the logic of experience. Understanding dialogues with ancestors as a form of participatory politics helps us to see that "authoritarianism" is not totalizing. Rather, there are many active ways to take charge of life and experience, to find voice, expression, and social participation in daily and political life. It is doubly important to recognize this in the context of an environment characterized by a centralized and exclusive economy, as well as by censorship and repression. Interacting with ancestors allows people to step outside of the hierarchy of state power, to step beyond that realm into the moral space of historical and cultural legitimation. When youngsters take their first steps, they will be blessed with the *bata* of grandparents and given advice about how to walk the good path in life. So, too, do families and communities receive the blessing of the ancestors, as they struggle to make their way into the future along the *ak zhol*.

AUTHORITARIANISM AND NATIONALISM

Ancestral rhetoric at the level of the state is part and parcel of widespread cultural or ethnic nationalist projects across Central Asia, which overlap with but also differ from more local appeals in their scope and intention. National leaders regularly invoke genealogy to link themselves to "great" leaders of times past to provide legitimacy for both themselves and their country. In Kazakhstan, the government, including the ministry of culture, under President Nursultan Nazarbayev has also embraced a mythic view of national history, elevating many exceptional figures from Kazakh history to the status of national hero-ancestors while at the same time seeming to encourage his own cult of personality in a highly centralized state.[3] Many films, music videos, and stories dramatize the mythology and central figures of Kazakh history for a popular audience.[4] The cinematic feature *Nomad* (Kaz: *Köshpendiler*) tells the story of Abylai Khan, the eighteenth-century leader credited with uniting the three Kazakh *zhuz*es to struggle against external political pressures, including China and Russia. (The obvious analogy to Kazakhstan's current geopolitical situation is difficult to miss.) Unification and a successful fight against Kazakh enemies are themes repeated in the aitys tradition by both poets and their sponsors, as I have described in chapters three and four. An appeal to the past to undergird a national sovereignty in the present is a widespread political strategy for most governments across Central and Inner Asia today.

In Uzbekistan, longtime president Islam Karimov repeatedly invoked the legacy of Timur (Tamerlane), the fourteenth-century conquerer of the Mongol Chagatai khanate in Khwarezmia. Kyrgyzstan's first president, Askar Akayev, actively promoted the epic poem *Manas* as a fundamental basis for ethnic national identity; Manas is a mythic warrior of a thousand years past, the totemic ancestor of the Kyrgyz people, whose life story and accomplishments are recited by bards.[5] Akayev placed himself firmly as an interpreter of the epic in his own book, where he also emphasized qualities and characteristics of the historic leader—namely harmony and cooperation—and invoked the "immortal spirit" of Manas that lives in the morality of Kyrgyz across generations (cited in Gullette 2010, 140). Appeal to historical figures and discourses—via statues, films, and speeches—is a source of entertainment, pride, and moral legitimacy for populations.

While celebration of culture and heritage has been a basic mechanism of ethnic nationalism, it has also been the symbolic legitimacy undergirding increasingly autocratic rule in Central Asian states since independence from Soviet rule (see Matveeva 2010). This strategy of rule is typically termed "authoritarianism" or "authoritarian patrimony," a top-down model of power that is often negatively contrasted to forms of democracy. For those studying politics in the region, the analytic model of authoritarianism is limiting in at least two fundamental ways: it first presupposes that strong (even paternal) rule is undesirable and, second, that such rule is fundamentally counterposed to forms of freedom or democracy (the latter perceived as inherently positive or possible).[6] The language of authoritarianism disguises that fact that the participation and voice of the people actually constitute a fundamental aspect of politicking across the region (Dubuisson 2014; Ismailbekova 2014b), and it also loses the logic that *just* governance is the necessary prerogative of Inner Asian spiritual ancestry—what Uzbeks in Osh, Kyrgyzstan, describe as *boqmoq* (see Liu 2005, 2012) and what might also be understood as the provision of social protection and welfare.

In her analysis of the contexts of Central Asian authoritarianism, Anna Matveeva (2010, 14) also stresses the concept of legitimacy, "the belief or opinion that existing institutions are morally proper," as well as the need to be "responsive to the people." The obligation toward accountability and care is particularly strong for those modern leaders tasked with guiding the "states" created by the great ancestors who came before: great leaders should inspire an awe for their rule.[7] This awe would be inspired by strength and stoicism in the face of enemies, as well as by accountability and justness in governance. This ideal, while valorized at many levels of family and community in everyday life, actually loses traction at the level of seated government, where "genealogy" is often reduced to nepotism. Under manipulated political conditions, where areas such as employment, property ownership, policing, and the judiciary are widely perceived to be corrupt (and often feared by people like the family whose story I tell in the introduction to this volume), law and governance are simply not experienced equally by all.[8] A primary source of uncertainty or instability in everyday life stems from the sharply decreased forms of social security offered by current state governments, as well as from the need to organize family life and labor in a coherent spiritual world. The voicing of social and political criticism thus becomes an imperative aspect of patriotism; rather than other modes of dissent or opposition for which they might be arrested, politicians can use ancestral rhetoric as a vehicle for these concerns in different national(ist) contexts.

What becomes interesting in a comparative analysis of politics across Inner Asia is that ancestral rhetoric is not limited to any one national environment. Rather, it is a constant across a geography connected by a broader social and cultural history. Comparing the contexts in which ancestors are consulted as a means of achieving physical, socioeconomic, and spiritual well-being, it becomes clear that these practices are similar in a variety of countries, from Uzbekistan and Kyrgyzstan to Mongolia, Russia (Altai), and China (Xinjiang). The perduring effects of cultural nationalities policies in socialist states, as well as the collapse of economic centralization under socialism, have led to certain commonalities of experience across a wide geographic area. While nations claim particular "heroes," ordinary citizens wrestle with issues of economic uncertainty and social welfare. In these conditions, I think, the deeper history or vision of khanates should not be taken merely as "reinvented tradition" but as a different kind of discursive space, one with greater pragmatic potential. Ancestors can provide the moral framework both for families in everyday life and for the cultural and political leadership of newly independent states.

While my own ethnography centers on the experience of Kazakhs living in Kazakhstan, I think it is ultimately imperative to look at practices of oral tradition and ancestral dialogue in comparative perspective across a wide geographic area.

MONGOLIA AND CHINGGIS KHAN

In the Kazakhstani context, it is typically the case that ancestors are dialogically invoked on a national level from the perspective of Kazakh nationalists, to criticize other seated government members for their failure to take care of the "Kazakh people." Language and culture become a metaphor, in a specific sense, for anticolonial or anti-Russian sentiments, as well as in a more general sense, for the interests of those disenfranchised by the Kazakhstani state. In the context of aitys poetry, for example, it is most often leadership at the city or regional level (*akimat*) as well as the parliament deputies (*mazhilis*) who are accused of poor governance, nepotism, and self-interest. Represented by poets and protected by the wishes of the ancestors, "the people" are criticizing government, from below, in that performative tradition. However, in one of the most dramatic comparative examples of ancestral discourse in recent years, a seated president (i.e., someone working from the top down) turned the tables, performing in epic style and calling upon the country's celebrated ancestor to criticize his own government members.

In March 2011, Mongolia co-organized with the World Economic Forum a session entitled "Partnering against Corruption." In the opening portion of his speech to the session, Tsakhiaghiin Elbegdorj, the president of Mongolia, directly invoked the figure of Chinggis Khan, the great spiritual forefather of the modern Mongolian nation. Elbegdorj said that the principles of law and justice under the code of Yassa (Mong: Ikh Zasag)—specifically, anticorruption and antibribery behavior among civil officials—had been firmly established under the government of Chinggis Khan hundreds of years ago.[9] It is the standard to which modern rulers must also adhere.[10] President Elbegdorj re-echoed that sentiment the following year, in a speech at the 850th anniversary of the birth of Chinggis Khan (a national holiday). There he stood as an orator, speaking in the style of an oral epic, telling the story and legacy of the great leader:

> Chinggis honored law in his State.
> He esteemed military art, esteemed that rule and discipline were an order in his army.
> He honored his people to uphold dignity.
> A man comes to this world crying, but has to live upholding rules.
> He was a man who deeply realized that the justice begins and consolidates with
>   equality of law, and not with the distinctions between the people.
> He was a man who knew that the good laws and rules lived longer than fancy palaces.
> Though he built the largest on earth empire, Chinggis Khaan had never rushed to
>   build statues to himself.[11]

President Elbegdorj placed a clear and unmistakable emphasis on certain qualities of the Great Khan, notably his modesty, fairness, wisdom, and adherence to the rule of law. These he presents as fundamental qualities of good leadership. In the first verse, excerpted above, Elbegdorj says that Chinggis Khan lives on in us through the state he crafted, his decrees, and his wisdom. In the remainder of this speech, Elbegdorj reiterated at length that the rule of law—as well as the equally important observance of the law by all people, regardless of other social differences, such as wealth—was the backbone of the state itself.

> He saw that the savior of the Mongol people was to unite the fractioned and
>   dissipated country.
> He knew that otherwise Mongolia would have collapsed.
> He honored unity and harmony at home, and dismissed internal disaccord
>   perpetuated by external provocations.
> And he did it:
> He did manage to establish the empire, a statehood, a state under rule of law.

> Firmly upholding the Golden State means an unwavering and equal adherence to the laws of the State.
> In modern language, it's about equality in front of law—laws must be upheld both by an ordinary citizen, and by a state's dignitary.
> Both rich and poor obey the law, that's what it means.
> If laws are breached, both an unmanageable official and a regular citizen should bear the responsibility, this is what it means.
>
> A man must answer for his deeds.
> The State should account for its actions.
> This is called Justice.
> The same ordinance was in place in Chinggis's times as well.
> And it must prevail today too.
> Such an established good order is known as a worth and value of the humankind.[12]

At the beginning and end of this elaborate speech, which I have only excerpted here, the president repeats that while the physical body of the great leader must die, his legacy lives, embodied in the principles and practices of all his living descendants in the state that he created. Here it is abundantly clear that the "Rule of Law and Order" is the evidence of Chinggis Khan's "wisdom" and the single most important organizing tool for the state he created to "flourish forever." It is clear that Elbegdorj is using the contexts of his presidency and national forums to rhetorically deliver a singular message to some audience either imagined or physically co-present—some audience that might need to be "reminded" about the centrality of justice and equality before the law in the contemporary "Golden State." In these speech-performances, Elbegdorj does not speak in the first person as the country's current "great leader" but rather defers or deflects the message back centuries, toward Uuelen's son Temujin, the historical "savior of the Mongol people."[13]

The invocation of Chinggis Khan as Mongolia's great leader is a basic tactic in contemporary state-making, as it is a strong historical source of pride and national legitimacy for Mongolians (see Kaplonski 2004; Sabloff 2001). The appeal to a great ancestor, as well as to the idea that the ancestor's legacy lives on in the lives and bodies of his descendants, has a deep and fundamental cultural resonance in Mongolia, where personal and cultural genealogies are "a constitutive part . . . of history, memory, and place-making" (Buyandelger 2013, 257). The great power of a speech invoking Chinggis Khan, as Elbegdorj's words demonstrate, is that a great ancestor would actively be concerned with the life and times of those who occupy the state he created in the steppe—the leaders who should be justly administering his law fairly across all levels of society, the leaders who should be focused not on "building statues for themselves" but on remaining accountable to ordinary citizens.

What stands in the way of good leadership and a strong state? Failure to uphold the rule of law, as well as silence in the face of systemic corruption. In his 2011 anticorruption speech, Elbegdorj says directly that "the biggest victims of corruption are ordinary citizens. Without fighting against corruption we do not do our best for our citizens, those [who] elected us." It is to these conditions of corruption in Mongolia that President Elbegdorj refers; he contrasts the current situation to the mythic legalism of Chinggis Khan.[14] Outside of any specific issue, these speeches illustrate in broad strokes several issues directly relevant to many: the invocation and rhetorical efficacy of ancestors, the personalistic nature of authority and rule, and the implication that current leaders may not be as just or strong as those of times past. An appeal to the great historical tradition of the "forefather of all Mongols" is an effective rhetorical strategy, one that simultaneously establishes Elbegdorj himself as a leader who champions his ancestors, while also borrowing ancestral authority to challenge other leaders who are not conforming to the ideals of law and justice established by Chinggis Khan.

An appeal to ancestral authority has had a heightened valence in the postsocialist era particularly because of the conditions of social and economic exclusion, as well as the cultural or ethnic nationalism characteristic of newly formed states. Ultimately, what I wish to point out is that, unsurprisingly, comparison shows us that ancestral discourse functions successfully as a model of morality in a variety of contexts across Inner Asia that share a social and cultural history. The more interesting question is to figure out *why*, beyond the rhetoric of any one nation, this language might resonate or be so appealing for citizens and to take very seriously the idea that ancestors do not just exist as an idea of the past; rather, their presence can have a concrete influence on the present. Outside of any political project, people are already accustomed to looking to their ancestors as arbiters of protection, welfare, and even social justice.

LOCAL LEGITIMACY

I see the concept of ancestors' care in dialogue as the basic link connecting broad-based political strategy to the everyday and to people's own understandings and interactions, which are often located within articulated genealogies. Within the generations of family relations, certain relatives stand out as particularly wise or good. These are not the khans or batyrs of empires but rather individuals with more modest or regular biographies who nonetheless are remembered positively for their leadership. For example, in one conversation with Meiramgul (whose words and story I share at length in chapter one), she described her uncle Zhengelbai Agha, the youngest of three sons. He had received a strong communist education and later became the director of the local state farm (*sovkhoz*) during the Soviet period. After his passing, his portrait was hung in the family home and has become something of an icon or source of spiritual energy. Meiramgul photographed the image on her cell phone so that she could carry it with her, and she described how even the new brides (*kelin*) coming into the family come to Zhengelbai's portrait to ask for bata, so that he can look after them, too.

In the story I excerpt below, Meiramgul talked of going to a distant relative's wedding in another town. When she arrived, she headed for the ordinary place she was originally assigned to sit among the family, toward the back of the crowd. But when the relatives realized that she was the niece of Zhengelbai, the grandmother who had organized the wedding changed her mind and brought Meiramgul to sit with other family members in a place of honor:

> MEIRAMGUL: Ho-ow she kissed my hands! She called me "Dear" [Kaz: *ainalaiyn*] like that, and she wanted to invite me again the next day, but I couldn't because I already had to leave home for work. They were even surprised—that I was from their generation!
>
> SALTANAT: Did they guess the year [that you were born]?
>
> MEIRAMGUL: Uh-huh, that's how they did it, and that's how they started to talk about Zhengelbai.
>
> SALTANAT: Mmm.
>
> AUTHOR: Mmm.
>
> MEIRAMGUL: And all of these, like for example Kazibek Bi, Aiteke Bi, Tole Bi— they . . . take [for example] a "judge" there—
>
> AUTHOR: Judges, mm-hmm.
>
> MEIRAMGUL: Everyone came to them for the last word. So it was, like that, that sort of thing. But this Kazibek Bi he started by *law;* by *law* they came to him as a *lawyer.*
>
> AUTHOR: Mm-hmm.
>
> MEIRAMGUL: His own brother, this—
>
> SALTANAT: Advisor?
>
> MEIRAMGUL: [This] lawyer was a like an advisor, the brother.
>
> SALTANAT: Yes.
>
> MEIRAMGUL: Kazibek Bi, he already knew how to bring the two sides together— political and legal. He didn't have his own legal education, but he could have tried. And just like that, [people came to] to our uncle also.
>
> SALTANAT: Mmm.
>
> MEIRAMGUL: Everyone approached him, and all the time they asked for his bata.
>
> SALTANAT: Mmm.
>
> AUTHOR: From Zhengelbai?
>
> SALTANAT: Zhengelbai Ata.
>
> MEIRAMGUL: So that this—
>
> SALTANAT (to MEIRAMGUL): And this is the family of Zhengelbai?
>
> MEIRAMGUL: No, this *ata* he was from the family Ysty, Karakhan Ysty?
>
> SALTANAT (to AUTHOR): From the family Ysty, you can also write that.
>
> MEIRAMGUL: From the Great Zhuz—
>
> SALTANAT (to AUTHOR): Great *zhuz.*

MEIRAMGUL: Just like that. And now these kinds of bata, you need to look in history, how they gave them, and that's all.
AUTHOR: Zhengelbai Ata, could you say that you consider him like an ancestor spirit [Kaz: *aruakh*], or how?
MEIRAMGUL: No, no. By generation.
AUTHOR: He's not considered an ancestor spirit, for example, so that I understand the meaning?
MEIRAMGUL: No. I want to say that from every generation like this, [one is] singled out from the family—like our Tole Bi, Aiteke Bi, there, he *led*.
AUTHOR: Mm-hmm.
MEIRAMGUL: Like that. There were those, as they say, people . . . oh, through a miracle, language too!
SALTANAT: Of course!
MEIRAMGUL: In Kazakh! <laughs>
AUTHOR: Please say.
SALTANAT: In Kazakh!
MEIRAMGUL: *Just* [Kaz: *adil*]. God's *just* [one]—
SALTANAT: Ah, very fairly.
MEIRAMGUL: Fairly, fairly, like that.
SALTANAT: Mmm.
MEIRAMGUL: I'm trying all the time!

Here Meiramgul explains that in the contexts of family and community life, certain individuals will emerge as particularly respected leaders; on the smaller scale of the collective farm, it was her own uncle who emerged as leader. On the larger scale of the Kazakh nation, it was famous figures such as Kazibek Bi, Tole Bi, or Aiteke Bi who have been valorized within the context of post-Soviet nationalism for their qualities of wisdom and justice.[15] Meiramgul calls these figures "ours," referencing a national genealogy, and also compares her biological uncle to these famous leaders of the past, stressing the quality of *adilet*, or fairness, that they demonstrated in their leadership, as well as their focus on care, unity, and the respect that they generated within communities. It is significant that Meiramgul, who had been narrating this story mostly in Russian to this point in the conversation, had trouble thinking of the word she wanted to use to describe her uncle's character and position in society (*adil*); it is clear that these ideas were part of a worldview that she associated more strongly with the Kazakh language. It is also significant that the three historical leaders she mentions (Tole Bi, Aiteke Bi, and Kazibek Bi), beyond local leadership, together worked at the level of the khanate of the Great Zhuz to create a law code (V. Martin 2001); thus "fairness" was elevated from daily interactions and relationships to a legalized standard of justice for *all* Kazakhs in the Great Zhuz.

Meiramgul touches lightly on this comparison between her own family and the more general Kazakh "ancestors," with the assumption that Saltanat and I (her interlocutors) are aware of these figures, their history, and their qualities—they do not need much explanation. Rather, this cultural history is invoked as a point of comparison to the more immediate case of her uncle, to explain why he was so special and why she (his biological niece) continues to be respected by their distant relatives even after his death. During his lifetime, people sought her uncle's blessing not only because he was a special community leader but also because his bata came together with (legal) advice and wisdom. His wishes blend together with those of similar ancestors. In this excerpt Saltanat wishes to understand the place of Meiramgul's uncle within a cultural genealogy (family, *zhuz*), which Meiramgul then explains to emphasize Zhengelbai's legitimate connection to greater structures of kinship, culture, and Kazakh history. Appeal to the past becomes a mode of explanation in Meiramgul's story, precisely because ancestry is recognizable and personal, a fundamental feature of moral and political legitimacy.

CULTURAL CONVERSATIONS AND POLITICAL ENGAGEMENT

Ancestral dialogue can function as rhetoric in contexts ranging from celebrations to pilgrimage and shrine visitation, from poetic competitions to nation-building projects, as well as in families to caution against behavior seen as undesirable. But why does the rhetoric work? What do these levels of experience have in common? In order to understand how notions of personal and political legitimacy are fundamentally connected, it is useful to look at the ways in which ancestry functions as a metadiscursive cultural framework, as well as the ways in which that worldview is embodied in language and the physical world. As the bata or blessing of a respected relative is received in the washing of the face (Kaz: *bet sipau*) by its recipient, so too may the deceased "eat" the smells of fresh fried or baked bread when they come to visit their living relatives. When people experience great sorrow or success, they may also offer bata and bread to those around them, to share the embodiment of their fortune. At sacred shrine sites, the holy qualities of those ancestors are seen to transmute the earth and the physical world, such that pilgrims may take away blessings in both word and, for example, water. Their experience is mediated by shrine caretakers, who have received their calling from the ancestors in a deeply embodied way: in dreams.

In all of these circumstances in this cultural worldview, we can see that ancestors care deeply and constantly about what happens to their living descendants and that, through principles of language and embodiment, those wishes can translate into actual change in the world. Here the term "descendants" refers equally to specific relatives within a family or lineage, as well as to those gathered under the figurative shangyrakh of a more distant ancestor. The wishes of the great heroes of times past are voiced by poets performing in oral and epic traditions throughout the Inner Asian world. In aitys poetry, social and political criticism is a feature of performance.[16] Poets, sponsors, and supporters alike often refer to the tradition as the "democracy of the steppe," a defense and a call to political engagement that brings to mind the notion of "dialogic democracy" developed by Rosemary Coombe (1998, 296–97, cited in Paley 2002, 487): "By involving 'social systems of signification' open enough to provide the 'cultural conditions for conversation' for a wide variety of people, dialogic democracy allows diverse groups to 'express identity, community, and social aspiration in the service of imagining and constructing alternative social universes." In the aitys tradition, I think "democracy" refers fundamentally to forms of participation and voice, the desire to establish a dialogue of accountability with leaders.[17] As great heroes and leaders watched over their people in mythic times past, so too should contemporary leaders care for today's populations.

The performative dimension of aitys poetry helps us to see in a more literal sense how the participant frameworks of ancestral dialogue—who is participating and how—expand to envelop multiple dimensions of time and space to collapse the claims of the past in the claims of the present (see Boyarin 1994). When ancestral rhetoric emerges on a national stage, all of these frames (family, pilgrimage, poetry) are referenced. This ethnography explores a basic question: in what sense do ancestors bear a responsibility for and the possibility of assuming the position or the words and actions necessary to serve as guardians, and how are they recognized or protected in turn? How can we understand this relationship of mutuality not only as a way to navigate along the right path in life but also as "the desire for some degree of collective self-legislation, the desire to participate in shaping the conditions and terms of life" (Brown 1995, 4), a basic form of "participatory politics" (see Wedeen 2008)? The perspective of dialogic emergence and ancestral worldview can help us to acknowledge the limits of the nation-state, as well as to avoid the false dichotomy of authoritarianism and democracy, in our analysis of social and political life in Inner Asia.[18]

NOTES

A NOTE ON THE COVER ART

1. Please see Suleimenova's website, https://saulesuleimenova.wordpress.com/about/, for a complete list of her work and exhibitions.

2. On the role of contemporary artists and the state in Kazakhstan, see the article by Zhanara Nauruzbayeva (2011).

3. On the role of Suleimenova and other female artists in the formation of the nation-state in Central Asia, see the article by Diana Kudaibergenova (2015).

4. For a recent artist profile of Suleimenova, see the New Eurasia website at https://www.neweurasia.net/culture-and-history/artist-profile-saule-suleimenova/.

A NOTE ON FIELDWORK AND METHOD

1. The members of the national aitys network are all public figures, and I therefore, with permission, use their real names.

2. I have used italics to show speakers' own emphasis in words and phrasing.

INTRODUCTION

1. In my use of the term "Inner Asia" I wish to emphasize the cultural, linguistic, and historical connections among peoples, including not only the five "stans" (typically referred to as Central Asia) but also Mongolia and western China to the east and a Turkic legacy to the west.

2. See the monograph by Agha (2007).

3. See the concluding chapter of this book for a critique of authoritarianism as an analytic rubric.

4. For a discussion of "cultural rights" as a fundamental part of heritage, see the collection edited by Kapchan (2014).

5. On the role of oral tradition and genealogical imagination in the structuring of history in a national present, see also the monograph by Shryock (1997).

6. Perhaps the most straightforward example is the case of reported speech, when a speaker quotes the speech of another social figure either directly or indirectly; see the book by Volosinov (1973).

7. The population of the Kazakh SSR was particularly heterogeneous, with large numbers of Russians, Koreans, Germans, and others sent to the territory at various points under Soviet rule, including during the deportations (see Westren 2012) and the Virgin Lands campaign. The national census data are from Das Länder-Informations-Portal, accessed 21 June 2016,

https://www.liportal.de/fileadmin/user_upload/oeffentlich/Kasachstan/40_gesellschaft/Kaz2009_Analytical_report.pdf.

8. The anthropology of "well-being" in Central Asia was the subject of a special issue (vol. 32, no. 4) of *Central Asian Survey*, and I echo the ethnography and discussion of those contributors in my own analysis.

9. I thank S. Yessenova for this point. On short- and long-term strategies of economic reform in Kazakhstan, see the work of Jones Luong (2000, 2004). For an ethnographic perspective on market reforms across postsocialist spaces, see the collection by Mandel and Humphrey (2002).

10. On contemporary politics in Kazakhstan, see the work of Cummings (2005, 2010) and of Dave (2007, 2010). For a regional perspective, see also works by Jones Luong (2004) and Schlyter (2005).

11. Beyer (2013b) gives a detailed ethnographic description of how a Kyrgyz village's local reorganization of the economic and moral order was a source of (post-Soviet) unity and security.

12. On Central Asian labor migration and remittance economy, see works by Abazov (1999), Nasritdinov (2007), Reeves (2012), Roche and Hohmann (2012), and Werner and Barcus (2009). For countries like Kyrgyzstan and Tajikistan, remittances can account for more than a third (up to half) of their nations' gross domestic product (Marat 2009).

13. Bissenova (2009, 2014) has written on both the construction "boom" and emergent middle class in Astana as well as on the city's master plan. On the materiality and aesthetics of growth in the city, see works by Buchli (2007) and Laszczkowski (2014). For a cross-national perspective on urban spaces across Central Asia, see the collection by Alexander, Buchli, and Humphrey (2007).

14. The correlation between joblessness, substance abuse, and gender-based violence is well documented in postsocialist spaces. Ethnographic examples include works by Ghodsee (2011), Caldwell (2009), and Tereskinas (2009).

15. For different narratives of "chaos," see books by Nazpary (2001) and McGlinchey (2011). For a critical ethnographic approach to postsocialist "transition," see the collection edited by Berdahl, Bunzl, and Lampland (2010); for ethnographies of postsocialist economic transformations, see the collection by Mandel and Humphrey (2002).

16. See contributions to the special issue (vol. 32, no. 4) of *Central Asian Studies* for ethnographic examples and strategies of well-being in Central Asia.

17. This quote is traditionally attributed to Stalin. On this ideology, see works by Slezkine (1994), T. Martin (2001), and Suny and Martin (2001).

18. On *hujum* in Uzbekistan, see works by Northrop (2004) and Kamp (2006).

19. On Kazakhstan's national musical identity, see works by Rouland (2005) and Rancier (2009).

20. On Kazakhstan and Kyrgyzstan, see works by Yessenova (2009) and Gullette (2010), respectively. For a regional overview, see the compilation by Cummings (2010).

21. On the December 1986 events in Kazakhstan, see works by Aitbaioly (2011), Dave (2007), Michaels (1996), and Olcott (1995).

22. On Kazakhstan's repatriation program, see works by Diener (2009), Werner and Barcus (2010), and Genina (2011).

23. I refer here to the death of Altynbek Sarsenbayev, the circumstances of which I discuss at greater length in chapter four.

24. The *kamcha* has a great deal of symbolic significance for homes and relationships across Inner Asia among peoples whose history and present center on horse riding and herding. The kamcha can be a metaphor for relations of gender and dominance and is often found decorating the home.

25. The center was related to the broader Ak Zhol (or Ata Zhol) movements in Kazakhstan, described in chapter one.

26. On the *aitysh* of Kyrgyzstan, see Mustafa Coskun's doctoral work, "Improvising the Voice of Ancestors: A Historical Ethnography of Oral Poetry Performances among the Kyrgyz" (forthcoming from Max Planck Institute of Social Anthropology, Halle).

27. On the relation between dombyra music and homeland among Kazakhs in Mongolia, see the article by Post (2007).

28. See Guldana Salimjan's doctoral work on the role of aitys and oral tradition in the context of gender and intergenerational history among Kazakhs in Xinjiang (dissertation forthcoming from University of British Columbia Institute for Gender, Race, Sexuality, and Social Justice).

29. The concept of an interpretive frame was developed as a rubric of sociological analysis by Goffman (1986). In his classic treatise on verbal art, Bauman ([1977] 1984) identified the interpretive frame as a basic metapragmatic condition of performance.

30. On patronage politics in Central Asia, see works by Prior (2000), Ismailbekova (2014b), and McGlinchey (2008, 2009, 2011).

ONE. BATA AND BLESSING

1. On bata in the Kyrgyz family context and its importance for childhood upbringing, see the piece by Tulebaeva (2015).

2. "Holy bata" seem to specifically include God as an interlocutor or benefactor in the blessing.

3. I thank Naubet Bissenov and Bota Zhussunova for their help with transcription and translation of this text and all the subsequent texts in this chapter.

4. Holidays corresponding to the cultural-religious calendar are all marked by this bata (Kaz: *kutty bolsyn*), which is the proper salutation for the feast of Eid or the spring new year, Nauryz.

5. Like most private homes in urban neighborhoods, the large square homestead is completely surrounded by a tall fence—brick on the back walls and an iron gate in the front facing the street.

6. Privratsky (2001, 125) remarks on "the transferability of blessing," comparing it to the Islamic concept *baraka*, "the spiritual power that dwells in material things."

7. From page 38 of a schoolbook (author unknown) issued in 2011 by the company Mekteptegi synyptan tys zhumystar in Almaty.

8. The material presented in this chapter is translated and transcribed from recorded interviews and fieldnotes taken in the summer of 2013.

9. *Zhar* is a wedding song, both fun and festive.

10. While a full discussion is outside the scope of this chapter, it should be emphasized that each of these events is potentially a great expense to the family. Most families will dedicate a sizable percentage of their income toward organizing the best possible version of these events. This is an important moment to display a family's wealth, social connections, and success (see Ismailbekova 2014a; Roche and Hohmann 2012; Werner 1998, 1999).

11. Toasting also gets wrapped up in ethnic cultural identity. See, e.g., the work of Roberts (2007) and Montgomery (2007).

12. Privratsky (2001, 22) refers to this as *bet sipau*, "the receiving of the blessing being implied in the act."

13. Personal interview, summer 2013.

14. This term "халекеті," meaning evil or damage, is spelled traditionally here, based on the Arabic or Persian word; in Kazakh, it is usually spelled "бәлекет," while in Uzbek it is "халоніт." I thank Naubet Bissenov for this note.

15. These phenomena—a mediated discursive relationship with ancestors and the revalidation and comparison of results—have an obvious correlation to other spiritual practices in Inner Asia, such as shamanism, which has been extensively described in the Mongolian context (Buyandelger 2007, 2013; Humphrey 2002; Pederson 2011; Swancutt 2008).

16. For an extended discussion of *ayan* as a revelation dream, see the book by Privratsky (2001).

17. I have chosen to use the subjunctive in translation here, for poetic effect.

18. On forms of marriage and the roles of women see, for example, the work of Ismailbekova (2014a) and Werner (1998, 2004).

19. They also did not necessarily hold these ideals so uncompromisingly when it came to their own daughters.

20. It is helpful to understand views of family within the context of cultural nationalism; see, for example, works by Yessenova (2005a, b, 2009).

21. The *mankurt* is a figure created by Kyrghyz novelist Chingis Aitmatov to describe a hero who has lost all sense of his own genealogy and culture—and therefore himself—and has thus become a slave to others under Russian imperialism. Somewhat ironically (given the meaning of this term), Gaukhar said *mankurt-ami*, combining the Kazakh or Kyrgyz lexical term with the instrumental case in Russian grammar.

22. On the conflation of nationality and Muslim identity, see the book by Privratsky (2001).

23. The story of Chingis Aimatov, the figure of the mankurt, and its significance as critique of the Soviet system are well described by Gullette (2010).

24. "List of occult and mystical organizations, activities which are prohibited on the territory of the Republic of Kazakhstan," Ministry for Religious Affairs and Civil Society for the Republic of Kazakhstan, accessed 4 August 2014, http://www.din.gov.kz/eng/press-sluzhba/spisok_okkultno-misticheskix_o/.

25. The concept of *shezhire* as a source of identity, connection, history, and strength has

been explored at length in urban and national contexts in Kazakhstan (Yessenova 2005a, b, 2009). Popular geneaology websites such as www.elim.kz allow people to explore this concept and to trace their own heritage. See also Gullette's (2010) work on *sanjyra* in Kyrgyzstan.

26. This was Gaukhar's own disclaimer, not my description.

27. I describe the museum and grounds of Zhambyl's home as a sacred site in chapter two (see also Dubuisson 2009).

TWO. GUARDIANS OF THE ANCESTORS

1. The largest single research collection about sacred sites has been compiled by the Kyrgyz ethnologist Gulnara Aitpaeva, who has also explored how the sites are related to healing practices in Central and Inner Asia. She is the founder and executive director of the Aigine Cultural Research Center in Kyrgyzstan, which has published extensively on sacred sites in Kyrgyzstan (see Aitpaeva 2009).

2. For comparison, see various works on Uzbek and Tajik political and identity categories and the nationalization of statehood (e.g., L. Adams 2010; Dagiev 2014; Heathershaw and Herzig 2012; Suyarkulova 2012).

3. On the perceived threat of Islamic extremism in Central Asia, see Rasanayagam (2006); see also the work by Montgomery and Heathershaw (2014).

4. For further reading on shrine site visitation, its Islamic legacy, and its place in a political economy, please see the book chapter by Schwab and Bigozhin (2016).

5. A *khoja* is one in a line claiming direct descent from the prophet Mohammed.

6. Further, these differences could be seen in comparative perspective to saints, shrines, and pilgrimage practice in other historically Sufi contexts; see the work of Werbner (2003) for one such example.

7. On the complexities of research on Islam in post-Soviet Central Asia, see the special edition of *Central Asia Survey* 25, no. 3. For an ethnography of Islamic life in Kyrgyzstan, see Montgomery (2016).

8. For extended and comparative discussions of *ziyarat* in Uzbekistan, see books by Rasanayagam (2012) and Louw (2007).

9. The evil eye tradition, or belief that the evil or jealous gaze of others can cause physical harm and must be guarded against, is widespread in many different cultural contexts. In the post-Soviet context, such jealousy (of success, marriage, material wealth, etc.) can be considered a negative expression of "spiritual health" and a common source of affliction.

10. While many long-term site caretakers have an established reputation and I have used their names in this chapter, this young man was an apprentice at the site and I have given him a pseudonym to protect his identity.

11. *Bagyshitau* refers to the prayers read, typically on Thursdays or Fridays and preferably by a mullah, for the spirits of deceased ancestors.

12. Here I intentionally use the terminology employed by Roman Jakobson ([1960] 1980) in his analysis of the functions of language; he argued that utterances have not just one but at least six ways of "acting" in the world, given the multidimensional construction of the communicative framework.

13. Louw (2007) describes shrine guardians (Uz: *domlo*) in Uzbekistan.

14. See the classical anthropological writing by Mary Douglas ([1966] 1984) on the various forms and meanings of cleanliness merged under the category of the sacred.

15. Margarethe Adams (2015) described the integration of this tour and others into a pilgrimage worldview in her presentation at the Forty-Third World Conference of the International Council for Traditional Music, held in Astana in 2015.

16. Like all other caretakers, Saghynbek is able to recite several formulaic *sure* in Arabic.

17. Personal interview and fieldnotes, summer 2013.

18. Poets Zhambyl and Abai both attended Russian schools and, in their capacity as leaders, urged harmonious relations between Kazakhs and their Russian rulers—Zhambyl was acclaimed in Moscow for his poetry praising Stalin. These figures were brought to prominence as Kazakh poets by the well-known folklorist and Soviet academic Mukhtar Auezov.

19. Zhambyl's granddaughter is the only female caretaker I have met, one of only two women I know to be actively associated with a site. The other is arguably the most well-known figure associated with a sacred site: the elderly woman at Ungurtas. Her name is Bifatima Apa, and she calls herself the last Sufi dervish in Kazakhstan. She is the subject of multiple national and international news reports, photo essays, and documentaries and is reputed to have inspired the central character of the Kazakh film *Shaman* (Kaz: *Baksy*) by Guka Omarova. But Bifatima is not a caretaker so much as a full-time healer for a steady stream of guests who come to live at her compound.

20. Over a period of twelve years, I have visited at least twenty-four sacred sites of various kinds, many of them multiple times. While I have prayed and had informal conversations with many caretakers, I have also interviewed five at length when visiting as part of a pilgrimage group.

21. In her ethnography *Spirited Performance*, the anthropologist Nienke van der Heide ([2008] 2015, 119–28) has described the way in which Kyrgyz epic poets (Kyg: *manaschi*) are called to oration through dreams, at the summons of the spirit of Manas, the epic hero himself.

22. Notes from personal interview, summer 2013.

23. On the role of the kobyz in Kazakhstan's national imaginary, see the article by Rancier (2009).

24. Raiymbek Batyr and his enemies, the invading Kalmak and Dzungar armies, are described at length in chapter three.

25. I thank Bota Zhunussova for this information. Bata and bread alike are to be "eaten" or embodied, as noted in chapter one.

THREE. ANCESTRY IN *AITYS* POETRY

Some of the material for this chapter was published previously in the *Journal of Linguistic Anthropology* (vol. 20, no. 1) in a special issue, "Performing Disputes: Cooperation and Confrontation in Argumentative Language," guest-edited by Valentina Pagliai. I am very grateful to Naubet Bissenov and Bota Zhunussova for their help and guidance in the Kazakh-English translations I present here.

1. For regional comparative work on the *aitysh* tradition among Kyrgyz poets in Kyrgyzstan, please see the paper by Coskun (2013), and on the tradition among Kazakh poets in Xinjiang (China), please see the article by Salimjan (2017).

2. When I finished my fieldwork in Kazakhstan, Yerman, in addition to dealing with the demands of the aitys network, was named head of Kazakh Radio, a prestigious post previously held by a famous Kazakh pop singer.

3. A primary figure behind Eurasianism is Lev Gumilev (1912–92), a twentieth-century historian whose controversial theories of ethnogenesis put him at the forefront of the "neo-Eurasian" intellectual movement. His theories, republished in Russia as *Ritmy Evrazii* (The rhythms of Eurasia) in 2003, became very popular in Astana in the 2000s and were explicitly adopted by Nazarbayev in his early ideological modeling of the new capital.

4. The center also has a publishing house, which released the biography *Murzatai Zholdasbekov: Shyn men Shyndau* (Truth and truth-telling). Zholdasbekov's center in Astana also published a book of Zhursin Yerman's poetry in 2005, *Khudiretke Zhüginuw* (Supplicating God).

5. Dariga Nazarbayeva headed the social movement Asar (Help for all), which then was transformed into a political party during elections in 2004. After a dispute with her father, the party was reabsorbed into the president's own party, Otan. She was appointed deputy prime minister in 2015.

6. Being able to name one's ancestors seven generations back is often invoked by Kazakhs as a marker of "real" ethnicity, though in practice knowledge of ancestry varies widely (see Schatz 2004). Ancestral knowledge is directly associated with language and history in the term *ataly suzder*, which refers to the words of those seven generations of forebears. Aitys akhyns are among those who are said to use this language.

7. The Union of Writers was once part of a broad-based union initiated by the Communist Party in 1932 as a means of guiding literary production throughout the republics. For more on the establishment, goals, and activity of Soviet writers' unions, see works by Fitzpatrick (1999) and Suny (2010). The Union of Writers in Kazakhstan now comprises ethnic Kazakh writers and literary poets who publish primarily in their own newspaper. Several of the aitys organizers in Almaty belong to this union, which has its own building in the city.

8. On the concept of "style" and enactment in language and interaction, see the essay by Irvine (2001).

9. Other national performative traditions include the singing of epic poetry (*zhyrau*) and other musical traditions, such as *terme* and *kyi*. Certain musical instruments are also considered to have a national quality, most notably the *kobyz* (see Rancier 2009).

10. A poet's group will usually be in the audience, but, in several performances I witnessed, members of the group actually came onstage to sit behind the poet so that he or she could consult with them during competition.

11. The Kazakh lineages often invoked in aitys performances include the six major groups of the Middle Horde (*orta zhuz*): Arghyn, Naiman, Kipshak, Khongyrat, Uakh, and Kereu.

12. In Almaty, part of the local mythology of Raiymbek Batyr is that he protects travelers in the city (see chapter two).

13. Along with its major river and basin, the Sary Arka region in the north figures heavily in a mythic Kazakh history and is the subject of a traditional instrumental song (Kaz: *kyi*) written by the famous Kazakh composer Kurmanghazy Saghyrbaioly in the nineteenth century.

14. Two lines have been reversed in position for clarity in translation.

15. These sponsors are discussed in more detail in chapter four.

16. For a brief overview of post-Soviet transboundary agreements, please see the article by Wegerich (2011).

17. It is important to note that Renat's wife is not actually Uzbek in her ethnic origin, as there are many Kazakh families living in Uzbekistan. She could be considered a "returnee." Here her country, not her ethnicity, becomes a symbol.

18. Felt has traditionally been used throughout the region (by nomadic herders) to make warm insoles for shoes.

19. On the issue of Kazakh repatriation from Mongolia, see works by Diener (2005, 2009), Dubuisson and Genina (2012), and Werner and Barcus (2009, 2010). On the constructed nature of Kazakh territorial homeland, see articles by Diener (2002) and Finke (2013). The repatriation affected large numbers of Kazakhs in Uzbekistan and China as well.

20. For a publicly available online biography of Al-Farabi, see the website of Kazakh National University, accessed 8 February 2013, http://www.kaznu.kz/en/11244/page.

21. I am grateful to my colleague and friend, the Kazakh historian Dr. Bakhytnur Otarbayeva, for her help and explication of this example.

22. Like Raiymbek and other Kazakh heroes and leaders, Ablai Khan has been memorialized in statues, boulevard renaming, and the naming of a university. He was also the subject of the popular international film *Nomad* (2005).

23. Discourses on tribalism and clan rivalry in Central Asian politics also appear in academic analysis, a trend that was rightly criticized by David Gullette (2012), who noted that tribalism and clan rivalry are overly general concepts often confused with the broader and more common political mechanism of patron-client relations.

24. See, for example, an advertisement for a museum exhibit of materials from the site on the official web page of Kazakhstan, http://prositeskazakhembus.homestead.com/101006.html.

25. For a highly positive overview of Kazakhstan's 2030 plan, see the essay by Utegenova (2010).

FOUR. DIALOGIC AUTHORITY

A version of this chapter was published originally as "Dialogic Authority: Kazakh Aitys Poets and Their Patrons" in the volume *Ethnographies of the State in Central Asia: Performing Politics*, edited by Madeleine Reeves, Johan Rasanayagam, and Judith Beyer, and published by Indiana University Press in 2014.

1. The culturally legitimated places of the powerful could be at the front of a crowded auditorium at an aitys performance, at the front of a celebration or political gathering (Is-

mailbekova 2014b), in a choice seat that is respected by others during a village court session (Beyer 2014), or at an exclusive spectacle or performance (L. Adams 2010).

2. As an analytic, the concept of *voice* I present here is social and political, most akin to Goffman's (1981) "principal figure"—a collective "someone" who is committed to what is being said—described in the introduction to this volume.

3. Daniel Prior (2000) provides an in-depth examination of how those relations of patron and poet shifted in the early Soviet period to become less personal and instead more nationalistic—current sponsorship conditions are an admixture of both—the argument being that Soviet authorities recognized and sought to control the "propaganda potential" (Prior 2000, 9) of epic and improvisational poetry.

4. See works by Gabullin (1968), Tebegenov (2002), Torsynov (1976, 2003), Umbetayev (1992), and Zharmukhamedoly (1976, 2001).

5. The definitive volumes on Kazakh literature compiled by the Academy of Literature and Arts include those edited by Mukhanov et al. (1964) and Ahmetov et al. (1988a, b).

6. Auezov's materials on the Kazakh poet Abai Turanbaiolu ([1988] 1997) were revised at the academy by a literature specialist, Margarita Madanova, and reissued as the popular volume *Path of Abai*, published in Kazakh, Russian, and English (Madanova 2004).

7. For a comparative historical perspective on the organization of cultural activity at the local level during the Soviet period, please see works by Grant (1995) and İğmen (2012).

8. Kundirbaeva's (1994) analysis does not make it clear when and if aitys ever had a glory day as a "real" oral tradition. She cites Auezov in saying that the tradition was beginning to die out in the late nineteenth century, but she regularly refers to aitys as one of "the most popular musical and poetic genres of the Kazakh people" (Kundirbaeva 1994, 105).

9. Personal interview, spring 2004.

10. This arrangement relates more broadly to economic relations among kin networks, which operate according to the principle of a revolving credit system: kin networks mobilize to provide cash or goods for some members, with the understanding that those members will in turn do the same at another time. In that configuration, money is at once a necessary but minimal aspect of the relations of social obligation (see Werner 1999).

11. On language, performance, and the attribution of responsibility in a political economy, see Irvine's (1989) article.

12. Zamanbek Nurkadilov, a former mayor of Almaty who in an open letter in 2005 accused the president of corruption and demanded his resignation, was killed in November of that year.

13. For coverage of the complicated fallout of the Sarsenbayev killings, see, for example, "Kazakhstan: A Shaken System," Radio Free Europe/Radio Liberty, 3 March 2006, http://www.rferl.org/content/article/1066325.html.

14. President Nazarbayev is still in office at the time of writing.

15. Personal interview, spring 2004.

16. One article on the matter was headlined, "Kazakh Folk Poetry Slams Corrupt Establishment!," *Central Asia–Caucus Analyst*, 21 February 2007, http://www.cacianalyst.org/?q=node/4465.

17. Beyer (2009, 2014) has shown that the dynamic of mutuality exists among politicians and elders (*aksakals*) during political events in Kyrgyzstan.

18. Personal interview, summer 2006.

19. Personal interview, summer 2006.

20. Personal interview, summer 2006. The sense of the term *yel* in Kazakh here is most like the English term "country."

21. At the time of writing, the country's internal linguistic politics and popular culture have shifted, and there seems to be a renewed interest in the development and promulgation of Kazakh language as a language of both government and the general public. Throughout the post-Soviet period, knowledge of the Kazakh language has been used strategically in the nationalization of government offices throughout the country (Cummings 2005; Dave 2007).

22. On the concept of language ideology as a cultural and political matrix and worldview for speakers and observers alike, see the article by Woolard and Schieffelin (1994), as well as the edited volume by Schieffelin, Woolard, and Kroskrity (1998).

23. Sponsors can also be local or regional politicians and businessmen, either established or trying to solidify their careers, but having a nationalist agenda tends to be a feature of those who are most successful.

24. Personal interview with Zhursin Yerman, summer 2004.

25. Personal interview, spring 2006. I thank Akbota Anuzkhanova for help with translation.

26. Personal interview, spring 2006.

27. The story of Isatai Taimanov and Makhambet Utemisoly is described in a variety of sources, ranging from a work by Shaxmatov ([1946] 2013) to one by Artykbayev (2004). Western Kazakh University in Uralsk is named in honor of Makhambet Utemisov.

28. *Molodets* is a Russian word typically said to children who do something well; it is a term of praise and encouragement.

29. Karima Akhyn, Shimkent Regional New Year's Aitys, 18 March 2006. Any faults in translation are entirely my own.

30. Kazakhstan's economy is largely based on natural resource extraction, primarily oil and gas, but also including coal, uranium, and gold. Profits from that mining activity remain centralized, under the control of the elite members of the president's administration.

31. Ak Zhol is also the name of political parties in both Kazakhstan and Kyrgyzstan.

32. Kazakhstan's government agreed to lease the active site to Russia until 2050 for $17 million per year. On post-Soviet weapons testing in Kazakhstan and Russia, see the essay by Werner and Purvis-Roberts (2014).

33. Abai Kunanbaioly (1845–1904) was a late Russian-era poet, writer, and leader who has been canonized in Soviet (and now nationalist) Kazakh folk mythology as a great cultural hero.

34. Zhyrau was the poet of Abylai Khan, the seventeenth-century ruler mentioned earlier.

35. Personal interview, summer 2006.

36. This extended example was originally published in an earlier article of my own (Dubuisson 2010).

37. It is important that Aibek is from Astana, the current seat of the national government; each poet represents his or her region of origin and bears a responsibility to address issues particular to that region. It would be far less likely for a poet from another city or region to use this particular *dat* form.

38. Like many poets, Aibek himself was raised in a rural village, and he is personally invested in calling attention to the great disparity between rural and urban life.

39. Here Aibek makes the same play on *akhtaban shubyryndy* (the historical period when Kazakhs were uprooted from their lands by invading Kalmyks) and "alcohol" that Orazaly did in the aitys described in chapter three.

40. In 2004, the politician Galymzhan Zhakiyanov was one such well-known symbol of the jailed opposition; the former akim of Semei, he joined the Democratic Choice Kazakhstan Party, an opposition group, in 2001 and was imprisoned in 2002. Subsequently, he was forced to renounce any effort to participate in political activity in the country.

41. This phrasing is taken from J. L. Austin's ([1962] 1975) classic work on performatives.

42. Adai and Berish are major lineages of the Kazakh Kishi Zhuz (Minor Horde).

43. In a personal interview with me in 2004, the prominent nationalist Beibit Koishybayev, director of the state-sponsored newspaper *Ana Tili* (Mother tongue), explained that from a nationalist perspective, without the compulsory usage of Kazakh alone as a government language, Kazakhs cannot *oizimmen oizim bolugha* (be in their own place)—the period of "independence" is simply a version of neocolonialism.

CONCLUSION

1. On other comparisons of capitals across Central Asia, see the collection by Alexander, Buchli, and Humphrey (2007).

2. Beyer (2013a) offers a compelling view of how, after multiple amendments and reforms, "the constitution" has become a quasi religious master symbol in Kyrgyzstan, viewed and interpreted as an object more than as a text that is a source of legitimacy and hope.

3. On neopatrimonialism and symbolism in contemporary Kazakhstani state-making, see the collection of essays edited by Laruelle (2016).

4. See the essay by Marat (2010) on "nation-branding" in Kazakhstan. On the role of music in nation-building in Kazakhstan specifically, see the article by Rancier (2009).

5. On the Manas epic, tradition, and use in political life, see the book by van der Heide (2008).

6. I would like to thank Zhanara Nauruzbayeva and the organizers and participants of the thirteenth annual SOYUZ symposium, "Authoritarianism and Beyond: Lessons from Postsocialist Societies," for extensive conversation on these themes.

7. As Laura Adams (2010) elaborates, modern Uzbekistan has tried to short-circuit the

awe factor in its staging of "spectacular events," participation in which confers the tacit recognition of state legitimacy. See also Cummings's (2010) collected volume on symbolism and state power in Central Asia.

8. For example, Reeves (2014) shows how a state's "border"' is not an artifact but can be a lived reality, a negotiation of local human relationships.

9. The unwritten Yassa law code was created under Chinggis Khan for the rule of the Mongolian Empire.

10. Speech of President Elbegdorj at introduction of Partnering against Corruption initiative (translator unknown), 3 March 2011, Public Relations and Communications Division, Office of the President of Mongolia, http://president.mn/eng/newsCenter/viewNews.php?newsId=492.

11. Speech by Tsakhiagiin Elbegdorj, President of Mongolia, at a Solemn Assembly, dedicated to the 850th Anniversary of Birth of Chinggis Khaan (translator unknown), 14 November 2012, Public Relations and Communications Division, Office of the President of Mongolia, http://www.president.mn/eng/newsCenter/viewNews.php?newsId=848.

12. Speech by Elbegdorj, 850th Anniversary of Chinggis Khaan.

13. Speech by Elbegdorj, 850th Anniversary of Chinggis Khaan.

14. Speech of President Elbegdorj at introduction of Partnering against Corruption initiative. I make no claim or judgment about Elbegdorj's own leadership, other than to note that he used this rhetorical mode referencing ancestry in the public space of presidential speeches.

15. "Tole-bi," HeritageNet Kazakhstan, accessed 17 October 2014, http://www.unesco.kz/heritagenet/kz/content/history/portret/tolebi.htm.

16. Well-known Kazakh writer Ghabbas Kabyshyly has defended the principle of "freedom" in the aitys tradition; for a discussion of aitys in his online forum in 2009, please see "Internet Conference: Ghabbas Kabyshyly," accessed 19 January 2017, http://old.abai.kz/content/internet-konferentsiya-gabbas-kabyshyly.

17. In her analysis of leaders across Central Asian states, Matveeva (2010, 19) argues that "communication between the rulers and the ruled" is a fundamental way in which "cultural coherence" and political legitimacy are achieved.

18. In my thinking on this issue of the false dichotomy of authoritarianism and democracy, I am deeply indebted to the anthropologist Zhanara Nauruzbayeva, who worked to convene the thirteenth annual meeting of SOYUZ (the research network for postsocialist cultural studies) on the theme "Authoritarianism and Beyond" at Columbia University's Harriman Institute in 2013.

REFERENCES

Abazov, Rafis. 1999. "Economic Migration in Post-Soviet Central Asia: The Case of Kyrgyzstan." *Post-Communist Economies* 11 (2): 237–52.

Abramson, David M., and Elyor E. Karimov. 2006. "Sacred Sites, Profane Ideologies: Religious Pilgrimage and the Uzbek State." In *Everyday Life in Central Asia: Past and Present*, edited by Jeff Sahadeo and Russell Zanca, 319–38. Bloomington: Indiana University Press.

Abu-Lughod, Lila. 1986. *Veiled Sentiments: Honor and Poetry in a Bedouin Society*. Berkeley: University of California Press.

Adams, Laura. 2004. "Cultural Elites in Uzbekistan: Ideological Production and the State." In *Transformations of Central Asia: From Soviet Rule to Independence*, edited by Pauline Jones Luong, 93–119. Ithaca: Cornell University Press.

Adams, Laura. 2010. *The Spectacular State: Culture and National Identity in Uzbekistan*. Durham: Duke University Press.

Adams, Margarethe. 2015. "Liquid Modernity and Shifting Belief: Music and Shrine Pilgrimage in Post-Soviet Kazakhstan." Paper presented at the Forty-Third World Conference of the International Council for Traditional Music, Astana.

Agha, Asif. 2007. *Language and Social Relations*. Cambridge: Cambridge University Press.

Ahmetov, Z., et al., eds. 1988a. *XIX Ghasyrdaghy Kazakh Akhyndary*. Almaty: Ghylym.

Ahmetov, Z., et al., eds. 1988b. *Kazakh Halykh Ædibieti*, volume 2, *Aitys*. Almaty: Kazakh SSR Ghylym Akademiasy.

Aitbaioly, Talghat. 2011. *Almaty 1986 Zheltoksan*. Almaty: National Chamber of Books, Republic of Kazakhstan.

Aitpaeva, Gulnara. 2009. "Sacred Sites in Kyrgyzstan: Spiritual Mission, Health and Pilgrimage." In *Nature, Space and the Sacred: Transdisciplinary Perspectives*, edited by S. Bergmann, P. M. Scott, M. Jansdotter Samuelsson, and H. Bedford-Strohm, 249–57. Farnham: Ashgate.

Alexander, Catherine, Victor Buchli, and Caroline Humphrey, eds. 2007. *Urban Life in Post-Soviet Asia*. London: University College London Press.

Artykbayev, Zh. O. 2004. *Istoriya Kazakhstana*. Astana: Elim. www.elim.kz/article/371/.

Attinasi, John, and Paul Friedrich. 1995. "Dialogic Breakthrough: Catalysis and Synthesis in Life-Changing Dialogue." In *The Dialogic Emergence of Culture*, edited by Dennis Tedlock and Bruce Mannheim, 33–53. Urbana: University of Illinois Press.

Auezov, Mukhtar. (1959) 1964. "Aitys." In *Kazakh Ædebietining Tarixy*, volume 2. Almaty: Kazakh SSR Ghylym Akademiasyn Baspasy.

Auezov, Mukhtar. (1988) 1997. *Put' Abaia*. Volumes 1–4. Almaty: Ana Tili.

Auezov, Mukhtar. 1997. *Ædebiet Turaly*. Almaty: Sanat.

Austin, J. L. (1962) 1975. *How to Do Things with Words*. Cambridge: Harvard University Press.

Bakhtin, M. M. 1981. *The Dialogic Imagination*. Translated by Caryl Emerson and Michael Holdquist. Austin: University of Texas Press.

Basso, Keith. 1996. *Wisdom Sits in Places: Landscape and Language among the Western Apache*. Albuquerque: University of New Mexico Press.

Bauman, Richard. (1977) 1984. *Verbal Art as Performance*. Long Grove: Waveland Press.

Bauman, Richard. 1992. "Contextualization, Tradition, and the Dialogue of Genres: Icelandic Legends of the *Kraftaskáld*." In *Rethinking Context: Language as an Interactive Phenomenon*, edited by Alessandro Duranti and Charles Goodwin, 125–47. Cambridge: Cambridge University Press.

Behar, Ruth. 1995. "Rage and Redemption: Reading the Life Story of a Mexican Marketing Woman." In *The Dialogic Emergence of Culture*, edited by Dennis Tedlock and Bruce Mannheim, 148–78. Urbana: University of Illinois Press.

Bellér-Hann, Ildikó. 2005. "The Micropolitics of a Pilgrimage." In *Central Asia on Display: Proceedings of the European Society for Central Asian Studies*, edited by Gabriele Rasuly-Paleczek and Julia Katchnig, 325–34. Münster: LIT Verlag.

Berdahl, Daphne, Mattie Bunzl, and Martha Lampland, eds. 2010. *Altering States: Ethnographies of Transition in Eastern Europe and the Former Soviet Union*. Ann Arbor: University of Michigan Press.

Bernstein, Anya, dir. 2006. *In Pursuit of the Siberian Shaman*. Feature-length ethnographic documentary (75 min.). Distributed by Documentary Educational Resources. www.der.org.

Beyer, Judith. 2009. "Authority as Accomplishment: Intergenerational Dynamics in Talas, Northern Kyrgyzstan." In *Eurasian Perspectives: In Search of Alternatives*, edited by Anita Sengupta and Suchandana Chatterjee, 78–92. New Delhi: Shipra (Maulana Abul Kalam Azad Institute of Asian Studies).

Beyer, Judith. 2010. "According to Salt: An Ethnography of Customary Law in Talas, Kyrgyzstan." PhD diss., Martin-Luther University, Halle-Wittenberg.

Beyer, Judith. 2013a. "Constitutional Faith: Law and Hope in Revolutionary Kyrgyzstan." *Ethnos* 80 (3): 320–45. doi:10.1080/00141844.2013.841270.

Beyer, Judith. 2013b. "Ordering Ideals: Accomplishing Well-Being in a Kyrgyz Cooperative of Elders." *Central Asian Survey* 32 (4): 432–47.

Beyer, Judith. 2014. "'There is this law . . .': Performing the State in Kyrgyz Courts of Elders." In *Ethnographies of the State in Central Asia: Performing Politics*, edited by Madeleine Reeves, Johan Rasanayagam, and Judith Beyer, 99–126. Bloomington: Indiana University Press.

Bissenova, Alima. 2009. "Construction Boom and Banking Crisis in Kazakhstan." *Central Asia–Caucasus Institute Analyst*, 8 June, 13–15. http://www.cacianalyst.org/publications/analytical-articles/item/11850-analytical-articles-caci-analyst-2009-6-3-art-11850.html.

Bissenova, Alima. 2014. "The Master Plan of Astana: Between the 'Art of Government' and the 'Art of Being Global.'" In *Ethnographies of the State in Central Asia: Performing Politics*, edited by Madeleine Reeves, Johan Rasanayagam, and Judith Beyer, 127–48. Bloomington: Indiana University Press.

Boyarin, Jonathan. 1994. "Space, Time, and the Politics of Memory." In *Remapping Memory:*

The Politics of Timespace, edited by Jonathan Boyarin, 1–38. Minneapolis: University of Minnesota Press.

Briggs, Charles L. 1986. *Learning How to Ask: A Sociolinguistic Appraisal of the Role of the Interview in Social Science Research.* Cambridge: Cambridge University Press.

Briggs, Charles, and Richard Bauman. 1990. "Poetics and Performance as Critical Perspective on Language and Social Life." *Annual Review of Anthropology* 19:59–88.

Brower, Daniel R., and Edward J. Lazzerini, eds. 1997. *Russia's Orient: Imperial Borderlands and Peoples, 1700–1917.* Bloomington: Indiana University Press.

Brown, Wendy. 1995. *States of Injury: Power and Freedom in Late Modernity.* Princeton: Princeton University Press.

Buchli, Victor. 2007. "Astana: Materiality and the City." In *Urban Life in Post-Soviet Asia,* edited by Catherine Alexander, Victor Buchli, and Caroline Humphrey, 40–69. London: University College London Press.

Burawoy, Michael, and Katherine Verdery, eds. 1999. *Uncertain Transition: Ethnographies of Change in the Postsocialist World.* Lanham: Rowman and Littlefield.

Buyandelger, Manduhai. 2007. "Dealing with Uncertainty: Shamans, Marginal Capitalism, and the Remaking of History in Postsocialist Mongolia." *American Ethnologist* 34 (1): 127–47.

Buyandelger, Manduhai. 2013. *Tragic Spirits: Shamanism, Memory, and Gender in Contemporary Mongolia.* Chicago: University of Chicago Press.

Caldwell, Melissa, ed. 2009. *Food and Everyday Life in the Postsocialist World.* Bloomington: Indiana University Press.

Caton, Steven. 1990. *"Peaks of Yemen I Summon": Poetry as Cultural Practice in a North Yemeni Tribe.* Berkeley: University of California Press.

Conquergood, Dwight. 1982. "Performing as a Moral Act: Ethical Dimensions of the Ethnography of Performance." *Literature in Performance* 5 (2): 1–13.

Conquergood, Dwight. 1998. "Beyond the Text: Toward a Performative Cultural Politics." In *The Future of Performance Studies: Visions and Revisions,* edited by S. J. Daily, 25–36. Washington, DC: National Communication Association.

Coombe, Rosemary. 1998. *The Cultural Life of Intellectual Properties.* Durham: Duke University Press.

Coskun, Mustafa. 2013. "Oral Traditions and Moral Citizens: Poets, Poetry and Politics in Transition." Paper presented at the Third Annual Conference of the Central Asian Studies Institute, American University of Central Asia, Bishkek.

Cummings, Sally. 2005. *Kazakhstan: Power and the Elite.* London: I. B. Tauris.

Cummings, Sally, ed. 2010. *Symbolism and Power in Central Asia.* London: Routledge.

Dagiev, Dagikhudo. 2014. *Regime Transition in Central Asia: Stateness, Nationalism, and Political Change in Tajikistan and Uzbekistan.* London: Routledge.

Das, Veena, and Deborah Poole. 2004. "State and Its Margins: Comparative Ethnographies." In *Anthropology in the Margins of the State,* edited by Veena Das and Deborah Poole, 3–34. Santa Fe: School of American Research Press.

Dave, Bhavna. 2007. *Kazakhstan: Ethnicity, Language, and Power.* New York: Routledge.

Dave, Bhavna, ed. 2010. *Politics of Modern Central Asia.* London: Routledge.

DeWeese, Devin. 1994. *Islamization and Native Religion in the Golden Horde: Baba Tukles and Conversion to Islam in Historical and Epic Tradition.* University Park: Pennsylvania State University Press.

Diener, Alexander. 2002. "National Territory and the Reconstruction of History in Kazakhstan." *Eurasian Geography and Economics* 48 (3): 632–50.

Diener, Alexander. 2005. "Kazakhstan's Kin State Diaspora: Settlement Planning and the Oralman Dilemma." *Europe-Asia Studies* 57 (2): 327–48.

Diener, Alexander. 2009. *One Homeland, or Two? The Nationalization and Transnationalization of Mongolia's Kazakhs.* Washington, DC: Woodrow Wilson Center Press; Stanford: Stanford University Press.

Douglas, Mary. (1966) 1984. *Purity and Danger.* New York: Routledge and Kegan Paul.

Dubuisson, Eva-Marie. 2009. "The Value of a Voice: Culture and Critique in Kazakh Aitys Poetry." PhD diss., University of Michigan.

Dubuisson, Eva-Marie. 2010. "Confrontation in and through the Nation in Kazakh Aitys Poetry." *Journal of Linguistic Anthropology,* special issue edited by Valentina Pagliai, "Performing Disputes: Cooperation and Conflict in Argumentative Language," 20 (1): 101–15.

Dubuisson, Eva-Marie. 2014. "Dialogic Authority: Kazakh Aitys Poets and Their Patrons." In *Ethnographies of the State in Central Asia: Performing Politics,* edited by Madeleine Reeves, Johan Rasanayagam, and Judith Beyer, 55–77. Bloomington: Indiana University Press.

Dubuisson, Eva-Marie, and Anna Genina. 2012. "Claiming an Ancestral Homeland: Kazakh Pilgrimage and Migration in Inner Asia." In *Movement, Power, and Place in Central Asia and Beyond: Contested Trajectories,* edited by Madeleine Reeves, 111–28. London: Routledge. Reprinted from *Central Asian Survey* 30 (3–4).

Duranti, Alessandro, and Charles Goodwin, eds. 1992. *Rethinking Context: Language as an Interactive Phenomenon.* Cambridge: Cambridge University Press.

Edgar, Adrienne. 2004. *Tribal Nation: The Making of Soviet Turkmenistan.* Princeton: Princeton University Press.

Fabian, Johannes. 1990. *Power and Performance: Ethnographic Explorations through Proverbial Wisdom and Theater in Shaba, Zaire.* Madison: University of Wisconsin Press.

Feaux de la Croix, Jeanne. 2010. "Moral Geographies in Kyrgyzstan: How Pastures, Dams, and Holy Sites Matter in Striving for a Good Life." PhD diss., University of St. Andrews.

Fierman, William. 2006. "Language and Education in Post-Soviet Kazakhstan: Kazakh-Medium Instruction in Urban Schools." *Russian Review* 65:98–116.

Finke, Peter. 2013. "Historical Homelands and Transnational Ties: The Case of the Kazakh Oralman." *Zeitschrift für Ethnologie,* special issue, "Mobility and Identity in Central Asia," 138 (2): 75–194.

Fitzpatrick, Sheila. 1999. *Everyday Stalinism: Ordinary Life in Extraordinary Times; Soviet Russia in the 1930s.* New York: Oxford University Press.

Gabullin, M. G. 1968. "Aitys." *Istorii Kazakskoi Literatury,* 1:324–51. Almaty: Nauka.

Galkina, Galina. 2002. "Zvyozda i smert' Maxambeta Utemisova." *Novoie Pokolenie* 50 (238).

Genina, Anna. 2011. "Claiming Ancestral Homelands: Mongolian Kazakh Migration in Inner Asia." PhD diss., University of Michigan.

Ghodsee, Kristen. 2011. *Lost in Transition: Ethnographies of Everyday Life after Communism.* Durham: Duke University Press.

Goffman, Erving. 1981. *Forms of Talk.* Philadelphia: University of Pennsylvania Press.

Goffman, Erving. 1986. *Frame Analysis: An Essay on the Organization of Experience.* Boston: Northeastern University Press.

Grant, Bruce. 1995. *In the Soviet House of Culture.* Princeton: Princeton University Press.

Grant, Bruce. 2011. "Shrines and Sovereigns: Life, Death, and Religion in Rural Azerbaijan." *Comparative Studies in Society and History* 53 (3): 654–81.

Grant, Bruce. 2012. "Recognizing Soviet Culture." In *Reconstructing the House of the Culture: Community, Self, and the Making of Culture in Russia and Beyond,* edited by Joachim Otto Habeck and Brian Donahue, 263–76. New York: Berghahn Books.

Grousset, René. 1970. *The Empire of the Steppes: A History of Central Asia.* Translated by Naomi Walford. New Brunswick: Rutgers University Press.

Gullette, David. 2010. *The Genealogical Construction of the Kyrgyz Republic: Kinship, State, and "Tribalism."* Kent: Global Oriental Press.

Hann, C. M. 2002. "Farewell to the Socialist 'Other.'" In *Postsocialism: Ideals, Ideologies, and Practices in Eurasia,* edited by C. M. Hann. London: Routledge.

Hann, Chris, Caroline Humphrey, and Katherine Verdery. 2002. "Introduction: Postsocialism as a Topic of Anthropological Investigation." In *Postsocialism: Ideals, Ideologies, and Practices in Eurasia,* edited by C. M. Hann, 1–27. London: Routledge.

Heathershaw, John, and Edmund Herzig, eds. 2012. *The Transformation of Tajikistan: The Sources of Statehood.* London: Routledge.

Hill, Jane. 1995. "Voices of Don Gabriel." In *The Dialogic Emergence of Culture,* edited by Dennis Tedlock and Bruce Mannheim, 97–147. Urbana: University of Illinois Press.

Hill, Jane, and Judith T. Irvine, eds. 1993. *Responsibility and Evidence in Oral Discourse.* Cambridge: Cambridge University Press.

Hirsch, Francine. 2005. *Empire of Nations: Ethnographic Knowledge and the Making of the Soviet Union.* Ithaca: Cornell University Press.

Humphrey, Caroline. 2002. "Shamans in the City." In *The Unmaking of Soviet Life: Everyday Economies after Socialism,* 202–22. Ithaca: Cornell University Press.

Hymes, Dell. 1981. *In Vain I Tried to Tell You: Essays in Native American Ethnopoetics.* Philadelphia: University of Pennsylvania Press.

İğmen, Ali. 2012. *Speaking Soviet with an Accent: Culture and Power in Kyrgyzstan.* Pittsburgh: University of Pittsburgh Press.

Irvine, Judith T. 1989. "When Talk Isn't Cheap: Language and Political Economy." *American Ethnologist* 16 (2): 248–67.

Irvine, Judith T. 1996. "Shadow Conversations: The Indeterminacy of Participant Roles." In *Natural Histories of Discourse,* edited by Michael Silverstein and Greg Urban, 131–59. Chicago: University of Chicago Press.

Irvine, Judith T. 2001. "Style as Distinctiveness: The Culture and Ideology of Linguistic Differentiation." In *Style and Sociolinguistic Variation,* edited by P. Eckert and J. R. Rickford, 21–43. Cambridge: Cambridge University Press.

Ismailbekova, Aksana. 2014a. "Migration and Patrilineal Descent: The Role of Women in Rural Kyrgyzstan." *Central Asian Survey* 33 (3): 375–89.

Ismailbekova, Aksana. 2014b. "Performing Democracy: State-Making through Patronage in Kyrgyzstan." In *Ethnographies of the State in Central Asia: Performing Politics*, edited by Madeleine Reeves, Johan Rasanayagam, and Judith Beyer, 78–98. Bloomington: Indiana University Press.

Jacquesson, Svetlana. 2016. "Genealogies as Craft: The Search for 'Truth' and Authority in Contemporary Kyrgyzstan." In *History Making in Central and Northern Eurasia*, edited by Svetlana Jacquesson, 100–121. Wiesbaden-Dotzheim: Reichart Verlag.

Jakobson, Roman. (1960) 1980. *The Framework of Language*. Ann Arbor: University of Michigan Slavic Publications.

Jones Luong, Pauline. 2000. "After the Break-Up: Institutional Design in Transitional States." *Comparative Political Studies* 33 (5): 563–92.

Jones Luong, Pauline, ed. 2004. *The Transformation of Central Asia: States and Societies from Soviet Rule to Independence*. Ithaca: Cornell University Press.

Kamp, Marianne. 2006. *The New Woman in Uzbekistan: Islam, Modernity, and Unveiling under Communism*. Seattle: University of Washington Press.

Kapchan, Deborah, ed. 2014. *Cultural Heritage in Transit: Intangible Rights as Human Rights*. Philadelphia: University of Pennsylvania Press.

Kaplonski, Christopher. 2004. *Truth, History, and Politics in Mongolia: The Memory of Heroes*. London: Routledge Curzon.

Kendirbaeva, Gulnar. 1994. "Folklore and Folklorism in Kazakhstan." *Asian Folklore Studies* 53:97–123.

Khalid, Adeeb. 1998. *The Politics of Muslim Cultural Reform: Jadidism in Central Asia*. Berkeley: University of California Press.

Khalid, Adeeb. 2007. *Islam after Communism: Religion and Politics in Central Asia*. Berkeley: University of California Press.

Khodorkovsky, Michael. 2002. *Russia's Steppe Frontier: The Making of a Colonial Empire, 1500–1800*. Bloomington: Indiana University Press.

Kudaibergenova, Diana. 2015. "Between the State and the Artist: Representations of Femininity and Masculinity in the Formation of Ideas of the Nation in Central Asia." *Nationalities Papers: The Journal of Nationalism and Ethnicity* 44 (2): 1–22.

Kuscu, Isik. 2008. "Kazakhstan's Oralman Project: A Remedy for Ambiguous Identity." PhD diss., Indiana University.

Laitin, David D. 1998. *Identity in Formation: The Russian-Speaking Populations in the Near Abroad*. Ithaca: Cornell University Press.

Laruelle, Marlene, ed. 2016. *Kazakhstan in the Making: Legitimacy, Symbols, and Social Changes*. Lanham: Lexington Books.

Laszczkowski, Mateusz. 2014. "State-Building(s): Built Forms, Materiality, and the State in Astana." In *Ethnographies of the State in Central Asia: Performing Politics*, edited by Madeleine Reeves, Johan Rasanayagam, and Judith Beyer, 149–72. Bloomington: Indiana University Press.

Levin, Theodore. 1996. *The Hundred Thousand Fools of God: Musical Travels in Central Asia (and Queens, New York)*. Bloomington: Indiana University Press.

Light, Nathan. 2011. "Genealogy, History, Nation." *Nationalities Papers* 39 (1): 33–53.

Liu, Morgan. 2002. "Recognizing the Khan: Authority, Space, and Political Imagination among Uzbek Men in Post-Soviet Osh, Kyrgyzstan." PhD diss., University of Michigan.

Liu, Morgan. 2005. "Post-Soviet Paternalism and Personhood: Why Culture Matters to Democratization in Central Asia." In *Prospects for Democracy in Central Asia*, edited by Birgit Schlyter, 225–38. London: I. B. Tauris.

Liu, Morgan. 2012. *Under Solomon's Throne: Uzbek Visions of Renewal in Osh*. Pittsburgh: University of Pittsburgh Press.

Louw, Maria Elisabeth. 2007. *Everyday Islam in Post-Soviet Central Asia*. London: Routledge.

Madanova, Margarita. 2004. *Path of Abai*. Institute of Literature and Arts named for M. O. Auezov, International Abai Club (Kazakh, Russian, and English versions).

Madison, Soyini. 2005. *Critical Ethnography: Method, Ethics, and Performance*. London: SAGE.

Madison, Soyini. 2012. *Critical Ethnography: Method, Ethics, Performance*. 2nd ed. Los Angeles: SAGE.

Mandel, Ruth, and Caroline Humphrey, eds. 2002. *Markets and Moralities: Ethnographies of Postsocialism*. London: Berg.

Mannheim, Bruce, and Dennis Tedlock. 1995. Introduction to *The Dialogic Emergence of Culture*, edited by Bruce Tedlock and Dennis Mannheim, 1–32. Urbana: University of Illinois Press.

Marat, Erica. 2009. "Shrinking Remittances Increase Labor Migration from Central Asia." *Central Asia–Caucasus Institute Analyst*, 11 February, 1–9. http://www.unece.org/fileadmin/DAM/hlm/prgm/cph/experts/tajikistan/Documents/CACI.shrinking.remittances.pdf.

Marat, Erica. 2010. "Nation-Branding in Central Asia: A New Campaign to Present Ideas about the State and the Nation." In *Symbolism and Power in Central Asia: Politics of the Spectacular*, edited by S. Cummings, 39–52. New York: Routledge.

Martin, Terry. 2001. *The Affirmative Action Empire: Nations and Nationalism in the Soviet Union, 1923–1939*. Ithaca: Cornell University Press.

Martin, Virginia. 2001. *Law and Custom in the Steppe: The Kazakhs of the Middle Horde and Russian Colonialism in the Nineteenth Century*. Richmond: Curzon.

Matveeva, Anna. 2010. "Legitimising Central Asian Authoritarianism: Political Manipulation and Symbolic Power." In *Symbolism and Power in Central Asia: Politics of the Spectacular*, edited by S. Cummings, 12–38. New York: Routledge.

McGlinchey, Eric. 2008. "Patronage, Islam, and the Rise of Localism in Central Asia." PONARS Eurasia Policy Memo no. 2.

McGlinchey, Eric. 2009. "Searching for Kamalot: Political Patronage and Youth Politics in Uzbekistan." *Europe-Asia Studies* 61:1137–50.

McGlinchey, Eric. 2011. *Chaos, Violence, Dynasty: Politics and Islam in Central Asia*. Pittsburgh: University of Pittsburgh Press.

Mekteptegi synyptan tys zhumystar (Textbook examples and work) 5. 2011. Almaty: Zhauapkershiligi Shekteuli Seriktestigi.

Michaels, Paula. 1996. "Ninety Winds of Change: The Alma-Ata Riots and the Mobilization of Kazakh Ethnic Identity." *Michigan Discussions in Anthropology* 12:39–50.

Montgomery, David. 2007. "Namaz, Wishing Trees, and Vodka: The Diversity of Everyday Religious Life Central Asia." In *Everyday Life in Central Asia: Past and Present*, edited by Jeff Sahadeo and Russell Zanca, 355–70. Bloomington: Indiana University Press.

Montgomery, David. 2016. *Practicing Islam: Knowledge, Experience, and Social Navigation in Kyrgyzstan*. Pittsburgh: University of Pittsburgh Press.

Montgomery, David, and John Heathershaw. 2014. "The Myth of Post-Soviet Muslim Radicalization in the Central Asian Republics." Russia and Asia Programme Research Paper. London: Royal Institute of International Affairs and Chatham House.

Mostowlansky, Till. 2013. "'The State Starts from the Family': Peace and Harmony in Tajikistan's Eastern Pamirs." *Central Asian Survey* 32 (4): 462–74.

Mukhanov, Sabit, et al., eds. 1964. *Aitys*. Almaty: Kazakh SSR Ghylym Akademiasy.

Nasritdinov, Emil. 2007. "Regional Changes in Kyrgyzstan: Bazaars, Open-Air Markets and Social Networks." PhD diss., University of Melbourne.

Nauruzbayeva, Zhanara. 2011. "Portraiture and Proximity: 'Official' Artists and the Stateization of the Market in Post-Soviet Kazakhstan." *Ethnos* 76 (3): 375–97.

Nazpary, Joma. 2001. *Post-Soviet Chaos: Violence and Dispossession in Kazakhstan*. London: Pluto Press.

Northrop, Douglas. 2004. *Veiled Empire: Gender and Power in Stalinist Central Asia*. Ithaca: Cornell University Press.

Olcott, Martha Brill. 1995. *The Kazakhs*. 2nd ed. Stanford: Hoover Institution Press.

Paley, Julia. 2002. "Toward an Anthropology of Democracy." *American Anthropological Review* 31:469–96.

Pederson, Morten Axel. 2011. *Not Quite Shamans: Spirit Worlds and Political Lives in Northern Mongolia*. Ithaca: Cornell University Press.

Post, Jennifer. 2007. "I Take My Dombra and Sing to Remember My Homeland: Landscape and Music in Kazakh Communities in Western Mongolia." *Ethnomusicology Forum*, special issue, "Musical Performance in the Diaspora," 16 (1): 45–69.

Prior, Daniel. 2000. *Patron, Party, Patrimony: Notes on the Cultural History of the Kirghiz Epic Tradition*. Papers on Inner Asia no. 33. Bloomington: Indiana University Research Institute for Inner Asian Studies.

Privratsky, Bruce. 2001. *Muslim Turkistan: Kazak Religion and Collective Memory*. Richmond: Curzon.

Rancier, Megan. 2009. "Resurrecting the Nomads: Historical Nostalgia and Modern Nationalism in Contemporary Kazakh Popular Music Videos." *Popular Music and Society*, special issue, "Popular Music in the Post-Soviet Space: Trends, Movements, Social Contexts," 32 (3): 387–405.

Rasanayagam, Johan. 2006. "I'm Not a Wahhabi: State Power and Muslim Orthodoxy in Uzbekistan." In *The Postsocialist Religious Question: Faith and Power in Central Asia and East-Central Europe*, edited by Chris Hann, 99–124. Berlin: Lit Verlag.

Rasanayagam, Johan. 2012. *Islam in Post-Soviet Uzbekistan: The Morality of Experience*. Cambridge: Cambridge University Press.

Reeves, Madeleine. 2012. "Black Work, Green Money: Remittances, Ritual and Domestic Economies in Southern Kyrgyzstan." *Slavic Review* 70 (1): 108–34.

Reeves, Madeleine. 2014. *Borderwork: Spatial Lives of the State in Rural Central Asia.* Ithaca: Cornell University Press.

Reeves, Madeleine, Johan Rasanayagam and Judith Beyer, eds. 2014. *Ethnographies of the State in Central Asia: Performing Politics.* Bloomington: Indiana University Press.

Roberts, Sean R. 2007. "Everyday Negotiations of Islam in Central Asia: Practicing Religion in the Uyghur Neighborhood of Zarya Vostoka in Almaty, Kazakhstan." In *Everyday Life in Central Asia: Past and Present,* edited by Jeff Sahadeo and Russell Zanca, 339–54. Bloomington: Indiana University Press.

Roche, Sophie, and Sophie Hohmann. 2012. "Wedding Rituals and the Struggle over National Identities." In *The Transformation of Tajikistan: Sources of Statehood,* edited by John Heathershaw and Edmund Herzig, 127–42. New York: Routledge.

Rouland, Michael. 2005. "Music and the Making of the Kazakh Nation, 1920–1936." PhD diss., Georgetown University.

Sabloff, Paula, ed. 2001. *Modern Mongolia: Reclaiming Genghis Khan.* Philadelphia: University of Pennsylvania Museum of Archeology and Anthropology; Ulaanbaata: National Museum of Mongolian History.

Sabloff, Paula. (2013) 2016. *Does Everyone Want Democracy? Insights from Mongolia.* Walnut Creek: Left Coast Press. Reprint, London: Routledge.

Salimjan, Gulnara. 2017. "Debating Gender and Kazakhness: Memory and Voice in Poetic Duel Aytis between China and Kazakhstan." Paper presented at the Sixteenth Annual Conference of the Central Eurasian Studies Society, Washington, DC.

Schatz, Edward. 2004. *Modern Clan Politics: The Power of "Blood" in Kazakhstan and Beyond.* Seattle: University of Washington Press.

Schieffelin, Bambi B., Katherine A. Woolard, and Paul V. Kroskrity, eds. 1998. *Language Ideologies: Practice and Theory.* Oxford: Oxford University Press.

Schlyter, Birgit, ed. 2005. *Prospects for Democracy in Central Asia.* London: I. B. Tauris.

Schwab, Dell, and Ulan Bigozhin. 2016. "Shrines and Neopatrimonialism in Southern Kazakhstan." In *Kazakhstan in the Making: Legitimacy, Symbols, and Social Changes,* edited by Marlene Laruelle, 89–109. Lanham: Lexington Books.

Shaxmatov, V. F. (1946) 2013. *Vnutrennaiya orda i vosstanie Isataiya Taimanova.* Almaty: Institute for History and Ethnology named for Valihanov. e-history.kz.

Shryock, Andrew. 1997. *Nationalism and the Genealogical Imagination: Oral History and Textual Authority in Tribal Jordan.* Berkeley: University of California Press.

Slezkine, Yuri. 1994. "The U.S.S.R. as Communal Apartment, or How the State Promoted Ethnic Particularism." *Slavic Review* 53 (2): 414–52.

Sneath, David, and Caroline Humphrey. 2009. *The End of Nomadism? Society, State, and Environment in Inner Asia.* Durham: Duke University Press.

Soucek, Svat. 2000. *A History of Inner Asia.* Cambridge: Cambridge University Press.

Suleimenova, Saule. 2009. *Kazakhskaia Xronika* (Kazakh chronicles). Almaty.

Suny, Ronald Grigor. 2010. *The Soviet Experiment: Russia, the USSR, and the Successor States.* 2nd ed. Oxford: Oxford University Press.

Suny, Ronald Grigor, and Terry Martin, eds. 2001. *A State of Nations: Empire in the Age of Lenin and Stalin.* Oxford: Oxford University Press.

Suyarkulova, Mohira. 2012. "Statehood as Dialogue: Conflicting Historical Narratives of Tajikistan and Uzbekistan." In *The Transformation of Tajikistan: Sources of Statehood,* edited by John Heathershaw and Edmund Herzig, 161–76. London: Routledge.

Swancutt, Katherine. 2008. "The Undead Genealogy: Omnipresence, Spirit Perspectives, and a Case of Mongolian Vampirism." *Journal of the Royal Anthropological Institute* 14 (4): 843–64.

Tebegenov, Temirhan Sakhaoly. 2002. "Akhyndykh Poeziadaghy Folklor men Adebiet Dasturi." PhD diss., Abai Atyndaghy Almaty Memlekettik Universiteti, Almaty.

Tedlock, Dennis. 1983. *The Spoken Word and the Work of Interpretation.* Philadelphia: University of Pennsylvania Press.

Tedlock, Dennis, and Bruce Mannheim, eds. 1995. *The Dialogic Emergence of Culture.* Urbana: University of Illinois Press.

Tereskinas, Arturas. 2009. "Social Suffering, Post-Soviet Masculinities and Working-Class Men." *Social Sciences/Socialiniai Mokslai* 2 (64): 79–86.

Torsynov, E. D. 1976. *Kazakh Auyz Ædebietin Zhasaushylardyng Baiyrghy Ükilderi.* Almaty: Ghylym.

Torsynov, E. D. 2003. "Dvernie Tipy Nositelei Kazakhskovo Folklora (Genesis i Tipologia)." PhD diss., Academy of Literature and the Arts, Almaty.

Tulebaeva, Baktygul. 2015. "Being a Kyrgyz Child." In *Contemporary Society: Tribal Studies,* Volume 10, edited by Deepak Kumar Behera. New Delhi: Concept Publishing.

Turner, Victor. 1982. *From Ritual to Theater: The Human Seriousness of Play.* New York: PAJ Publications.

Umbetayev, M. 1992. *Pirim-Mening—Suinbai.* Almaty: Kazakh Universiteti.

Utegenova, Ailuna R. 2010. "Kazakhstan's 2030 Development Strategy: Significance and Results." *Yearbook of the Institute for Peace Research and Security Policy,* 133–43. Hamburg: University of Hamburg.

Uzendoski, Michael A., and Edith Felicia Calapucha-Tapuy. 2012. *The Ecology of the Spoken Word: Amazonian Storytelling and Shamanism among the Napo Runa.* Urbana: University of Illinois Press.

van der Heide, Nienke. (2008) 2015. *Spirited Performance: The Manas Epic and Society in Kyrgyzstan.* Bremen: Rozenberg.

Verdery, Katherine. 1991. *National Ideology under Socialism: Identity and Cultural Politics in Ceauşescu's Romania.* Berkeley and Los Angeles: University of California Press.

Volosinov, V. N. 1973. *Marxism and the Philosophy of Language.* Translated by Ladislav Matejka and I. R. Titunik. Cambridge: Harvard University Press.

Wedeen, Lisa. 2008. *Peripheral Visions: Publics, Power, and Performance in Yemen.* Chicago: University of Chicago Press.

Wegerich, Kai. 2011. "Water Resources in Central Asia: Regional Stability or Patchy Make-Up?" *Central Asian Survey* 30 (2): 275–90.

Werbner, Pnina. 1996. "Stamping the Earth with the Name of Allah: Zikr and the Sacralizing of Space among British Muslims." *Cultural Anthropology* 11 (3): 309–38.

Werbner, Pnina. 2003. *Pilgrims of Love: The Anthropology of a Global Sufi Cult.* Bloomington: Indiana University Press.

Werner, Cynthia. 1998. "Household Networks and the Security of Mutual Indebtedness in Rural Kazakhstan." *Central Asian Survey* 17 (4): 597–612.

Werner, Cynthia. 1999. "The Dynamics of Feasting and Gift Exchange in Rural Kazakhstan." In *Contemporary Kazaks: Social and Cultural Perspectives*, edited by Ingvar Svanberg, 47–72. London: Curzon.

Werner, Cynthia. 2004. "Women, Marriage, and the Nation-State: The Rise of Non-Consensual Bride Kidnapping in Post-Soviet Kazakhstan." In *Transformations of Central Asia: From Soviet Rule to Independence*, edited by Pauline Jones Luong, 59–89. Ithaca: Cornell University Press.

Werner, Cynthia, and Holly Barcus. 2009. "Mobility, Immobility and Return Migration: The Impact of Transnational Migration on the Kazakh Diaspora in Mongolia." *Migration Letters* 6 (1): 49–62.

Werner, Cynthia, and Holly Barcus. 2010. "The Kazakhs of Western Mongolia: Transnational Migration from 1990–2008." *Asian Ethnicity* 11 (2): 209–28.

Werner, Cynthia, and Kathleen Purvis-Roberts. 2014. "Cold War Memories and Post–Cold War Realities: The Politics of Memory and Identity in the Everyday Life of Kazakhstan's Radiation Victims." In *Ethnographies of the State in Central Asia: Performing Politics*, edited by Madeleine Reeves, Johan Rasanayagam, and Judith Beyer, 285–312. Bloomington: Indiana University Press.

Westren, Michael H. 2012. "Nations in Exile: 'The Punished Peoples' in Soviet Kazakhstan, 1941–1961." PhD diss., University of Chicago.

Woolard, Katherine, and Bambi Schieffelin. 1994. "Language Ideology." *Annual Review of Anthropology* 23:55–82.

Yerman, Zhursin. 2005. *Khudiretke Zhüginuw.* Almaty: Gridan Poligraf.

Yessenova, Saulesh. 2005a. "Routes and Roots of Kazakh Identity: Urban Migration in Postsocialist Kazakhstan." *Russian Review* 64 (4): 2–20.

Yessenova, Saulesh. 2005b. "Knowing the Road That Leads You Home: Family, Genealogy, and Migration in Post-Socialist Kazakhstan." *Journal of Guangxi University for Nationalities, Philosophy, and Social Sciences Edition* 27 (7): 40–48.

Yessenova, Saulesh. 2009. *The Politics and Poetics of the Nation: Urban Narratives of Kazakh Identity.* Saarbrücken: Lambert Academic Publishing.

Zharmukhamedoly, Mukhamedraxim. 1976. *Aitystyng Damu Zholdary.* Almaty: Ghylym.

Zharmukhamedoly, Mukhamedraxim. 2001. *Aitys Ølenderining Arghy Tegi men Damuy.* Almaty: Morattas.

Zholdasbekov, Murzatai. 2002. *Shyn men Shyndau: Makhalar, Surlasular, Lebizder.* Astana: Khoghamdykhsayasi Basylym.

Zholdasbekov, Murzatai, ed. 2004. *Kazirgi Aitys (1–2).* Astana: Kultegin.

INDEX

Note: Page references in *italics* refer to figures.

Abai Kunanbaioly, 69, 126, 150n18, 154n33
Abai Turanbaiolu, 153n6
Ablai Khan, 102, 152n22
Abramson, David M., 60, 61, 68
Abu-Lughod, Lila: social production and, 3–4
Abylai Khan, 115, 135, 154n34
Academy of Literature and Arts, 107, 108, 109, 113, 153n5
Academy of Sciences, 108, 110
accountability, 4, 21, 89, 107, 100, 132, 134, 136, 139; dialogue of, 144; mutual, 135; poets and, 114; politics of, 22
Adai, 131, 155n42
Adams, Laura: spectacular events and, 155n7
Adams, Margarethe, 68, 150n15
Aibek Akhyn, 155n37, 155n38; *akhtaban shubyryndy* and, 155n39; criticism by, 131, 132; dat of, 129, 130, 131; youth of, 155n38
Aida, 78, 82; Saltanat and, 79, 81
Aiteke Bi, 19, 141, 142
Aitmatov, Chingis, 148n21, 148n23
Aitpaeva, Gulnara, 149n1
aitys, 20, 21, 49, 108, 112, 115, 116, 117, 128, 134, 143; audiences for, 86–89, 90, 91, 92, 93, 96, 97, 98; commodity of, 107; competition, 93, 96, 98, *111*, 114, 121, 126, 127; cultural production of, 110; defined, 106; as dialogic, 92; excerpts from, 97; judging, 87–88, 119;

national network and, 84–86, 111, 145n1, 151n2; not for sale, 120–24; oral art of, 22, 84; patronizing, 114; performance of, *88*, 89–92, 118, 120, *126*, 144; property metaphor in, 67, 119; as protective framework, 105; real, 109, 118; repopularization of, 85; as shared talk, 91; social purpose of, 88; sponsoring, 114, 119, 125; status of, 129; theater, 98

aitys poets, 85, 89, 113; cultural organizers and, 22; Kazakh history and, 96; sponsors and, 20–21
aitys tradition, 90, 100, 110–11, 117; history of, 97; sponsorship of, 106–7
aitysh, 20, 147n26, 151n1
aitysu, 20, 84, 92, 106
Ak Orda (White Horde), 122; *aitys* and, 119, 120; religion and, 118; sponsorship and, 124
Ak Zhol (White Way), 17, 124, 135, 147n25, 154n31
Akayev, Askar, 136
Akhmetov, Daniel, 104
akhtaban shubyryndy, 103, 155n39
akhyn, 70, 90, 92, 125, 130, 151n6
akim, 125, 127, 133
akimat, 77, 137
aksakals, 107, 154n17
akyly sozder, 122

Al-Farabi (Abu Nasr Mohammed Farabi), 100, 101, 152n20
Al Fatiha, 49, 53
Alash-Orda government, 97
Alash political party, 97
alcohol, 51, 67, 82, 103, 130; discouraging, 17, 19
Almaty, 10, 48, 50, 64, 74, 77, 86, 92, 99, 100, 109, 112, 113, 114, 128, 129, 147n7, 153n12; *aitys* in, 127, 151n7; competition in, 96; performances in, 88, 117; protests in, 14
Amanzhol, 92, 93, 94
Ana Tili (newspaper), 155n43
ancestors (*ata-babalar*), 6, 58, 64, 75, 76, 136; authority of, 65–66; *bata* of, 55; blessing from, 4, 19, 71; caretakers and, 66, 79–80, 82; channeling, 18; connecting with, 67; conversation with, 21, 133–35; distant, 143; dreaming of, 71; enshrined, 134; famous, 5, 21, 41, 69; God and, 62; influence of, 72; Kazakh, 17, 21, 69, 76, 92, 93–94, 143; legacy of, 139; living and, 3, 4–5, 7, national, 56–59; nongenealogical, 50; path of, 47–55; pictures of, 90; presence of, 55; protection of, 78; relationships with, 6, 19, 53, 84; reverence for, 119; rhetorical frame of, 86, 140; sacred sites and, 56; spirit, 15, 30, 63, 82, 142; taking care of, 51; wishes of, 52, 83; worshiping, 61
Ancestors' Path, 47–48
ancestry, 100; dialogic emergence of, 3–6, 88; Kazakh, 71, 99, 143; religious identity and, 57; spiritual, 136
art (*uner*), 108
aruakh (ancestor spirit), 63, 142
Astana, 10, 89, 92, 110, 129, 133, 155n37; middle class in, 146n13
Ata Zhol, 47–48, 49, 50, 58, 65, 68, 75, 76, 147n25; *bata* and, 51
audiences, 6, 20, 21, 27, 68, 84, 85, *88*, 100, 102, 104, 105, 108, 111, 118, 119, 120, 121, 123, 125, 127, 130, 135, 139, 151; *aitys*, 86–89, 90, 91, 92, 93, 96, 97, 98; enthusiasm of, 110; poets and, 125; voting of, 88
Auezov, Mukhtar, 108, 150n18, 153n6, 153n8
aul, 10, 74, 129
aumin, 25, 33, 34, 69
Austin, J. L., 155n41
authoritarianism, 4, 9, 145n3; democracy and, 144, 156n18; nationalism and, 135–37
authority, 96, 133; moral, 44; paternalistic form of, 107; personalistic nature of, 140; social, 3, 114; spiritual, 54
avliyo, 65
A. Y. *See* Yermegeayev, Amangeldi

Bab, Arstan, 60
bagyshitau, 63, 149n11
Baidibek Ata, 74
Baitursunov, Ahmet, 120
Bakhtin, Mikhail: heteroglossic voice, 5, 6
baraka, 60, 68, 147n6
Basso, Keith, 60
bata, 4, 6, 31–34, 51, 59, 69, 74, 78, 81, 141, 142, 143, 147n1, 147n4, 150n25; Allah and, 66, 67; ancestors in, 41, 44, 50, 52, 55, 71, 72; blessing of, 26, 39, 82; changing, 30–31; classifications of, 37; collection of, *45*; as comfort/distress, 34–44; contexts of, 28–31, 33; defined, 25, 26; education and, 45; family, 26, 46–47; form of, 50; future and, 25–26, 31; giving, 7, 18, 19, 20, 23, 29–30, 34, 36, 39, 48, 54, 67, 72; healing, 39, 49; life-cycle, 46–47; life-training and, 28; past and, 25–26; performative power of, 8; pilgrimage and, 48, 49, 58; prayers and, 57; receiving, 27, 31, 40, 55, 76; research on, 62; role of, 32; symbolism of, 34; weddings and, 31; wishes of, 65
batyrlar (*batyrs*), 5, 22, 37, 70, 92, 94, 95, 102, 134, 140
bazaars, 12, 35, 43, 58, 70, 77, 86
beginning action, 31, 52
Berish, 131, 155n42
Bes Atalar (Five Forefathers) pilgrimage, 68, 69, 70, 73
bet sipau, 143, 148n12
Beyer, Judith, 107, 146n11, 154n17, 155n2
bi figures, 19, 141, 142
Bifatima, 150n19
black stripes, 38–39
blessings, 5, 6, 8, 19, 25, 26, 39, 51, 58, 68, 75, 135, 148n12; altering/changing, 30–31; forms of, 71, 82; seeking, 60; taking away, 143; transferability of, 147n6
boqmoq, 9, 12, 136
Boyarin, Jonathan, 4
bread, 3, 5, 18, 29, 30, 35, 39, 63, 67, 68, 70, 71, 80, 140, 143, 150n25
Buddhism, 59, 62
Bukayev horde, 121
Bukhar Zhyrau, 115, 128
burial sites, 18, 60, 64, 66, *78*, 80

care, 71, 82; cycles of, 4, 72; levels of, 6–8
caretakers, 9, 74; ancestors and, 66, 79–80, 82; miracle stories by, 68; role of, 66–68, 68–72
carolers, 26–27
Caton, Steven: social production and, 3–4
censorship, 9, 85, 97, 107, 112, 113, 128, 135
Chagatai khanate, 135
channeling, 18, 50

Chinggis Khan, 3, 69, 133; Mongolia and, 137–40; Yassa law code and, 156n9
clean people, 66, 67, 69
cleansing, 31, 50
collaboration/collusion, 22, 104–5, 117, 123, 132
collective infrastructure, reorganization of, 10–11
communication, 21, 65, 149n12
Communist Party, 35, 152n7
community, 83, 106, 142; building, 133, 134; cultural, 120; literary, 86; moral, 44–47
construction, 60, 76, 77, 100, 108, 146n13
Coombe, Rosemary, 144
coping, 4, 6, 13, 34, 41, 43
corruption, 16, 20, 22, 99, 103, 129, 133, 137, 138; fighting, 140; systemic, 140
cosmology, 67, 72
costumes, Kazakh, 90
criminality, 44
criticism, 107; indirect, 104; kinship and, 96–102; as nationalism, 129–32; sociopolitical, 21, 84, 88, 96, 97, 112, 113, 129, 137, 143
cultural affairs, 86, 92, 108, 109, 110, 111, 128
cultural forgetting, metaphor of, 47
cultural legitimacy, 107, 114
cultural organizers, 22, 85, 88, 108, 126, 128
cultural production, 108, 110
culture, 6, 54, 57, 59, 65, 88, 101, 119, 135, 143; authentic, 53, 132; celebration of, 136; commoditization of, 85; conversation with, 4, 143–44; expressive, 6, 134; Kazakh, 8, 15, 16, 21, 88, 90, 108, 114, 115, 116–17, 129, 137; knowing, 85; loss of, 47; national, 13, 61, 86; religion and, 57; Soviet, 13; understanding of, 5; voices in, 22

dastarhan, 29, *30*, 39, 45, 68, 70, 126–27
dat, 129, 130, 131, 155n37
death, 3, 16, 35, 38, 40, 43, 44, 46, 50, 63, 64, 71, 76, 113, 121, 143
decorations, 37, 90
democracy, 136; authoritarianism and, 144, 156n18; dialogic, 144; understandings/forms of, 10
Democratic Choice Kazakhstan Party, 155n40
descendants, 3, 5, 51, 63, 66, 72, 77, 92, 95, 96, 101, 103, 105, 134, 139, 143; generalized, 56
dialogic authority, 22, 106–32
dialogic emergence, 6, 144
dialogism, 5, 107, 135
dialogue: ancestral, 83, 132, 133–35, 137; collusion in, 104–5; life-changing, 107; metaphoric, 44; moments of, 5
Dina, 66; *bata* and, 29, 31, 32, 34, 35, 36; conversation with, 28, 30; Saltanat and, 38

dombyra, 20, 70, 89, 90, 147n27
Douglas, Mary, 150n14
dreams/dreaming, 38, 39, 40, 59, 60, 62, 64, 73, 74, 80, 133, 143; ancestors in, 41, 44, 50, 52, 55, 71, 72; *ayan* as, 148n6; *bata* and, 7, 34; interpreting, 61; oration and, 150n21; relationships and, 58
drugs, 17, 45, 67
dynastic genealogies, narrators of, 96
Dzungars, 102, 103, 150n24

ecology, 4, 59
economic uncertainty, 6, 9, 10–13, 59, 137
education, 8, 13, 14, 20, 28, 71, 111, 116; *bata* and, 45; cultural, 6, 44; Islamic, 57, 62; moral, 133–34; upbringing and, 25–28
Elbegdorj, Tsakhiaghiin, 138, 139, 156n10; on corruption, 140; partnering against Corruption initiative and, 156n14; quote of, 133
elders, 6, 7, 8, 9, 22, 26, 28, 30, 31, 32, 39, 40, 90, 119, 135, 154n17; *bata* from, 31, 34, 37, 46, 55; community, 15, 126, 127; cultural resources of, 55; legal guidance from, 15; politicians and, 154n17; relationships with, 34; religious, 33; respect for, 7, 8, 9, 44, 47, 120, 127; spiritual, 41
elites, 6, 9, 10, 110, 111, 113, 117, 120, 129; communist, 8; economic, 106, 107; growth of, 11; political, 107; sponsors, 20, 85, 129
enemies, 22, 26, 34, 36, 77, 121, 136, 150n24; Kazakhs and, 92–96, 134, 135
energy, 82, 88, 104; dark, 51, 73; negative, 38–39, 40, 42, 50; spiritual, 140
Engels, Friedrich, 131
environment, 9, 11, 75, 133, 134, 135; cultural, 22; historical, 22; multicultural, 33; national, 137; political, 20, 22; postsocialist, 3, 8; regional, 133; social, 83; steppe, 14
epics, 5, 105, 136, 138, 143
ethnicity, 12, 13, 14, 56, 57, 69, 89, 113, 122, 152n17; real, 151n6
ethnography, 5, 12, 22, 65, 107, 137, 144
evil eye, 51, 62, 149n9
expression, 129, 135; cultural, 21; negative, 149n9

fairness, 50, 72, 123, 124, 138, 142
family life, 35, 86, 98, 101, 142, 144; *bata* and, 26; patriarchal, 12; problems with, 45
Feaux de la Croix, Jeanne, 59
folklore, 14, 107–12, 116
fortune-telling, 18, 39, 40
frameworks, 4, 22, 25, 65, 98, 100, 105, 115, 130, 132; ancestral, 84, 96; communicative, 149n12; cultural, 143; dialogic, 88, 92;

frameworks (cont.): ethnic, 93; ideological, 84; interpretive, 147n29; moral, 137; narrative, 67; participant, 6, 30–31, 41, 144; performance, 111, 114, 129; political, 97; rhetorical, 86, 131

Gaukhar, 28, 47, 53, 54, 55, 149n26; *bata* and, 46, 49, 50; blessing and, 51; Saltanat and, 52; social ills and, 52
genealogy (generation), 13, 18, 51; connection to, 6; cultural, 139, 143; dynastic, 96; nepotism and, 136; personal, 139; symbolic importance of, 3
geography: moral, 59; political, 47; sacred, 59–61, 66; social, 92, 93; spiritual, 76
God (Allah), 50, 52, 61, 62, 63, 73; *bata* and, 66, 67
Goffman, Erving, 6, 21, 153n2
Gorbachev, Mikhail, 14
governance: good, 54, 105, 134; national, 83; poor, 137
Great Zhuz, 141, 142
grief, past/present/future and, 102–4
guests, 16, 17, 70, 73, 74, 130, 150n19; place for, 29; receiving, 67, 68, 79, 124; table for, *30*; toasts by, 31, 33
Gumilev, Lev: Eurasianism and, 152n3

halykh (people), 123
Hann, C. M., 6
harmony, 12, 61, 65, 136, 138
healing, 19–20, 48, 50, 61, 72, 82; *bata* and, 39, 49; physical, 58–59; sites, 61; spiritual, 47, 58–59, 68
hearth, 119; cult of, 61
hegemony, Russian, 14, 95, 116, 117, 129
heritage, 4, 59, 136
heroes, 22, 53, 84, 95, 96, 135; connection to, 6; cultural, 19; real, 130
Hirsch, Francine, 13
history: cultural, 7, 37, 86, 89, 96, 100, 137, 140, 143; family, 16–20; gender, 147n28; intergenerational, 147n28; Kazakh, 19, 21, 77, 96, 102, 127, 135, 143; multinational, 99; mythic, 21; national, 19; religious, 59, 61; social, 5, 95, 137, 140; symbolic importance of, 3
Holy Bata, 26
hospitality, 12, 17, 29, 30, 39, 124, 127, 130; Kazakh, 16, 125
household economy, 12, 17

identity, 148n11, 149n2; ancestry and, 57; cultural, 14, 85, 112, 113; ethnic, 12, 13, 14, 56; historical, 19; musical, 146n19; Muslim, 57, 119, 148n22; national, 3, 56, 92; religious, 12

ideology, 6, 12, 133; language, 90, 116, 154n22; social authority and, 3
Ideology Department (Kazakh SSR), 85
imperialism: Russian, 13, 148n21; Soviet, 13
independence, 8, 10, 11, 15, 47, 103, 105, 136, 155n43
interaction, levels of, 6–8
International Council for Traditional Music, 150n15
internationalism, 15, 89, 115, 116
Islam, 14, 57, 61, 62

Jakobson, Roman, 149n12
jokes/joking, 27, 64, 68, 78, 79, 82, 89, 93, 96, 97, 98, 121, 125, 126, 129
Journal of Linguistic Anthropology, 150
judges, 9, 19, 70, 87, 92, 119; advice of, 22
jury, 87, 91, 109, 121, 122

kabyrstan, 64, 76
Kabyshyly, Ghabbas: freedom and, 156n16
Kainazar Ata, 50, 68, 69
Kalmyk, 93, 150n24, 155n39
Karaganda, protests in, 14
Karasai, Batyr, 70, 71
Karima Akhyn, 106, 119, 120, 122, 132; *aitys* of, 123, 124
Karimov, Elyor, 60, 61, 68
Karimov, Islam, 136
Kazakh History Department, 85
Kazakh Languages and Literatures Department, 85
Kazakh National University, 100, 101
Kazakh New Year, 109, 120
Kazakh Radio, 151n2
Kazakhs, 61, 88, 153n8; enemies of, 92–96; identification by, 8
Kazibek Bi, 19, 141, 142
Kazirgi Aitys, 86
kelin, 46, 141
Kendirbaeva, Gulnar, 109
Kenzhebai Akhyn, 92, 94, 96, 127; dialogic authority and, 128; pilgrimage with, 77; purpose of, 95
Kenzhibek Akim, 127
Khabar (Television news station), 86, 96, 117
Khan Zhangir, 121
khanates, 89, 114, 137
khandai, 114–17, 124. *See also* paternalism
khans, 5, 22, 89, 115, 130, 132, 140; Kazakh, 125; patrons and, 114; poets and, 21, 127–29; regional, 93
Khudiretke Zhuginuw (Yerman), 151n4
kinship, 20, 30, 90, 143; criticism and, 96–102; dialogic frames of, 88; networks, 106, 153n10

Kishi Horde, 115, 155n42
knowledge, 100, 151n6; cultural, 90; linguistic, 90
kobyz, 73, 74, 75, 150n23, 151n9
Koishybayev, Bebit, 155n43
Koishyghary, 113
Kolbin, Gennady, 14, 15
kolkhoz, 80
Koran, 17, 19, 53, 61, 63, 69; reading, 3, 33, 35, 38, 40, 41, 42, 50, 80
Kunayev, Dinmukhamed, 14
Kundirbaeva, 109, 153n8
Kydyrali Ata, 71
kyi, 134, 151n9, 152n13
kymyz, 70, 79, 81, 82, 118
Kyz Zhibek (film), 37
Kyzylorda, 125, 128

labor migration, 11, 12, 13, 146n12
land, 124; protecting, 76–82; resources and, 9, 10, 11, 98, 99, 115, 124, 129, 154n30
landscapes, 4, 58; affective, 56; ancestral, 8, 59; cultural, 7; spiritual, 60
language: Chinese, 116; English, 116; Kazakh, 15, 21, 88, 90, 115, 116–17; 120, 129, 130, 132, 137, 154n21; Russian, 116, 130, 132; Turkish, 116; understanding of, 5, 22
leadership, 72, 90, 106, 117, 125, 140; alternative model of, 21; ancestral, 4, 133; correct form of, 134; dialogic, 20–23; inclusive, 135; informed/dependent, 114; Kazakh, 15, 84, 117; quality of, 124; reality and, 10; Russian, 15; spiritual, 71
legitimacy, 12, 13, 48, 89, 90, 107, 109, 130, 132, 135, 136, 139, 155n2; cultural, 114; historical, 88, 107, 113, 135; local, 140–43; political, 6, 22, 260, 143, 156n17; symbolic, 136
Lenin, Vladimir, 70, 131
life cycle, 7, 12, 25, 27
Light, Nathan: idealized narratives and, 96
literature: Kazakh, 107, 116, 120, 121; Russian, 116
Liu, Morgan: *boqmoq* and 33, 160, 187; informants of, 9; state paternalism and 33, 131
Louw, Maria Elisabeth, 57, 58

Madanova, Margarita, 60, 153n6
Makhambet Utemisoly, 121, 131, 154n27
Manas (mythic warrior), 3, 69, 136, 150n21, 155n5
Mangistau, 120, 121, 122
mankurt, 47, 130, 148n21, 148n23
Mannheim, Bruce, 5
marriages: *bata* and, 31; beginning of, 32–33

Marx, Karl, 131
Marzhan Akhyn, 121, 124, 126, 131, 132; *aitys* and, 123, 127; issues and, 122; performance and, 120
Matveeva, Anna, 136, 156n17
mausoleums, 18, 19, 62, 64, 69, 73
Mecca, 59, 70, 118, 120
media, 57, 85, 128; censorship of, 97, 112; reform of, 113
Meiramgul, 52, 53, 140, 141, 143; bad ancestor spirit and, 44; *bata* and, 31, 36, 37, 39, 40, 42, 44, 45, 46–47, 49, 50, 142; conversation with, 28; coping by, 43; family life and, 45; mysticism and, 41; narrative process and, 41; obligation and, 47; pilgrimages and, 49; proverbs and, 42; Saltanat and, 38; story of, 38–39, 42–43
Mels Akhyn, 129, 131
Middle Horde, 102, 151n11
Minor Horde, 155n42
miracle stories, 7, 68, 72
Mira Apai, 118
Miras, 76; Saltanat and, 63–64; speech by, 63, 64
Mohammed, Prophet, 63, 149n5
Montgomery, David; Islamic life in Kyrgyzstan and, 149n7
moral order, 12, 42, 44, 146n11
moral welfare, lack of, 9
morality, 8, 22, 65, 119, 136, 140
Mostowlansky, Till, 12
mullahs, 33, 35, 40, 80, 81–82, 119, 149n11; *bata* and, 39
music, 15, 73, 74, 84, 108, 135, 147n27; Kazakh, 86, 108, 155n4; national styles of, 14; pop, 109, 113
Muslims, 58, 61; Bukhara, 57; orthodox, 65
mutuality, 4, 22, 68, 71, 73, 82, 86, 109, 114, 117, 132, 135, 144
mysticism, 41, 48, 49, 60, 148n24
mythology, 68, 75, 77, 115, 135, 151n12; cultural, 124; folk, 154n33

Naghyz Ak Zhol (True White Way), 112, 113
namas, 31–34, 38, 63, 124
Naqshbandi Sufi shrine, 20
narratives, 7, 46, 51; idealized, 96; moral, 121; mythic, 3; nationalizing, 22; short, 74
nation-branding, 96, 155n4
nation-building, 3, 143
nation-state, 23, 96, 114, 144
nationalism, 47, 57, 58, 65, 93, 100, 122, 134; authoritarianism and, 135–37; criticism as, 129–32; cultural, 13–15, 58, 140, 148n20; ethnic, 13, 14, 56, 84, 85, 90, 92, 103, 140;

nationalism (cont.): Kazakh, 15, 69, 89, 104, 115, 116, 127, 129, 132, 137; Russian, 89
nationalities, 56, 123, 148n22; cultural, 137; Soviet, 13–14
nationalization, 6, 8, 70, 135, 149n2, 154n21
Nauruzbayeva, Zhanara, 155n6, 156n18
Nazarbayev, Nursultan, 15, 50, 86, 113, 115, 118, 128, 133, 135, 151n3; quotes from, 42
Nazarbayeva, Dariga, 86, 151n5
Nefrit Ata, negative energy from, 38–39
nepotism, 130, 136, 137
networks, 11; national, 84–86, 111, 145n1, 151n2; performance, 110; personal, 107
Nomad (film), 135, 152n22
Nur Otan, 152
Nurbek (caretaker), 79, 80–81, 82
Nurkadilov, Zamanbek: Almaty and, 153n12
Nurlan Akhyn, 120, 121, 122

Oirats, 93
Omarova, Guka, 150n19
oralman, 99–100
oral tradition, 3, 5, 6, 20, 89, 129, 137, 138, 147n28, 149n7; potential of, 22–23; real, 153n8
Orazaly Akhyn, 99, 102, 155n39; *aitys* and, 96, 97, 101, 105; grief/loss and, 103; housing and, 100; joke by, 98
Orta Zhuz (Middle Horde), 102, 115, 151n11
Ospanov, Bakhytzhan, 118
Otan (Patriotic fatherland) party, 97, 114, 117, 132, 151n5

Pagliai, Valentina, 150
"Partnering against Corruption," 138, 156n14
paternalism, 8–10, 12, 107, 114, 117
Path of Abai (Madanova), 153n6
patriotism, 21, 100, 109, 120, 137; for hire, 89
patronage, 88, 106, 111, 114, 124. *See also* sponsorship
performance, 85, *88*, *91*, 104, 107, 108, 114, *115*, 117, 120, 122, *126*, 130, 134, 144; *aitys*, 89–92; conditions of, 128–29; cultural, 21–22; frameworks, 92, 111, 115; international, 20; judging, 87–88; networks, 110; nonpolitical, 126; public, 23, 83; Soviet internationalist, 89; sponsorship and, 124; success/failure of, 87, 91
performativity of words, 4, 5, 6, 8, 20, 21, 22, 50, 65, 83, 97, 107, 144, 151n9
piety (*imanshylykh*), 120; poetry and, 118–19
pilgrimages, 18–19, 19–20, 57, 59, 60, 61, 65, 70, 75, 76, 118, 120, 143, 144, 149n6;

bata and, 48, 49, 58; daylong, 68; guides for, 72; informal, 77; undertaking, 56
poetry, 18, 85, 89, 108, 116, 124, 144; action/cultural practice and, 4; competition, 84; epic, 134, 151n9; national styles of, 14; performance of, 23; piety and, 118–19; political consequences of, 4; popular forms of, 109; social task in, 93; sponsors and, 117
poets, 85, 86, *91*, 100, 125, 132; accountability and, 114; *aitys*, 84, 108; audiences and, 125; classical, 102; competition of, 91–92; cultural/historical legitimacy and, 107; duty/mission of, 89; khans and, 21, 127–29; patrons and, 111, 114; performances by, 22, 87, 91, 108; recruiting, 109; rehearsing by, *111*; relationships with, 111; social/artistic ideals and, 110; social purpose of, 88–89; sponsors and, 20–21, 117; warriors and, 92
political economy, 10, 111
political parties, 9, 106
political problems, 4, 12
politics, 8, 13, 22, 90, 96, 97, 98, 100, 110, 114, 119, 134, 140, 143–44; comparative analysis of, 137; Kazakh, 16, 104, 144; linguistic, 154n21; local, 92; national, 14; participatory, 23, 132, 144; patronage, 106; performance of, 23
postsocialism, 6, 11, 83
poverty, 11, 26, 51, 120
prayers, 5, 20, 50, 56, 66, 73, 74, 75; *bata* and, 57; Muslim, 25, 33, 53, 67; reading, 39, 67
Prior, Daniel, 153n3
privatization, 8, 10, 11
Privratsky, Bruce, 59, 60, 147n6, 148n12
prizes, 87, 91, 92, 109, 110, 118, 119, 120, 122, 127
propaganda, 48, 57, 153n3
property metaphor, 67, 119
prostitution, 45, 51, 52
purges, 13, 14
Pushkin, Alexander, 126

Raiymbek Batyr, 77, 92, 93, 95, 102, 150n24, 151n12, 152n22; *aitys* audiences and, 96; celebration of, 127–28; as Kazakh *batyr*, 94
Rasanayagam, Johan: ethnography of Islam and, 65, 188
relationships, 4, 41, 47, 63, 71, 91, 110; call-and-response, 88; dialogic, 132; dreams and, 58; in-law, 46; interpersonal, 126; kinship, 92; mentorship, 90; passionate/volatile, 35; performing, 84, 111; personal, 107; social, 5, 16, 114; sponsorship, 110, 132
religion, 65, 75, 129; culture and, 57

INDEX

Renat Akhyn, 84, 97, 99, 100, 152n17; *aitys* and, 96, 101, 105; criticism by, 102; national government and, 103; performance by, 104; politics and, 98; stealing and, 104
Republican Theater, 96
respect, 4, 30, 39, 48, 71, 101, 102, 106, 123, 124; for elders, 7, 8, 9, 44, 47, 120, 127; encouraging, 17; for holy people, 63; for language/traditions, 120; mutual, 132; politics of, 22
revelation (*ayan*), 40, 41, 52, 148n6
rhetoric, 5, 7, 22, 51, 57, 63, 64, 83, 84, 86, 95, 96, 102, 103, 122, 131, 139; ancestral, 135, 137, 140, 143, 144; master narrative, 133; strategy, 134, 140
Ritmy Evarzii (Gumilev), 151n3
rituals, 7, 25, 30, 33, 50, 58; *bata* and, 26
rule of law, 10, 139, 148

Sabilianov, Nurtai, 132
Sabit Akhyn, 122, 123
sacred sites, 60, 65, 72, *78*, *79*, 82; ancestors and, 56; mythology of, 75; spiritual dimensions of, 58; as testimonies, 80; visiting, 61, 67–68
Saghynbek, 68, 69, 150n16
Saghyrbaioly, Kurmanghazy, 152n13
saints, 61, 62, 65, 71, 149n6; blessing by, 68
sale, metaphor of, 107–12
Saltanat, 43, 51, 53, 54, 55, 72, 80, 90, 141, 143; Aida and, 79, 81; bad ancestor spirits and, 44; *bata* and, 29, 31, 32, 33, 34, 35, 36, 39, 40, 42, 46, 49, 50, 62, 66, 78; bazaar and, 58; caretakers and, 66, 79; clean people and, 67; conversation with, 28, 30; cross-border trade and, 35; dark energy and, 73; Dina and, 38; divorce and, 46; family life and, 45; feedback from, 51; Gaukhar and, 52; Meiramgul and, 38; Miras and, 63–64; mother's diary of, *37*; mullahs and, 81–82; mysticism and, 41; obligation and, 47; story of, 38
Samarkand, 59, 61, 65
Saribai Ata, 50
Sarsenbayev, Altynbek, 147n23; murder of, 112, 113, 153n13
Satypaldy, Kairat, 118
Second Mecca, 59
security, 104; social, 10, 11, 12, 137
Shaman (film), 150n19
shamanism, 61, 62, 148n15
shangyrakh, 70, 90, 101, 134, 143
shezhire, 13, 49, 149n25
Shimkent, 97–98, 120, 121, 122, 126; performances in, 118; protests in, 14

show business, 107–12
shrines, 57, 62, 66, 70, 71, 76, *81*, 149n6; experiences/narratives of, 58; pilgrimages to, 48, 60; visiting, 61, 67, 143
shyrakhshy, 59, 67, 68, 71
silencing, 112, 114, 129
social commentary, 97, 100, 119
social conventions, 6–7
social criticism, 97, 137, 143
social fabric, unraveling of, 47
social interaction, 5, 22
socialism, 6, 10, 11, 137
social justice, 140
social life, 5, 9, 45, 144
social problems, 4, 6, 52, 59
social welfare, 9, 10, 15, 100, 104, 136, 137, 140
sociopolitical affairs, 21, 84, 97, 129
Solomon's Mountain, 59
songs, 14, 89, 134
sovereignty, 21, 84, 89, 99, 102, 103, 105; ethnic, 134; national, 19, 95, 136
sovkhoz, 140
SOYUZ, 155n6, 156n18
Specialized Inter-District Economic Court, 48
spirits, 55, 136; ancestor, 30, 38–39, 44; evil, 18
spiritual dimensions, 58, 61
spiritual landscape, Inner Asian, 60
spiritual worlds, 41, 137
sponsors, 128, 132; *aitys* poets and, 20–21; local/regional, 111; poets and, 20–21, 117; social purpose of, 88–89
sponsorship, 22, 88, 106–7, 111, 119, 125, 127; bad, 117; climate of, 124; ethnic nationalist, 134; external, 110, 114; performance and, 124; private, 110. *See also* patronage
Stalin, Joseph, 131, 146n17, 150n18
state farms, 35, 140
stereotypes, 16, 29, 120
strategy: cultural, 6; economic, 10; financial, 128; political, 140
style, 5, 14, 46, 51, 53, 70, 76, 88, 90, 100, 116, 126, 138, 151n8
substance abuse, 11, 146n14
Sufism, 58, 60
Suinbai Ata, 50, 70, 71
Sulbanalyoly, Usen, 70, 71
Suleimenov, Olzhas, 14
Sunnism, 14, 58, 61
support: ancestral, 48; mutual, 82; spiritual, 49; state, 12
sure, 19, 42, 150n16
symbolism, 3, 34, 155n3, 156n7
Syr Darya river (Zhetisu), 60, 93, 94, 98

175

Taimanov, Isatai, 121, 154n27
Taldykorgan, protests in, 14
tamada, 33, 125
Tamerlane (Timur), 60, 69, 136
Tarbai Ata, 68
Tasmagambetov, Imangali, 104
Taushen, 119
tax police, 17
Tedlock, Dennis, 5
Temujin, 139
Tengrism, 59, 61, 62
toasts, 31–34
Toktybai Ata, 50, 72–76, *75*, *76*
Tole Bi, 19, 141, 142
tombs, 60, 61, 104
tourism, 58, 67–68, 69, 76
tradition: cultural, 33; ethnic, 56; Islamic, 33; Kazakh, 26, 53, 108, 120; patriarchal, 46; poetic, 5, 112; reinvented, 137; religious, 56, 62. See also *aitys* tradition; oral tradition
transformation, 19; economic, 11, 146n15; moral, 9; political, 11
tribalism, 102, 152n23
ture, 125
Turetam, 124–27; *aitys* in, 126, *126*, 127
Turkestan, sites in, 3, 57, 59, 61, 65, 69, 84, 97, 99, 136, 137
Turoly Akhyn, 125, 127

Ulken Horde, 115
unification, 94, 115, 134, 135
Union of Writers, 151n7
University of Astana, 113
upbringing, 54, 71; education and, 25–28; moral, 25–26, 44
Uzbekistan, 3, 57, 59, 61, 65, 69, 85, 97, 99, 136, 137; Kazakh-Uzbek relations and, 98; water issue and, 98

values: ancestral, 48; cultural, 29, 46
Verdery, Katherine, 13
violence: criminal, 44; gender-based, 146n14; male, 11; political, 112

visitation, 57, 58, 61, 62, 71, 143, 149n4
voice (*un*), 135; cultural, 20, 107; political, 112–14; social, 112–14

Wahhabi, external threat of, 57
warriors, 22, 134; poets and, 92
water spring, 78, *79*
weddings: *bata* and, 31; length of, 32–33
well-being, 12, 137, 146n8
wishes, 25, 52, 56, 61, 65, 83; good, 26, 30, 42
wishing tree, *79*
World Economic Forum, 138
worldview, 8, 67, 75; ancestral, 5, 20, 58, 66, 144; cultural, 5, 7, 57, 143
words (*suzder*), 90, 151n6

Yasawi, Khoja Ahmed: Yasawi *tariqah* and, 60
Yassa, 138, 146n9
Yawasi legacy, 60
yel (country), 72, 94, 115, 123, 154n20
Yerman, Zhursin, 85, 86, 96, 118, 120, 151n2, 151n4
Yermegeayev, Amangeldi (A.Y.), 114–15, 125, 128, 132; sponsors/poets and, 117
Yessenova, Saluesh, 13, 146n9
yurts, 79, 80, *81*, 90, 101

"Zhai Ramazan" (song), 26
Zhakiyanov, Galymzhan, 155n40
Zhambyl Zhabaev, 50, 68, 69, 70, 150n18, 150n19; *bata* and, 72; home of, 149n27
zhek pe zhek genre, 85, 96, 119, 120
Zheltoksan, 14, 15, 85
Zhengelbai Agha, 140, 141, 142, 143
zhol ashu (opening the road), 77
Zholdasbekov, Murzatai, 85
Zhulduz, 56, 72, 73, 76; pilgrimages by, 74–75
zhuz (Kazakh horde), 77, 135, 141, 143
ziyarat, 61, 62, 149n8
ziyaret, 61–66